Hans van Ewijk / Jef van Eijken / Harry Staatsen (Eds.)

A good society is more than just a private affair

Citizenship based social work in practice

EHV)

Hans van Ewijk / Jef van Eijken / Harry Staatsen (Eds.)

A good society is more than just a private affair

Studies in Comparative Social Pedagogies and International Social Work
and Social Policy, Vol. XXI

EHV

www.eh-verlag.de

Ewijk, Hans van; Eijken, Jef van; Staatsen, Harry (Eds.)

A good society is more than just a private affair
Citizenship based social work in practice

Studies in Comparative Social Pedagogies and International Social Work and Social Policy, Vol. XXI

Editor of the series: Peter Herrmann

Editorial board : Beatriz Gershenson Aquinsky, Maria Anastasiadis, Christian Aspalter, Torben Bechmann, Nuria Pumar Beltran, Yitzhak Berman, Kezeban Celik, Hsiao-hung Nancy Chen, Geoffrey Cook, Judit Csoba, Leta Dromantiené, Wendy Margaret Earles, Franz Hamburger, Arno Heimgartner, Alpay Hekimler, Peter Herrmann, Sibel Kalaycioglu, Francis Kessler, Jerzy Krzyszkowski, Yeun-wen Ku, Nadia Kutscher, Juhani Laurinkari, Wan-i Lin, Jussara Maria Rosa Mendes, Letlhokwa George Mpedi, Julia O'Connor, M. Ramesh, Mae Shaw, Dorottya Szikra, Stephan Sting, Sven Trygged, Hans van Ewijk, Paul Ward, Luk Zelderloo
www.socialcomparison.org

1. Edition 2012
ISBN: 978-3-86741-805-8
© Europäischer Hochschulverlag GmbH & Co. KG, Bremen, 2012.
www.eh-verlag.de

EHV

Hans van Ewijk

Jef van Eijken

Harrie Staatsen

Lia van Doorn

Maarten van der Linde

Jo Hermanns

Anneke Menger

Doortje Kal

Stijn Verhagen

Ben Fruytier

Rob Gründemann

Jean Pierre Wilken

This edition is a translated and revised version of *Samenleven is geen privézaak*, Den Haag: Boom Lemma, 2012.
Chapters 1, 3, 4, 5, 7, 8, 9 and 11 have been translated by Mark Bos and Kriti Toshniwal. Chapter 2 has been translated by Marja van Soest. Chapters 6 and 10 have been translated by the authors. All chapters have been edited by Mark Bos and Kriti Toshniwal.

Contents

Foreword

Peter Herrmann

Samenleven is geen privézaak – initially reading the title in the original Dutch, it had been then a little bit irritating reading in the translation about good society. My knowledge of the Dutch language is very limited – and perhaps this had been at that moment of advantage, allowing associations and interpretations that are possibly not immediately coming up while using terms without reflecting on them. Isn't *Samenleven* as living together something that society is about – or what it should be about? In this light society is by no means a 'given externality', a social fact sui generis; instead it is definitely first and foremost a process, permanently establishing and re-establishing itself – or failing to do so. And isn't this living together very much characterised by two sides – from migration studies we know the push and pull effects. And in a similar vein society – and membership in a society – is nothing that can be taken for granted.

In some respect all this seems to be a platitude. But the real challenge may come from the second point: we are not dealing with a private affair. The one line of differentiation seems to be clear – if it is not private it must be public. But this brings us quite obviously to another tensional line, namely that between individual and social.

The questions are of course as old as any considerations that are made about human beings, considering them as social beings. And already this formulation seems to be telling – in the strict sense we cannot have any a-social or non-social beings. As Marx highlighted in his Outline of the Critique of Political Economy, the human being can individuate itself only in the midst of society. (Marx, Karl, 1857: Outline of the Critique of Political Economy (Grundrisse); passim)

Thinking systematically further, it is obvious that anti-social behaviour is actually at the very same time self-destructive.

Since some time now we see frequently the emphasis of relationality – the idea of it is that, looking at the social, we are entering a field without beginning and end, without clear lines of demarcation, without a clear beginning, end or destination – the work on social quality (see www.socialquality.eu) works with a definition of the social that reflects exactly this. It understand the social – as noun – as outcome of the interaction between people (constituted as actors) and their constructed and natural environment. Its subject matter refers to people's interrelated productive and reproductive relationships. In other words, the constitutive interdependency between processes of self-realisation and processes governing the formation of collective identities is a condition for the social and its progress or decline. (van der Maesen, Laurent J.G./Walker, Alan, 2012: Social Quality and Sustainability; in: van der Maesen, Laurent J.G./Walker, Alan [Eds.]: Social quality: From Theory to Indicators; Basingstoke: Macmillan: 250-274l here: 260)

This seems to be hopelessly confusing – aren't we as human beings inclined to lead an orderly life and also to maintain an overview of clear orders, defining everything and seeing everything in clearly definable ways. As true as this may be at first glance, we easily overlook that this leads us into a zone of deceiving comfort.

The present book, when proposed for publication, caught my special attention. It opens a door to face exactly this challenge. And it does so by emphasising that professionals who are working in the social field are in particular challenged by two matters: they are part of society – and cannot develop or suggest any abstract values as guideline for any society and for living together. And they are part of society only if and insofar as society is understood and accepted as space of inter-action. Society has to be understood as process – changing itself and allowing people to change themselves. I suppose that living together will only then actually be able to develop towards a good society.

In this light the book elaborated by Hans van Ewijk and his colleagues is surely an important contribution to a necessary debate, allowing to consider afresh the politisation of social work and working out the 'personal dimension' of social policy.

1. Social workers and modern citizens

Jef van Eijken

1.1 Introduction

The last years we have witnessed a transformation from a welfare state to a participation state. In a participation state citizens are supposed to take care of themselves and help others. Only when self-care and mutual care appear insufficient, does professional care come into the picture. The idea amongst politicians and policy makers is that citizens jointly strive for the perpetuation and improvement of the quality of life in their immediate surroundings. In a society where traditional social structures are subject to erosion, for some this self-driven strife is a utopia, for others a challenge, for social workers a task at hand. In the transformation to a more participatory society, social work sees the revitalization of a broad traditional professional vision. In this vision, the goals of social work are aimed at improvement of self-help, social participation, and social integration. In this vision, social workers make use of the social structures in districts and neighbourhoods, and support existing citizens' initiatives aimed at improving the quality of social life. They connect to social networks and cooperate with informal care and volunteers. This vision criticizes the overplayed individualism and wants to achieve a more caring society.

This book is about social work that wants to enhance active citizenship. We make a connection between the profile and practice of social work on the one hand, and an agenda for research and knowledge generation aimed at developing and supporting active citizenship on the other. Jan Steijaart et al. (2005) describe active citizenship as follows: 'Active citizenship refers to the social behaviour and self-help of citizens, and the way in which service providers and policy invite and support citizens with this.' Active citizenship manifests itself in both the public as well as private domain, states Jakop Rigter (2004); it recognizes a moral compass of values and norms, and requires skills to transform motivation into effective behaviour. Hans van Ewijk (2010a) developed a concept of social work that he described as *contextual-transformative.* The contextual-transformative approach is aimed at improving and supporting the social functioning of people by reaching out and embedding, based on active and participative citizenship. Thus, the contextual-transformative approach stands for changing the immediate context; be it in relation to behaviour, relations and patterns within a family, neighbourhood, school, or work place. Professional social workers offer support to individuals as well as social networks, and actively produce connections between persons, groups, and social resources. According to Van Ewijk (as elaborated in chapter 3), in the local social zone this calls for stimulating and maintaining active citizenship, taking care of, mostly, long-term support to the most vulnerable citizens and responding adequately to critical situations in and around people's homes.

How do we understand social work then? Jean Pierre Wilken describes social work, in chapter 10 of this book, as the whole field of social care and welfare work. Social care is aimed at supporting people with self-care and social participation. Welfare work is service provision aimed at supporting citizens in their individual and collective welfare. This implies, for example, the building and maintaining of vital social networks and communal arrangements and provisions. Within the bounds of social work we find many related occupations, such as community workers, community educators, youth workers, pedagogues or social-pedagogic community workers. Social workers can be found in many parts of society: districts and neighbourhoods, companies, health care institutions, and youth care. They engage in a wide variety of activities, such as aid, housing support, work integration, guided education, debt relief, supporting social networks, and neighbourhood development. Social workers also focus on prevention. Their role extends beyond just improving the social networks of people who need support, says Stijn Verhagen in chapter 8. By creating strong social environments, one can prevent people from becoming all too vulnerable and therefore needing specialist care. Even people without the immediate need for support, thrive in vital social environments.

Social work is also a term for a binding field of knowledge and actions for related professions and types of work. Despite the knowledge and skills needed for executing the tasks entailed by specific professions, one can identify a common professional foundation of basic competencies that make someone a social worker. This common knowledge base is a subject of permanent research and further development. This will be the topic of the book's final chapter.

In this introductory chapter though, we will first take a closer look at active citizenship against the backdrop of social and political developments. We will then look at a concise description of the development of social work in relation to active citizenship, a view of its future, and we will conclude with an introduction to the contributions of the different authors included in this book.

4

1.2 Social work and citizenship

In the Netherlands, but also at other locations in Europe, social work has always been closely related to the design of social policy by the government. Over the years the municipalities have started playing a key role in this sphere. The active participation and responsibility of citizens in the creation and implementation of local social policy has gone through a development, which has recently come under strong criticism: it seems that little has been realized with regard to the centrality of citizens in social policy besides paying lip service to its importance. The current social situation calls for an approach where the commitment of citizens is assigned a central place and influence.

I began my career as a young community worker in Amsterdam South-East, the Bijlmer; a controversial new city district, which was in the 1970s still in the beginning stages of its development. In this (then) still largely virgin territory, new active residents had high expectations about what 'the city of the future' could give them and what they could contribute to it. They saw themselves as pioneers. Community workers supported them in their often unruly and sometimes anarchist initiatives. This was still during the period before the first government initiatives arose, with which local governments started to strengthen their grip on the capricious citizens' initiatives. These government initiatives were aimed at providing the government more grip on, at that time, the very religiously compartmentalized field of private welfare supply. In the district welfare planning that the government had in mind, citizens were to have a voice in the creation of the social welfare offered. In this manner, social work had to come to stand 'closer to the citizens'. The report 'Citizen Strength' (Dutch: *Burgerkracht*, 2011) published recently by the Council for Social Development, an important advisory body of the Dutch government, states that this initiative has been of little success It mentions that in the last few decades, social work has failed to realize this central position that the citizens need to hold. The main explanation given in this regard is that the government began to determine more and more what is good for the people, and went shopping for 'products' at welfare organizations, which started operating in the fashion of manufacturing companies. According to the authors of the report (De Boer & Van der Lans, 2011) the ability of citizens to solve their own problems could not develop within this context. A consequence of this development for social workers is that they often seem to have little insight into the social fabric from which civilian strength arises, and are not accustomed to citizens as being co-creators of what should happen in the social arena. This is elaborated further by Van Ewijk in Chapter 3 of this book.

In my first years as a community worker there was no such underestimation of citizens. I got to experience what active and vital citizenship could mean, through the fruitful dialectic that existed between citizens and the government in the development of residential areas as well as in halting developments unwanted by the residents. The training programmes for social work in those days had not yet seen the kind of rampant growth that eventually led to the fragmentation of the field into specialized subject areas and courses, depriving the view of the social function of social work as a whole. When, in the mid-seventies, I became involved as a teacher in a training for social work in the Netherlands, there was still talk of a broader methodological training for social workers throughout the four training years, that involved both the field of social casework as well as that of group work and community work. Although several teachers and students embraced the so-called 'politicizing care' as a new methodology, there was no discussion on the importance of a broad knowledge base for social work. In the fifties, important frontmen of social work in the Netherlands such as Marie Kamphuis en Jo Boer, inspired by developments in, amongst others, the United States, had laid down the solid foundation for this broad knowledge base: social workers must assist people to function adequately in different social roles and relationships, but must be simultaneously active in cultivating these connections themselves. These pioneers had big ambitions for the profession. It led them to the view of a broader-oriented professional who helps people in solving their problems themselves and choosing the right paths. It was obvious that the social worker had to be a professional person-centred worker, but in addition, also a skilled group worker and a person who was active and critical towards the institutions of society. These pioneers were part of a long tradition of such broadly-oriented thinkers in the profession of social work. In this context, it is inspiring to read Maarten van de Linde's contribution, Chapter 5 in this book, on how socially critical the pioneers of social work were in the early nineteenth century.

This wider professional image is being revitalized in a contemporary manner by Hans van Ewijk (2012b). Van Ewijk considers the power and essence of social work as the focus on people's social functioning, improving their social skills. Man is responsible not just for himself, but also as a citizen: 'In the social functioning of individuals and their relationships lies the silent strength of a strong society, and in that domain lies the strength of social work as well,' says Van Ewijk. In taking this position, he mainly reacts against excessive disorder-oriented, therapeutic approaches such as those that became dominant in social work in the eighties.

From the seventies onwards, in the field of social work in the Netherlands, more and more specialized trainings and vocational courses emerged with fewer theoretical and substantive connections between them. In the ideological disruption in the field of professional knowledge of social work, which caught up during the course of the seventies, social casework as an adjustment methodology was put aside, and social work and community work came to stand opposite each other. For community work in particular, this cost dearly. Community development ended up in a climate of political activism and largely disappeared from the social work agenda. A large share of the social workers sought refuge in marital- and family methodologies blown over from America. They became increasingly less involved with community-based activities, thus giving the work an almost clinical therapeutic image that was far-removed from the ideas of the 'originals' from the field. Such a narrowing of the image of social work didn't do the profession much good. It didn't do justice to the multifaceted needs of clients, the intertwining of their tangible and intangible problems. It deprived social workers of opportunities to be more broadly committed and work more in a more educational and community-oriented manner. The more business-related aspects of the work, such as the increasingly complex laws and regulations, were easily given away to newly created professional groups such as socio-legal service providers. In chapter 4 Lia van Doorn shows that this therapeutic approach with its focus on motivated clients with a well-articulated demand for care and an adequate degree of independence, ignored the often complex needs of the more socially vulnerable, who thus remained hidden from the eye of the professional.

This trend did not go unpunished. The clients' criticism of social workers were often centred around the professionals lacking important knowledge and information on the latest developments. With the growing complexity of their lives, the citizens' expectations of social workers changed: not only did social workers need to have strong communication skills, they also needed to possess sufficient business skills. They had to defend the clients' interests, be thoroughly informed on current matters, and be able to adequately refer to other professional if the need should arise. The average citizen began to increasingly realize the complexity of his daily life tasks and all that this requires of him. Richard Sennett relates this to the development of modern capitalism. Modern capitalism in recent years, says Sennet, has changed, weakening the previously predetermined narratives of people's lives. New technologies, global markets, and new bureaucratic organizations deregulate the experience that people have of time and cause erratic changes in their lifestyle. It compels people to shape their own life stories in order to be able to stay in control in an erratic and unpredictable world (Sennet 2010). Van Ewijk (2011b) gives a similar perspective in his inaugural speech where he mentions: the social world, by exponential growth of knowledge and economy, has in a short time become much more complex, leading to the fact that for most people the multiplicity of perspectives and realities has significantly increased, while their social embedment is subject to erosion. This makes it a major challenge for many people to maintain themselves socially and to handle the complexity.

Assertive citizens through the years

This vision of people struggling to be part of the social domain seems somewhat at odds with the image that the world is populated by empowered citizens constantly formulating their own needs for help, where demand-driven institutions then clearly know how to answer these demands. In 2001 Jan Willem Duyvendak, in contrast to the happy world of assertive citizens, rightly elaborated the image of the overburdened citizen, of whom, based on his knowledge and skills, too much is expected. (Duyvendak, 2002). In this view he criticizes the neoliberal political climate which placed the competent citizen on a pedestal. The exaggerated emphasis on this familiarized, autonomous person who knows better what is good for him and who prefers to minimize the involvement of a patronizing government and equally patronizing workers, reflects a development in which citizens, through higher levels of education and access to various sources of information, became more enterprising and often appropriately qualified. Yet this underestimates the complexity of the issues facing those same citizens and deprives the particular view on the position of citizens who do not ask for help and are unable to articulate such requests.

Evelien Tonkens, a professor working with the subject of active citizenship, explains in various publications that the definition of the term 'articulate citizens' has changed significantly over the years (Tonkens, 2009a; Tonkens, 2009b; Hurenkamp & Tonkens, 2011). She places citizenship against the background of developments in politics, economy, and society. After the Second World War, during the construction of the welfare state, the emphasis was implicitly on a kind of passive citizenship: citizens were given new social- and economic rights and facilities. The emphasis was on the care, insurance, and uplifting of citizens. The individual religious 'pillars' ensured the connection of citizens. Social cohesion was further strengthened by the strong family culture, the common task of reconstruction, and the relative scarcity in those years in which almost everyone needed to share. In those years of relative poverty the fear of being mistaken for an antisocial family prevailed. The mothers in large families especially, tried to escape this stigma and remain decent citizens. It was the social workers who were deployed to teach these citizens, the 'anti-socials', the basic skills of living and childcare (Dercksen & Verplanke , 1995).

In the seventies, says Tonkens, the common idea was that citizens who had been given rights and facilities, were also to have control over these. The ideal of the articulate citizen arose, with a right to participate, not only in relation to the government, but also within companies, schools, and care facilities. The power and authority of professionals and other experts were confronted head on. All forms of authority were subjected to criticism and there was the rise of a fervent anti-professionalism.

Around 1980 there emerged a broader criticism on the welfare state and the social sector. The welfare state was construed as too expensive, wasteful, too soft, and too vague. The new ideal was that of a withdrawing government and personal responsibility on the part of citizens. In the professional care and support sector, the emphasis was on making citizens active with regard to employment and social participation for the prevention and elimination of social exclusion. In the years thereafter many areas took to market-driven principles and privatization. The market was deemed as the best means to serve the citizens and make them actively involved. The thinking on the role of citizens was placed in a neo-liberal market framework; propagating the idea of individual, free-choosing citizens. It was considered that policymakers and professionals should not interfere too much with these mature, freely choosing citizens. Only in cases where the freely choosing citizens stood in each other's way (nuisance, lack of safety and crime), was the engagement of professional required. It was in this period, says Tonkens, that the care and support sectors mainly lost their recognisability, because they retreated behind their own front door and fragmented into an increasing number of specialities and functions, coupled with bureaucratic procedures, referral systems, and waiting lists.

In recent years we have entered a new phase. Everything now, says Tonkens, revolves around participation. There is a rediscovery of the social, which has its own dynamics. Politicians and scientists have discovered the importance of people's views on moral and intangible issues. However important employment and income are, policymakers should listen more to the concerns of citizens regarding liveability, safety, and integration and coexistence in multicultural neighbourhoods. The importance of social infrastructure as a base for social participation of citizens has come into view once again. It has been discovered that the lack of a human dimension in the public domain is in itself a major cause of existing social problems (Council on Social Development (RMO), 2001).

It is clear that neither the economy, nor the ideal of the articulate citizen has proved capable enough to adequately resolve social problems. Despite the higher level of welfare, social inequality has increased. The attention for the population of deprived neighbourhoods has turned out to be insufficient in the previous years. The emancipated individual did also not turn out to be social by himself, but often exhibited anti-social and egocentric behaviour. Several monitors show that most citizens are satisfied with their own lives, but dissatisfied with society and their fellow citizens. It is not for nothing that the image of the responsible citizen emerged as the antithesis of the self-centred, consumerist citizen. In recent years citizens are strongly invited by the government to be active. Solution to social problems are considered only together with citizens, and with minimal coercion. It is clear that not only moral and idealistic, but also economic and financial factors are involved here. While the financial scope of the government will be significantly reduced, in a few years the city must spend resources on a much broader spectrum than today; next to welfare and social care, work, income, and participation, also on youth care, youth protection, probation, and youth mental health care, as well as the care for the mentally disabled (De Boer & Van der Lans, 2011). This means that besides providing for the continued availability of professional assistance and services, the quest for what citizens can mean for each other as carers and volunteers in the fields of care, assistance, and support, has to be brought back again in full swing.

1.3 Active citizenship, a brief theoretical exploration

Active citizenship is seen as a cornerstone on which social work can be based. But what exactly do we mean by this concept; how normative and time-bound is it anyway? How critical should social workers be when an appeal is being made for citizenship?

Active citizenship is closely connected with civil society. Civil society refers to all activities of citizens outside the public sector and the market, which not only refers to the existence and operation of non-governmental organizations, but more to the entirety of activities of citizens such as caring for one another, contributing to mutual trust, striving for security in their own environment, commitment as a volunteer, and taking responsibility for administrative functions (also see chapter 9).

Active citizenship is based on three principles: (1) the responsibility of the citizen for his own behaviour and the fulfilment of rights and obligations as a responsible citizen; (2) the existence of human and social rights which citizens can invoke, such as education, work, shelter and health, mobility and accessibility, which entail duties to be fulfilled on the part of citizens in order to be able to continue enjoying these rights; (3) the principle of social responsibility of the citizens for the community, the people around them, and, besides freedom and equality, the forgotten principle of brotherhood (Van Ewijk, 2010a). Social work based upon active citizenship supports the citizens to take responsibility for themselves and their immediate surroundings and fellow citizens.

Political citizenship and social citizenship

While defining citizenship a distinction is usually made between political citizenship and social citizenship. Political citizenship represents forms of political activism, whereby citizens stand up for civil rights and political ideals. In the Netherlands, says Kennedy (2009), political citizenship is rather weakly developed. Throughout most of the twentieth century, the Dutch were encouraged to leave political activism to politicians and administrators. The idea that citizens should be vigilant about possible tyranny by the government is less developed in the Netherlands than in America for example. On the other hand, the Netherlands, with its extensively developed culture over the decades of communal associations and clubs, is quite familiar with the tradition of social citizenship. A study of Tonkens and Hurenkamp (2009) on visions of citizenship shows that amongst the Dutch, social citizenship is more dominant than political citizenship. When it comes to rights and duties, citizens think mainly of duties, especially in the local community: good contact with one's neighbours, helping one's neighbours. For Dutch citizens, good citizenship is, foremost, social participation: helping others, being committed to the neighbourhood, and doing this across ethnical boundaries and not specifically for their own group. Kennedy notes that it is not that the Dutch contribute less to society, but they do so in a different way. In recent decades the number of volunteers has remained stable. Donating time and money however, has gained a more arbitrary character. For many of the Dutch, citizenship is now less a form of life-long commitment to a cause or organization, but more an intense though brief participation in activities or projects. Duyvendak calls this 'mild forms' of social citizenship.

Citizenship is directly related to the degree of connection between citizens. This involves connection with each other, connection with other cultures, connection with the neighbourhood or with the public interest. Sociological research uses terms such as social capital in this context. Social capital consists of networks, trust, and shared norms and values (Putnam, 2000). According to Putnam, social capital is the main engine for collective action in a society. While in most other countries social capital; measured in terms of the club and association memberships and reciprocal relations; has declined sharply, according to researchers, social capital in the Netherlands has, in many ways, remained constant. In the scientific discussion three types of social capital are distinguished: bonding, bridging, and linking. Bonding stands for contacts between people with the same background, who know and recognize each other, where norms of reciprocity and trust are important. Bridging stands for the relationships between different groups of citizens, for example between people with different ethical backgrounds. Linking refers to the relationship between citizens and institutions. Professionals can use both bonding and bridging to help bring socially-marginalized back into mainstream society. Jean Pierre Wilken worked out these elements in the so-called rehabilitation and support approach and sees them as key challenges for social workers (see chapter 10).

The culturalization of citizenship

An interesting point in this context is the impact of globalization on citizenship. From the perspective of globalization, social cohesion is not threatened by the loss of legitimacy of politics or lack of interconnections, but by the lack of a shared identity and loyalty. Citizens come from different countries and recognize very little of each other in the shared environment. People feel insufficiently at home in the area where they live; country, city, or district. Increased citizenship can solve this in the form of culturalization; highlighting similarities and differences between citizens in cultural categories: religion, behaviour, habits, feelings of belonging, and loyalty. Citizens must not only act as citizens, but also (be able to) feel as citizens.

Duyvendak, Tonkens and Hurenkamp (2011) question the consequences of this culturalization of citizenship for the relationships between native Dutch and Muslim immigrants. What happened in a country like the Netherlands, which for years was known as an oasis of tolerance and is apparently no more so? Many studies that they quote, emphasize that tensions between communities are mainly due to the multicultural policy, which as a legacy of religious compartmentalization, for decades awarded group rights to newcomers without asking them to explore their new country's norms and culture.

What became clear from the seventies is that the Netherlands, as one of the most secularized countries in the world, showed little affinity to newly arrived religions like Islam and new religious movements. In the heightened tensions from the nineties, culturalization of citizenship played a major role. The Dutch progressive culture was increasingly portrayed as a product of timeless consensus, which had to be protected against external influences, and to which migrants were increasingly expected to prove their loyalty. Since the sixties, mention Duyvendak et al., the majority of the population in the Netherlands, as in Denmark, developed remarkably uniform progressive ideals. Although studies on Dutch newcomers show that these progressive views are also more common among them than in other (Western) European countries, the value gap between Islamic groups and the majority of the Dutch population is also larger than elsewhere in Europe. The majority of the Dutch population increasingly sees cultural differences as problematic. This polarization contributes to further culturalization of citizenship, which assigns to culture a more central role in the debate on social integration.

Vulnerable citizens

There is, as Duyvendak concluded in 2001, enough reason to subject the appeal to citizenship to a constant critical scrutiny. Conceptions of citizenship reflect the on-going changes in relationships and attitudes in society. Under the influence of social and political developments the concept of citizenship remains in constant motion. Modern citizenship is embedded in a context of globalization, urbanization, and a polarized political and social climate. A striking example is the changing views on the socio-cultural integration of newcomers and government policies relating to integration. They show an entirely different perception and handling of the concept of citizenship than was the case fifteen years earlier (Prins, 2010).

Conceptions of citizenship are inherently prescriptive and can easily derive an ideological connotation. By treating all citizens as the same from a normative perspective, there is the risk of wronging particularly vulnerable citizens. Active citizenship is a discriminatory term when used to assess people through a single frame of reference with no accounting for differences between people. For example, people with disabilities cannot fully participate in society without social support targeted at furthering their abilities, support that the completely valid do not need. This calls for a contextual interpretation of citizenship, attuned to diversity among citizens (Van Ewijk, 2010a).

In the light of these observation, Doortje Kal points out that the policy of socialization, implemented from the eighties onwards, which seeks to re-integrate people with psychiatric problems into society, is undermined by the merging of psychiatry with the medical-biological discourse. Thus the potential integration of people with psychiatric disorders in society is not increased. The policy did not lead to a greater understanding and tolerance for people with a psychiatric background. In chapter 7 Doortje Kal defends the notion that the pursuit of integrating people with a psychiatric background or other 'non-standard citizens' confronts society with conflict, friction, and discomfort. This asks society to be critical of what is seen as 'common', in order to meet that strange other. *Kwartiermaken* [1]for people who are different therefore, focuses on creating a hospitable society with the aim of enabling 'alternative' citizenship.

Vulnerable citizens are a motley cross-section of our society: young people with complex multiple problems, single parents, people on the edge of subsistence, people with debt problems, socially isolated older people, disabled people, certain groups of women from immigrant families, the homeless, people with severe psychiatric problems, low literacy, and more. These people often suffer from a multitude of problems. It is the case for each of them that their situation stands seriously in the way of self-development and social participation. As Lia van Doorn states in chapter 4, vulnerable citizens deserve special attention from both governments as well as other fellow citizens and

---

[1]   See chapter 7, footnote 1 for an explanation of the term *Kwartiermaken.*

social workers. Chances are high that these citizens will be further marginalized because of the reduced level of social services. Research by Machielse and Hortulanus (2011) on socially isolated older people in Rotterdam shows that older people who are structurally isolated, are less likely to come into the picture of regular care. These elderly are often retired, do not ask for help and show care-avoiding behaviour. In order to reach these elderly and to have them reach their full potential, an outreach process is needed, which means that these older people need to be actively traced and contacted. This requires a functional signalling network in which social workers work together with intermediaries such as GPs and home-care workers. Research on improved student counselling for young people with complex multiple problems (Admiraal, Wopereis, 2011) also shows the importance of early detection, and the availability of a nearby professional who works in an outreaching way and has the trust of pupils, parents, and other professionals. By providing timely help this counsellor prevents the youth and the parents from getting lost in the care chain or being caught within it unnecessarily long, making the youth lag behind in their education.

In the mid-nineties, the outreach approach developed from the care and support professions in response to the self-created distance by the care professional from the citizens who needed care and help the most. This *'Eropaf!'* approach also has a long tradition in social work, as Maarten van der Linde shows in chapter 5. The outreach approach has now gained a central place in many social work professions, and for a good reason. The living environment of citizens is often a reference to social problems that are complex. Much of what takes place behind the front door remains hidden from the perception of neighbours and professionals. The offer of care and support is for many citizens opaque, too remote and fragmented. They avoid it. The neighbourhood is not simply a quiet, safe environment where people know each other, and have the courage to talk to each other. Issues in the neighbourhood are the subject of controversy. Often, there is polarization between citizens. Social workers who work in the neighbourhood, cannot avoid the conflicts that divide these citizens. They must have confidence and must be equipped and supported to deal with moral dilemmas (Van Doorn, 2008). Professionals who 'go towards it' (follow the *'Eropaf!'* approach) need support with forming their moral judgements, while dealing with cases that exceed the limits of the permissible, and with the moral dilemmas that they face in interaction with clients.

1.4 Anno 2012: social work and active citizenship

In 2012, the economic and financial crisis has spread widely. There are plenty of cutbacks; the government must withdraw large quantities of previously offered public support, thus necessitating an even bigger role for the citizens, say the authors of the report *Citizen Strength* (De Boer & Van der Lans, 2011). Their estimate is that the crisis is so severe that there will finally be an end to the era in which mainly just lip service was rendered to the role of citizens and the strength of society. The dynamics of modern society requires different behaviour between governments, citizens, professionals, and institutions. The scarcity of public funds is a catalyst in that transformation.

More responsibility is attributed to citizens than they are used to or perhaps can cope with. Modern citizens are often willing to do something for others, but sometimes do not feel capable of it. The many tasks in everyday life that need to be fulfilled consume them. Social workers must understand and empathize with the lifestyle of modern people, which they themselves are anyway. Citizens, more so than in the past, rely on themselves for solving various problems. They are forced to take control themselves over the services they need, over the networks they want to build and maintain. These networks have become very diverse, less location-specific. Modern media plays a major role herein; these are not only of individual interest, but increasingly a significant social and political force.

The amount of initiatives that citizens develop in their own lives or towards their immediate environments, appears to not have reduced in the Netherlands over the years. On the other hand, the problem of, for example, elderly people in social isolation, and people with mental and intellectual disabilities who live independently in residential areas, shows that the mantra of the government to achieve more and more care by the district itself, is still far-removed from what modern citizens see as their task. For social workers a constantly recurring problem is to investigate what the real meaning of the local community is, and what they see as their individual and collective interests. On this basis, citizens can possibly be motivated and encouraged to help others.

The role that social workers fulfil to support citizens is subject to reconsideration due to financial shortage, government withdrawal, and transfer of responsibilities to citizens. The Citizen Strength report by RMO makes clear that something fundamental has gone wrong with the Dutch welfare policy in recent decades when it comes to the position of citizens. Citizens do not always find a platform in existing welfare institutions. Policy processes have become an oppressive clique between welfare organizations and municipalities, states the report. The buying and selling of 'welfare products' has, intentionally or unintentionally, become the essence of welfare. Welfare organizations are like manufacturing facilities, which are mandated by the municipality. The institutional logic of the welfare policies, which entails that the government should determine what is good for the people, is structurally in the way of the ability of citizens to solve problems themselves.

The RMO report calls for more distance between welfare supply and the government. Welfare organizations should, through smart business, try to tap into other financial sources, such as insurance companies, citizens themselves, funds and philanthropists.

Thus the view is: no more welfare supply unless the demand of citizens for this welfare comes first. It advocates 'development companies' that provide a combination of employment and social activities, such as service jobs, cleaning doorways, street surveillance, household care and welfare services at reasonable rates. Local governments would have to play a lesser role in all this. They should instead concentrate on how best to regulate access to their own facilities for those who really need these facilities, and to offer a comprehensive approach for very vulnerable people. In providing access to facilities, the city of Enschede is cited as an example where these counter-like functions are taken care of by so-called district coaches . In caring for the very vulnerable, a territorial approach of integrated social community teams with mandated professionals can regulate the rush for specialists. 'Social frontline teams' can also have the task of stimulating citizens to be more concerned with their vulnerable fellow citizens through social support systems (Giltay Veth, 2011).

Social workers require a contemporary profiling that meets the necessity and the need for innovating the relationships between government, citizens, institutions, and professionals. This new form of social work is complementary and supportive of many initiatives of citizens themselves, like those started in the recent years: buddy and mentoring projects, linking skilled people to social projects, community-based art projects, and forms of neighbourhood mediation (Van Bergen, 2010). In chapter 10 of this book, Jean Pierre Wilken outlines a contemporary profile of the social worker. At this point I restrict myself to some, and in my view, essential elements, that should characterize this new type of social work:

- The venturing out into the world of the citizen and staying less in the system world (Habermas) of organizations.

- Clarifying of and focusing on the demand of citizens, individually or collectively, rather than the supply by professionals or organizations.

- Staying away from bureaucracy and focusing on connecting individuals with other people, connecting people with authorities, and connecting the disadvantaged with the successful.

- Connecting the positive qualities and abilities of people with existing social networks and trying to strengthen and link these.

- Actively daring to approach citizens who have an unsolicited need for support.

- The building of well-functioning networks between informal and formal care.

- Strengthening of competencies that develop citizenship.

This last aspect I want to explain separately. Upbringing and education would have to lay a strong foundation in the development of citizenship skills. Mischa de Winter (2011) provides an inspiring perspective, inter alia in his book *Improve the world, start with parenting* (*Verbeter de wereld, begin bij de opvoeding*). Education and upbringing should be the foundation for what citizens see in later life as their role in relation to fellow citizens. Actively participating in society is seen as a learning process and assumes that it complies with certain conditions. Stroobrants, Calis, Snick and Wildemeersch (2011) name three such conditions: (1) challenge: feeling challenged and encouraged to act, and feeling responsible to commit oneself to something; (2) ability: feeling of having a grip on the challenge and to make a difference, having the knowledge, skills, and experience to achieve something; (3) connectedness: being continuously open to the different / the other, i.e. concrete solidarity with other people, ideas, organizations. For those who want to promote active citizenship it is important, say Stroobrants et. al., not to formulate the challenge in advance, but together with the people whom it concerns, to formulate challenges and connect them with individual challenges, and to treat participants as competent people with their own ideas and experiences. This is consistent with the empowerment concept that Wilken applies in chapter 10 to the care and support professions: good care and support should aim to make people stronger and help them in their coping- and development process. This begins with the recognition of the strengths of the person and focuses on strengthening capabilities. Clients appreciate professionals who have an optimistic view, who provide encouragement and inspiration, says Wilken.

Social workers should see the task of enhancing social skills as an obvious part of their task (Van Eijken, 2005). Social competence is increasingly important in our personalized and polarized society; the absence of it is a problem in the relations between citizens. A large part of the Dutch are inclined to agree with this observation, as shown by many studies. Social competence is not self-evident. People must constantly learn to take responsibility for their own environment. These are personal qualities that need to be developed and need constant maintenance, such as developing self-confidence in addition to confidence in others, the willingness to take responsibility in addition to the willingness to share responsibility, being open about one's own motives as well as being open to those of others, and the ability to influence others besides the ability to being open to other's influence on oneself.

Prins (2010) cites the philosopher Nauta, who mentions three competencies which citizens should have which strengthen social cohesion: (1) identification: the ability to identify with others; (2) representativeness: knowing how you ought to behave in a situation; (3) accountability: taking responsibility for your decisions and your actions. In addition, modern citizens need resilience, says Nauta, the ability to speak for themselves and yet have the ability to question prevailing codes and common habits. As a counterpart, they must also be tolerant, deal with differences, have the ability to admit to something which might be difficult on reasonable grounds, whereby we rely on our capacity for tolerance, precisely when we have difficulty tolerating something.

1.5   What is discussed in this publication

As early as in 2003, professors Wilken and Van Ewijk chose to link knowledge development in the field of social work to broad social issues and tasks. They were inspired by developments in the practical field of social work and in social policy, and also felt the need to bring more substantial coherence to the then severely fragmented field of social professions and related trainings.

In 2003 Van Ewijk distinguished the following three social tasks: (1) educating the public; a task for society to ensure that children and young people can grow up in a stimulating environment; (2) care and support for vulnerable citizens; (3) care for social cohesion, a reasonable quality of life and social relations. Over the years new research areas opened up, such as in the field of legal assistance, new labour relations, participation of youth and vulnerable citizens, and dealing with debt problems.

In the following chapters, a number of these topics from these research areas are thematically discussed. They give a good overview of the work that the professors and their staff carry out within the Research Centre for Social Innovation.

In chapter 2, Hans van Ewijk, professor Social Policy, Innovation and Professional Development and professor of Foundations of Social Work at the University of Humanistic Studies, argues that the essence of social work lies in promoting people's social functioning. Every citizen needs to be self-reliant and responsible, but also needs to be given the chance to do so. Herein social workers provide a supporting and guiding role. In the positioning of social work, Van Ewijk reacts against approaches that are too focused on target groups or disorders, against the dubious organization of care and support, which have made the Netherlands a country of institutions par excellence, and against the dramatic growth of specialized care, such as youth care, mental care, etc. Instead he pleads for a social worker, who takes the possibilities and capabilities of the individual as the starting point, and uses and strengthens the social networks of people to help them deal with complex life challenges that they encounter.

In chapter 3, Hans van Ewijk first examines the misfits that have led to the process of de-institutionalization in the Netherlands. The Netherlands is a country of institutions par excellence. In contrast to other countries, de-institutionalization rarely started at the demand-end of the care process, ensuring that people remain in their own environment by creating a coordinated local structure of mild to intensive care. In recent years, the research group Social Policy, Innovation and Professional Development, which he led, carried out several studies on the possibilities of bringing about such a structure, by means of the interplay between the public and professionals at the local level. These topics and reflections on the related experiences thus form the main theme of his contribution.

In chapter 4, Lia van Doorn, professor Innovative Social Services, argues that social work should pay more attention to people with complex problems. Current societal developments compel social workers to engage more with vulnerable citizens with complex problems, based on the expectation that the client base of social work will radically change in the near future, and will increasingly consist of people with complex problems, with a small support network and limited financial resources. Chapter 4 also shows in what way the research group Innovative Social Service Provision contributes to this through research and training of professionals.

In chapter 5, Maarten van der Linde, professor History of Social Work, shows that the so-called outreach- or *'Eropaf!'* approach, which was (re)discovered by the end of the twentieth century as being part of the core business of the broad field of social work, is part of a centuries old tradition. He illustrates clearly what was driving pioneers of social work from the early nineteenth century onwards, such as Elizabeth Frey, Thomas Chalmers, Daniel von der Heydt, Octavia Hill and Johanna ter Meulen, how they shaped their work in various fields, what they achieved, how they used it to inspire others and by which ideals and values they were motivated.

In chapter 6, Anneke Menger and Jo Hermanns, professors Working With Mandated Clients, treat the topic of reducing recidivism among offenders who return to society after a prison sentence. The relapse rate is high (70%). The authors show that behavioural intervention based on 'What Works' principles only limitedly help to reduce recidivism. Its success will significantly increase when behavioural interventions take place within a real life context. The combination of this behavioural intervention with a more social-ecological approach: the wraparound care approach, provides better prospects because of its effective, individualized and multi-system procedure.

In chapter 7, Doortje Kal, professor *Kwartiermaken*, discusses this concept of *Kwartiermaken*: creating space for the otherness of people with disabilities. Disintegration of social life can lead to rigid boundaries between insiders and outsiders Doortje Kal introduces *kwartiermaken* as a practice which seeks to influence social contexts of intentional and unintentional exclusion by working on hospitality for otherness. This otherness, which is associated with friction and discomfort, asks the community to be critical of their concept of the common in order to reach out to that foreign other. *Kwartiermaken* therefore focuses on the hospitality of society with the purpose of 'alternative' citizenship.

In chapter 8, Stijn Verhagen, professor Participation and Social Development, addresses the issue of promoting inter-ethnic relations by strengthening social networks. He illustrates this with the case 'Connecting through football', a project in the *Rivierenwijk* district of Utrecht, that worked on several goals: to promote respectful behaviour, to encourage volunteering and to promote inter-ethnic contacts. In the view of Verhagen, the role of new social professional extends beyond strengthening the social network of people who need support. People without the need for support also have an interest in vital social environments.

In chapter 9, Rob Gründemann and Ben Fruytier, professors Organizational Configurations and Work Relations, give a detailed analysis of the social participation of the lower-educated in the Netherlands. The socio-economic situation of the lower-educated remains structurally less developed than that of the medium- and higher-educated. The chapter looks at labour market opportunities, position within the workplace, and health and living situation. The chapter concludes with a discussion of the proposed programme 'Working and learning in the neighbourhood' (*Werken en leren in de wijk*), in which this research group works in collaboration with professors of the Research Centre for Social Innovation and the Research Centre for Education, and together with residents of two disadvantaged neighbourhoods in Amersfoort and Utrecht.

Chapter 10 attempts to outline a contemporary profile of the social worker, based on supporting active citizenship. Jean Pierre Wilken, professor Participation, Care and Support, outlines the body of knowledge related to the goals and tasks of social workers (as outlined by Van Ewijk), aimed at promoting independence, social participation, and social cohesion. Jean Pierre Wilken elaborates on three dimensions being typical of the professional actions of the social worker: (1) the relational dimension: the ability to use the relationship as a vehicle of change; (2) the contextual dimension: the ability to work in different contexts, switch between them, and the ability to make connections, and (3) the normative-reflective dimension: the ability for ethical and theoretical reflection.

In the concluding chapter 11, Harrie Staatsen, former professor and educational developer at the Faculty of Society & Law, describes what, according to him, is the core task of social work, in what way social work is constructed, and its significance in the light of the normative imperative of active citizenship. He ends his contribution with a brief sketch of the learning tasks on which, according to him, the training of social workers should be based.

Bibliography

Admiraal, L., Wopereis, (2011). *Geen Kind over Boord! A study into care arrangements for overburdened children and young people in the framework of the Regional Innovation Programme 'Regional Youth Center'. Final Report.* Utrecht: Utrecht University.

Bergen, A. van (2010). *De nieuwe professional.* Utrecht: Movisie.

Boer, N. de & Lans, J.van der (201:). *Burgerkracht.* The future of social work in the Netherlands. Den Haag: Council for Social Development

Dercksen, A. & Verplanke, L. (1995). *Geschiedenis van de onmaatschappelijkheids-bestrijding.* Amsterdam: Arbeiderspers.

Duyvendak, J.W. (2002). *Maatschappelijk (opbouw)werk, de actualiteit van Marie Kamphuis en Jo Boer.* Marie Kamphuis Lecture 2001. Bohn Stafleu.

Duyvendak, J.W., Tonkens, E. & Hurenkamp, M. (2011). Globalisering en culturalisering. In M. Hurenkamp & E. Tonkens, *De onbeholpen samenleving, burgerschap aan het begin van de 21ste eeuw.* Amsterdam: Amsterdam University Press.

Doorn, L. van (2008). *Sociale professionals en morele oordeelsvorming. Public class* Innovative Research Group social services.

Doorn, L. van (2009). *Dringen achter de voordeur, Outreachend werken in de wijk.* In E Tonkens, *Tussen onderschatten en overvragen, actief burgerschap en activerende organisaties in de wijk.* SUN Trancity - the city district Studies

Eijken, J. van (2005). Social Work education and training at the Hogeschool Utrecht. In J. van Eijken & H. van Ewijk, *Re-inventing Social Work.* Utrecht: Hogeschool Utrecht.

Ewijk, H. van (2003). *Redelijke sociale verhoudingen, redelijk sociaal gedrag. Public class research group Social policy, innovation and professional development.* Utrecht: Hogeschool Utrecht.

Ewijk, H. van (2010a). *European Social Policy and Social Work.* Londen: Routledge.

Ewijk, H. van (2010b). *Maatschappelijk werk in een sociaal gevoelige tijd.* Oration Universiteit voor Humanistiek. Amsterdam: SWP.

Giltay Veth, D. (2011). DGV Holding. In N. de Boer & J. van der Lans, *Burgerkracht, de toekomst van het sociaal werk in Nederland.* Den Haag: Council for Social Development.

Hurenkamp, M. & Tonkens, E. (2011). *De onbeholpen samenleving, burgerschap aan het begin van de 21e eeuw.* Amsterdam: Amsterdam University Press.

Kal, D. (2011). *Kwartiermaken. Werken aan ruimte voor anders zijn.* Public lecture. Utrecht: Hogeschool Utrecht.

Kennedy, J. (2009). Actief burgerschap in Nederland, overpeinzingen van een Amerikaan. In E. Tonkens, *Tussen onderschatten en overvragen, actief burgerschap en activerende organisaties in de wijk.* SUN Trancity - City District Studies.

Lans. J. van der (2010). *Eropaf! De nieuwe start van het sociaal werk.* Amsterdam: Augustus.

Machielse, A. & Hortulanus, R. (2011). *Sociaal isolement bij ouderen, op weg naar een Rotterdamse aanpak.* Amsterdam: SWP.

Prins, B. (2010). *Vreemdelingenverkeer, samen leven en laten leven.* Inaugural lecture professor Citizenship and diversity.den Haag: Haagse Hogeschool.

Putman, R (2000) Bowling alone: The collapse and revival of American Society, New York, Simon and Schuster

Council for Social Development. (2001). *Instituties in lijn met het moderne individu.* Den Haag: Council for Social Development.

Rigter, J. (2004). Kleine burgers, grote burgers, actief burgerschap als leerdoel in het onderwijs. In R. Diekstra, M. van de Berg & J. Rigter (red.), *Waardenvolle of waardenloze samenleving.* Uithoorn, Kraker publishers eg

Sennett, R. (2010). *De mens als werk in uitvoering.* Spinozalecture. Boom.

Steijaert, J. et al. (2005). *Actief Burgerschap.* Fontys Hogescholen.

Stroobrants, V., Calis, R., Snick, A. & Wildemeersch, D. (2001). Actief burgerschap, een leerproces. *Sociale Interventie,* 4, Citizenship theme issue.

Tonkens, E. (2009a). Uitsluiting en afzijdigheid. In E. Tonkens, *Tussen onderschatten en overvragen, actief burgerschap en activerende organisaties in de wijk.* SUN Trancity – City District Studies.

Tonkens, E. (2009b). *Mondige burgers, getemde professionals(revised edition).* Amsterdam: Van Gennep.

Verhagen, S. (2008). *Participatie en maatschappelijke ontwikkeling.* Public lecture professor Participation and social development. Utrecht: Hogeschool Utrecht.

Wilken, J.P. (2002). *Tussen illusie en werkelijkheid, over de maakbaarheid van de maatschappelijke reïntegratie.* Public lecture professor Social reintegration en community support. Utrecht: Hogeschool Utrecht.

Wilken, J.P. (2010). *Recovering care, a contribution to a theory and practice of good care.* Utrecht: SWP.

Winter, M. de (2011). *Verbeter de wereld, begin bij de opvoeding, vanachter de voordeur naar democratie en verbinding.* Amsterdam: SWP.

2.   Social work in socially sensitive times[2]

Hans van Ewijk

In the social domain you cannot take refuge in your own esoteric field of expertise, as doctors, lawyers, and engineers can do. You are accountable to your peers and your superiors. It remains to be seen whether the social worker knows better than the client.

The justification of social work is highly dependent on the recognition and acknowledgement by the client, financier and society. I would like to take you along on a quest for the essence of the social domain and social work, and in particular of case work. I will argue that these are socially sensitive times, difficult for the socially inept, and that the core of social work is not in combating social deprivation or remedying disorders, but supporting people in their social functioning.

2.1   From a state of progress to a state of complexity

25% of the Dutch population is facing severe problems in daily functioning. Approximately one million of them apply to secondary mental health care. Another million turn to their general practitioner, social work, and primary mental health services (GGZ, 2009). 14% of our young people are referred to some form of assessment care or special education (Hermanns, 2009). Most users of these provisions have socio-psychological problems; we cannot simply attribute this large appeal to psycho-social care to an aggressive market for well-being and happiness, or to pampering vulnerable citizens. I will argue that we are dealing with the transition from a state of progress to a state of complexity, resulting in increasing social sensitivity and vulnerability.

Until approximately the 1970s, the western welfare state could be described as a state of progress, and western thinking in general as a thinking in terms progress. Even two world wars did not deflect the western man from the notion that the future would bring a better world. This belief was based on the effects

of modern science and technological innovation. The progressing state wanted to combat poverty, illiteracy, and barbarism; and built its systems of education, health care, public housing, labour market, and social security (Beveridge 1942). A healthy economy and a strong (care and)

---

[2]   I use 'social work' as the umbrella of the different social work professions. Referring to specific social work 'social case work' is used.

welfare state would produce prosperity, well-being, and cohesion, precisely in that order. The underlying idea was: once the state is well organized, social cohesion and social well-being will follow naturally. When I began working as Extraordinary Professor in Tartu, Estonia, I realized that in the Soviet Union, to which Estonia belonged until 1991, there was no social work because social problems simply could not exist in the communist state. Social work, developed in the 1920s, was abolished after the annexation by the Soviet Union in 1945, and was not reintroduced until the 1990s (Kiik 2006). But the European Union as well, repeatedly stated that social cohesion will be a result of a competitive knowledge economy, and as such does not require a lot of attention (EC 2004, 2010). However, this assumption is an illusion. A highly developed society in particular, requires the most of people in order to maintain itself socially.

The old social quest of overcoming poverty, illiteracy, and barbarism, which resulted in the cultural offensive, is now changing into the postmodern social issue of people's (dys)functioning in an increasingly complex context. Looking back, I feel the 1960s and 1970s were an era in which we tried to enforce radical progress, while we were actually already on a stepping stone towards complexity. In retrospect, these years were ringing out the progress state. Ever since, we have been managing complexity.

One of the greatest complexity philosophers of our day is Edgar Morin. Morin links new knowledge and insights from natural science, biology, and the social sciences. His proposition is that modern science is attempting to unfold complexity by reduction, a search for one single cause, one law that applies to everything, to the functioning of parts instead of the whole. Nowadays, this rational, empirical approach runs the risk of getting stuck or even ending in catastrophe because we have lost our grip on the whole and the cohesion. We have tried to explain man and the universe in parts, studying them separately, and we have gained a lot, but it provided little insight into man as a self-organizing being, or, in the words of Morin, an eco-organizing being. By this he means that man produces himself in interaction with his surroundings. This self-organizing and producing being, that each one of us is as a human being, is an extremely complex phenomenon. In our brains alone, six billion cells work together to keep things going. We resemble complex machines, like computers, but we are living machines that develop themselves. Morin almost regrets that our brains are located inside a skull and can communicate by means of merely five senses. Only if we recognize and attempt to understand the complexity of the universe, man and his world, can we prevent reductionism from becoming overpowering and devastating (Morin 2008).

To me, thinking and acting on the basis of complexity seems a fruitful approach in the social domain. Our social world, with its exponential growth of knowledge and economy, has become much more complex in a short span of time. More knowledge and prosperity result in more differentiation in occupations, in institutions, in information, and in opportunities. We are able to do more, we know more, we are allowed more, we are obliged to do more, and we definitely want to decide for ourselves. At the same time, we do this in a world with an open horizon (Taylor 1989). The progressing state had a certain direction, a road to follow. It could have been communist, fascist, corporatist or social-democratic, but everyone had a sense of direction linked to great values such as equality or freedom. The battle was about the right direction, not about the question, if there was one at all. At school I was taught that as a Christian two roads were open to you: the broad road with a McDonalds on every corner, and the narrow road with health food shops. In my village we were very much in favour of the narrow road, but we mainly walked the broad one. These days, roads turn every other way, somewhere and nowhere, towards a something and nothing. Our days have no marked paths, we no longer know where progress is - in which direction we can find "it" and/or what "it" actually is? From a faith in progress, we ended up in a world of complexity, in which the management of this complexity takes up all our attention. Instead of a battle between major value systems and a struggle for the right direction, we must cooperate in a world with multiple values and more uncertainties. Instead of the former "either, or", we ended up in the days of "and, and" and the popular "win, win" (Seligman 2003). Not only do we lack direction, we are also at risk of losing a common context within which to position ourselves. World religions and political ideologies in all their diversity, had many similar structures and a mutually recognizable language. In the state of complexity there is a Babylonian confusion, a multitude of perspectives, constructions, and realities, in which it is difficult to identify recognizable structures. Finally, our social embedding too is being eroded. Man has freed himself from the clear, familiar multifunctional living communities such as the village and smaller town, the classes and the guilds. We have become residents of 'communities', each with its own composition, purpose or function. The individual himself must make the connection and adapt continuously to these different and changing relations. We divorce, we move house, we change our jobs, and if we do not change our jobs, the jobs themselves change. Citizens, politicians, business, and science have their hands full, managing complexity. It is opportunism rather than mission, however grand the mission statements of governments, universities, and business corporations may be. Complexity has entered our social worlds, it is in our living rooms, classrooms, on the job, united and divided. Keeping together a family, a department, class at school, or a group of friends, requires a great deal of expertise. The increasing complexity of postmodern society is also reflected in our hesitant and searching inner selves. Hence my argument that the old social issue of combating poverty has been moved aside by the social issue of finding direction and getting a grip on social complexity. We responded to the old social issue by building robust national systems with equal opportunities and equal treatment for everybody. The new social issue cannot be solved by systems or equality principles. On the contrary, maintaining oneself socially and being able to handle complexity is situational and context-bound. It is tailor-made instead of ready to wear, or in the words of the predecessor to my post Geert van der Laan (2006): We must know how to act in concrete and unique cases. Everyday complexity requires of postmodern man, great skills to provide a profile for himself and find a position in society. This is mainly a social skill, the art of dealing with yourself and your environment in such a way that you are seen, recognized and acknowledged. Decisive for your own future and position, is the ability to relate to others correctly and the opportunism to avail yourself of your options and opportunities in society. Social skills, so highly valued these days, have thereby become a ground for exclusion at the same time. This excluding effect can be illustrated painfully by the position of people with an autistic disorder. National research shows that of this group only 10% have a regular job (Health Council 2009). The Health Council believes that many more people with autism should be able to have regular jobs. They state that, 'the most often mentioned impediment to a successful job was the inability to meet the social requirements of the job.'(2009). By the way, they might have concluded that the job was insufficiently capable of adapting to the employees' idiosyncrasies. Therefore inadequate social functioning is the main ground for the exclusion of this group. Presumably, autistic people had fewer problems in the past because in many jobs, professional skills were rated higher than social skills. Furthermore, social ineptitude of people in higher positions was simply taken in one's stride. Another example is the increase of problem behaviour among young people with learning disabilities (CBZ 2004). This increase has everything to do with a society that no longer unambiguously attributes positions and roles to people within a familiar community, as used to be the case with mentally handicapped people in a village. In addition, the village had clear social control and social correction. In the state of complexity, a person has to reassign a role and position to himself over and over again. To a certain extent lacking the social skills of self-representation is now a ground for exclusion more than ever before. In the early history of our society, man's position and prospects were mainly determined by birth. You became what your father had been, you did what your mother did, and you lived where your parents lived, you were buried at the same cemetery as your relatives. In early industrial society, financial capital was the leverage that dethroned the aristocracy of old and crowned Marx and Adam Smith. Education became the main determinant of social success. In our postmodern days, social capital counts heavily (Putnam 1993, 2000). Every job profile and education profile puts communicative and social skills first, whether your aim is to be a surgeon, plumber, lawyer, or nurse. Almost 70% of the Dutch population works in a team every day (Kyzlinková et al. 2007), and contemporary education employs teaching in small groups. We expect our employees, children, and friends to be flexible, enjoy nothing more than social activities, and behave in a socially acceptable manner. Perhaps there may be a latent resistance against this social dominance, resulting in a kind of social hypochondria (Schinkel 2007) and right-wing populism.

This so far is my argument on the shift from progress philosophy to being able to handle complexity. It is not the perspective of a better world that drives us, but the struggle to be able to handle complexity. I will now move on to part two of my argument, on the persistent striving for disconnection and its effects on social work.

2.2   The persistent striving for disconnection

Let me begin by once more presenting some figures to you. During the past decade mental health care, youth care, schools for children with severe behavioural problems, the income regulation for disabled young people, and care for young people with learning disabilities have increased by 10% on average in the Netherlands, meaning they have doubled in ten years time (Kwartel 2010, FCB 2009 a,b, CBS 2010, UWV 2010). It is also remarkable that the Netherlands is preeminently a nation of institutes. In Europe we rank in the top ten amongst the charts of hospital beds in mental health care (WHO 2010) and children in special education (CBS 2010). More mentally-handicapped people have been placed in an institution in the Netherlands than in the UK and Scandinavia together (RMO 2003). With regard to the prison system, the Netherlands was at the bottom in Western Europe in the seventies; now it stands at second position (Eurostat 2010a,b). The number of people in detention has even multiplied tenfold in this same span of time. We are seeing a dramatic increase in expensive specialized care that can be attributed entirely to those unable to behave or maintain themselves socially (Hermanns 2009, CPB 2007). During the same time period, the deployment of street-level social workers remained more or less stable or even decreased slightly, and this in the age of localization and the Social Support Act (FCB 2009c). Policy and fact are rather far apart. How can this increase in expensive specialized care be explained and interpreted? Let me take you along on the path of my second argument on the persistent inclination to disconnect.

The success of the state of progress was partly due to the ability of the knowledge industry to divide labour processes into separate actions, and to specialize these separate actions further and make them more effective (Schön 1983, Morin 2008, Polyani 2009). Thus, numerous subdisciplines were created in which the specialists knew a great deal about very little, and precisely these extremely learned men received the most respect. The general practitioner bowed to the specialist, the internist to the specialist on one particular body part, the body part specialist to the specialist on a part of the body part, and they all bowed to those who knew everything about cells and genes (freely rendered from Schön). Social work, too, has been affected by this disconnection. A fine fabric of provisions, professions, and legislature have been developed. We have torn asunder practice, diagnosis, and management, and in the past few decades, social work and mental health care have been extensively subdivided into products and projects that can be paid for and planned per item. However, it still remains to be seen if social work is suited to being subdivided, and if disconnection increases the quality of the job. Elsewhere I have termed this inclination towards subdivision and disconnection in tasks and time units, 'organized discontinuity' (Van Ewijk 2007). I will now present to you two dominant processes of reductionism or disconnection, i.e. thinking on the basis of deprivation, and thinking on the basis of disorders. These disconnections have greatly influenced the position of social work.

The deprivation approach is linked to the fight against poverty, illiteracy, and barbarism of the 19th and 20th century. The national systems of education, health care, public housing, labour market, and social security, were tested for their accessibility and their contribution to a productive and egalitarian society. This resulted in a disconnection with general policy and a move towards a specific target group policy for each time a group would be disadvantaged. It started with the working classes and women, but was soon followed by the non-working classes, children, the disabled, young people, older people, people with mental problems, new migrants, original migrants, returners to the job market, homosexuals, former delinquents, and numerous further specializations. Only the highly-educated heterosexual white male between 27 and 55 years of age was never a target group, and so always had been better off. All these groups were deprived in some respect and were given their own policy and preferably their own ministerial department, laws, and provisions. The target groups also organized themselves and formed liberation movements. The public and the private sector thus, largely organized themselves along lines of target groups or deprived groups. Social work provided material and immaterial support and allied itself with the fight against deprivation, particularly to the various liberation movements. By raising awareness and promoting self-organization, the systems and society were confronted. This movement in our line of work can be identified under such appealing names as 'critical social work' and 'anti-oppressive practice' (Dominelli 2002), and the effort for social justice; a difficult task, and one beyond the strength of social work, needlessly throwing it into the political arena. Combating social disadvantages and social inequality is possible by means of education and employment mainly, and in the political arena. I hold the opinion that social workers had better stay out of it.

The disorder approach, on the other hand, is driven by the inclination to identify disorders, diseases, and handicaps in people, diagnose them and treat them, preferably through evidence-based protocols. The diagnosed disorder leads the conceptualization of what the problem is and what must be done about it. Often, those who are diagnosed take over the label and unite in organizations of the chronically ill, patients, and disabled persons in their many-hued variations. And so, here too we see the creation of a configuration of interest groups, managerial departments, and specific legislation that magnify the original handicaps and disorders in their own policy areas, client organizations, and door-to-door collections. The remedy focuses on the treatment of the severe disorders, and results in overconcentrating on the disorder itself, and through this in reduction. We might even call this a triple reduction or disconnection. We remove the individuals from their immediate surroundings to the surgery or institution, where within the individual we isolate the disorder, and we further tackle the disorder with a protocol treatment in which tight methods determine the interaction between individual and professional. In the sixties and seventies this social-medical perspective became predominant in social work (casework), that developed into a more therapeutic approach and tried to settle itself among the para-medical professions, for example by intended registration in the BIG Act[3] (van der Laan 1999). In this 'cure'-oriented approach, social work does not have much to gain or find. Where disease, disability, and disorder treatments are at stake, physicians and psychologists are the indicated professionals.

The strength and essence of social work, I feel, does not lie in combating deprivation or curing disorders, but in focusing on the social functioning of people, or the promotion of social independence. It is the task of the modern man to function in everyday life and in relation to others in such a way that life stays reasonably manageable. We know that mobility, participation, and social contacts help to lower the appeal to medical care, make it easier to find jobs, provide fewer conflicts, and even stimulate progress (Putnam 1983, 2000). In the social functioning of individuals and their relations lies the silent strength of a strong society, and it is in this very domain that the strength of social work is situated. Thus social work is in the middle of the state of complexity. A competent social worker recognizes both the complexity as a whole and its separate components, without disconnecting these components from the complexity. In many diagnoses we observe the assessment of how the person is doing in various areas of life, and in which areas help is needed. There are participation ladders by means of which we measure the extent to which people are active in the social environment. There are instruments to check the resilience, coping strength, burden, and, of course, social case workers and other social workers must have insight into and knowledge of disorders, disadvantages, cultural backgrounds, and their impact on individuals and their surroundings. However, it is characteristic that in social functioning we look at reality from different perspectives and unravel the problem without disconnecting the various areas of life. Social work is based on the individual as a self-organizing and self-producing being. All individuals, in spite of disorders or disadvantages, mainly form themselves in continuous interaction with their surroundings. It all happens inside the individual's head, but all these heads combined must somehow manage together. Until now I have

---

[3]   As a quality control measure, the BIG Act (Professions in Individual Healthcare Act) requires all individual health care professionals to register.

primarily described social functioning as the ability to position oneself with regard to others, and to relate in a way that manages complexity. More substantially, and intrinsically, we can link social functioning to social or active citizenship. The European Union and its separate member states are aiming for citizens that are personally responsible and co-responsible (Chanan 1997). In its simplicity, this is a strong foundation for postmodern society. Personal responsibility is not the same as sheer individualism or just looking out for one's self alone (Kunneman 2009). It emphasizes taking responsibility for one's personal life, employment, and behaviour. The individual as a personally responsible citizen is a counterbalance against the individual who is after his/her personal gain only. Co-responsibility presupposes that the citizen is not just responsible for his immediate environment, family, colleagues, and network of friends, but also for his physical and economic environment. Here we can observe a counterbalance against highly collectivistic systems in which the state takes over any co-responsibility. I will make three comments on this notion of citizenship – a notion that appeals to me. The first is that citizenship presupposes a decent care and welfare state with accessible systems. The second is that personal responsibility and co-responsibility should always be accompanied by the particular individual's capability. This we call relative citizenship, that extends beyond the notion of the standard individual (Lister 2007). My third comment is that citizenship also comprises relational citizenship (Lawy and Biesta 2006). Citizenship is not merely a personal task, but will only work if and when the society and government put in an effort on behalf of their citizens (van Ewijk 2010).

As a round up to the argument I have presented above, let me, in another way, present to you people who have difficulties in our society, sometimes to such an extent that stepping in or supporting them becomes inevitable.

The wanderer. In almost every family or circle of friends there are people who have trouble meeting the demands of daily life. They seem to be without direction, drive, and motivation, and appear to let life take its course. Perhaps they are neither able, nor willing to take on the pressure of everyday complexity and continuous expectations, which is for family and friends, often nerve-wrecking.

The one who is stuck. It can happen to just about anybody that they get stuck in a pattern they are unable to get out of. We all recognize this in our mutual relationships as partners, parents, or children. The relationship is in a rut somehow or the other, and the need to change things is strong, while at the same time is very painful to do so. Sometimes, set patterns can be overpowering, and oppressive even. This may be the case for a young person in a criminal gang, a couple permanently at war, a parent and child between whom relations are paralyzed, a neighbourhood that holds its residents in an iron grip, an addiction, or severe debt problems.

The ignored one. In the demand-oriented approach, the client can choose if and how to participate. However, many vulnerable people are afraid to get out of their lodgings or homes, because they are ashamed or feel shame in the presence of other residents. Older people get lonely in nursing homes. We know that many people with a mental handicap or disorder may have relatives, and sometimes see professionals, but are without friends.

The abused one. Every day the fear of being bullied, beaten, abused at home, on the job, or in the streets. We know that abuse is often kept silent, by victim and offender alike. Social work often deals with people seeking protection against abuse.

The derailed one. In contrast to the abused one, is the one who 'abuses', someone who is addicted to criminal behaviour; people of whom we cannot understand that they seem so totally without conscience, so hard on others and themselves. Social work encounters such persons too, and must play its part when confronted with them.

These five examples are not intended to create more categories. I show these types to illustrate that a great many questions on human functioning are not primarily about deprivation policy or treating disorders, although these may play a part. If you talk to a case worker or general practitioner, very soon you will encounter a broad range of people and problems where the case is not about mobility and disorders, but about people who are stuck; temporarily or permanently, the problem is in social dysfunctioning.

It is this very social dysfunctioning that is the problem of our times. It is a fact that more and more people are increasingly having trouble maintaining themselves socially. The question is, how do we respond to this, what support are we providing? Who is going to do what, why, when, and how? When do we decide that it is the individual's own business, and when do we feel that the family should solve things, and when does the situation become untenable, requiring professionals? A question that we seem to be unable to cope with in our society, resulting in widespread failure through impotence, ignorance, and divided structures. So much so that in fact, the complexity in which the client finds himself is increased by the very complexity of the support system.

Up to now I have argued that we find ourselves in a state of complexity, and in socially sensitive times that have shifted the social issue to people's social functioning in everyday environment. Then I demonstrated that the tendency of reduction or disconnection had quite devastating results in the social domain. I would advocate that we take complexity as the point of departure, and focus on connection as opposed to disconnection. Having said this, it is time to move on to the third and final part of my argument on the role and position of social work.

2.3 The positioning of social work

Where does social work stand right now? The latest elaborate Dutch professional profile describes the mission of social work as 'promoting that people are given their due, as human beings and as citizens', and further on, that 'people can develop to the best of their ability in interaction with their social environment' (NVMW 2006). In this respect the profile is very ambitious, too ambitious. Development and giving people their due, I would sooner define as government goals. The previous profile, from 1987, had the more modest formulation goal: 'to improve social functioning between individuals and their social environment' (NVMW 1987). This is closer to the core of my argument. If possible, I would like to be even more modest and observe that, often, social workers are mainly trying to make sure that things are not getting out of hand, that some degree of stability is reached, complexity is managed to a certain extent, and that worse things are prevented. I already described social functioning in the general sense. It is time to be little more precise and see what social workers are aiming for and have to offer. I like to use the keywords 'activating' and 'embedding' in this respect. Activating is the effort to help people get back to work, back to school, back to being there for their families, their friends and their surroundings, and also for themselves. When people are active, they make less of an appeal to expensive provisions, find jobs sooner, feel better. With regard to activation, we might also say that the social worker helps people find their bearings, to break through set patterns, to solve material and immaterial problems, helps to bring people together, to protect them, and to set them right. Activation, by any definition, is a frequently recurring concept in the history of social work, and very popular in contemporary politics. However, I would also like to call attention to embedding as an essential condition to keep up activation.

Embedment attempts to get the immediate environment to function in such a way that it becomes easier for a person to function socially, for example, adapting the workplace, the family, the classroom, the nursing home, the neighbourhood to an individual's characteristics. Embedding can be supported by a professional social infrastructure in the vicinity. I would like to elaborate three basic skills in the profession of social work in this regard. The first is that of assessing what is the matter, or the art of 'problem setting' (Schön 1983). If you define the problem incorrectly, the approach is not going to work either. This may seem obvious, but it actually is one of the most difficult things in professions in which complexity is the main issue. Where in this complexity, that I am facing as a professional, are the difficulties and opportunities situated? Which areas of life are hardest to handle? To what extent are disorders, handicaps, disadvantages, and cultural backgrounds an issue? How much resilience and coping strength does the person have, and what is the burden to his immediate surroundings, the family, colleagues, teachers? Is the problem a lack of direction and motivation, set patterns, being abandoned, drastic violations of personal existence, or of being derailed? What would be the best starting point at present, and is the time ripe for a breakthrough, or would it be best not to force anything just now? The next question is, in the apt terms of Regenmortel, adequate response (2008). A I phrase it: How can I get things to run as best as possible with a minimum of professional time? The question is, whose turn is it to do what at this moment and why? Therefore adequate response must be followed by adequate mobilization. How can I, as a professional, mobilize others to activate and to embed? For professionals are nothing more than extensions and tools.

It is now time for me to introduce my law, I will call it Van Ewijk's law, for want of a better term. It is a variation of Baumol's law and states that professions that benefit less from mechanization and technology are getting more expensive proportionately. Labour productivity per hour in social professions seems to increase at a much smaller rate than in the nearly fully-automated car industry or banking. It is my hypothesis, by way of correction and variation on this law, that in social work, labour productivity increases considerably when and where the professional activates the client and the surroundings. Let me expand on this. In specialized care, ranging from mental health care to youth care, from the prison system to institutionalized care for the disabled, for every client two to three professionals are employed, and only limited use is made of volunteers, relatives, and friends. On the other hand, a social worker usually cooperates with dozens of volunteers, and makes an effort to mobilize family, friends, and colleagues. If we disconnect less and connect more, this will have a positive net result, both in the economic sense and in the context of human relations. Investing in primary care social workers and de-investing in specialized care is – in my view- a cost-effective and socially rewarding operation. The most difficult thing is the funding system of the social sector. Specialized care is partly realized through insurances and partly through the national or provincial authorities. Primary care social work –welfare work, social care, case work- is the concern of the municipalities. A municipality that invests in social functioning may be less of a burden to the national system, but does not benefit itself, rather, such an investment will cost the municipality considerably more money. A second obstacle is the diffuse image of the local social worker, of who there are so many very different kinds. In addition to this, the main need is for experienced and well-trained generalists and few local social workers meet this profile. A third obstacle is that numerous provisions, institutions, and professionals are kept up by other laws and funds, largely due to the disconnection I mentioned earlier. In that sense it is time to really turn things round and to reassess, define, and place the basic social professional at the centre. This professional can be compared to the old-fashioned general practitioner, vicar, and headmaster, who knew the people in their village or town, visited them at regular intervals, and were always approachable. However, these professionals have retreated to the health centre, the comprehensive school system, or restrict themselves to their ever-decreasing flock. Much can be said for having, at the very least, one basic professional in the social domain who knows the neighbourhood and its people and is known himself. Recent Swedish research showed the need of clients for what they called 'a professional friend' (Berggren 2010); a combination of someone familiar and trusted as well as knowledgeable. Someone who can help manage the complexity, who helps to get whatever is necessary out of the systems and specialized institutions. The British government created the 'lead professional' as a professional who –with the client involved- makes sure that things are moving, that the help needed is given, who prevents overlap and positions himself as a reliable and faithful partner next to the client in need (DfES 2005). Both cases are not primarily concerned with a professional who provides care and support individually, but with a professional who mainly tries to make the surroundings and the provision of care run well. In the field of social care, we use the term *kwartiermaker* (see chapter 6 voor an explanation of the term). On the same note, public health care recently advocated life supervisors, an advice taken over by the Health Council (Health Council 2009). The essence is always that complexity is not being reduced to one single cause or disorder, that the solution is not looked for in one single method or professional, but that justice is done to complexity by mobilizing matters and binding them, activating and embedding them at the same time. I could rephrase that: because of the degree of complexity, people – who for whatever reasons have severe difficulties in social functioning- need a reliable partner to tackle this complexity. Sometimes this partnership is needed briefly, sometimes it has to last a lifetime. Often the partner is someone from the environment, sometimes a trained volunteer, and sometimes an expert professional. By the way, my plea does not imply that we won't need specialists and treatment experts in secondary care anymore. It does however imply that we are now in a state of imbalance because the frontline has been neglected and fragmented too much, and that is where the strength of reinforcing and preventing is situated.

I have now reached the conclusion of my argument, where I must confess that I have alternatingly spoken of social case workers, social workers, and even at times of social professionals. This is a delicate matter in the branch. There is confusion of concepts and there are clear points of view on the wider or smaller range of professions. In this inaugural lecture, I kept well away from this controversy. But I hope that my plea will appeal to both the social case worker and the social worker alike, and that they will recognize themselves in my outline. My argument is mainly that these different social professionals recognize themselves in a similar framework, language, and movement, and put in a general effort on behalf of social functioning in complex situations. Most of them are needed in the frontline, but we cannot do without the expertise of specialist and treatment experts.

Bibliography

Berggren, U.J. 2010. *Personligt ombud och förändringsprocesser på det socialpsykiatriska fältet*. Götenborg: Linnaeus University Press.

Beveridge, W. 1942. *Social Insurance and Allied Services: A Report by Sir William Beveridge*. CMD. 6404. London: HMSO.

Bourdieu, P. 1984. *Distinction, a social critique of the judgement of taste*, Cambridge (US): Harvard University Press.

CBS, Centraal bureau voor de Statistiek, 2010
http://statline.cbs.nl/StatWeb/publication/?VW=T&DM=SLNL&PA=37264&
D1=0-6&D2=0&D3=a&D4=0&D5=(1-9)-1&HD=090706-
1319&HDR=G3,G1,G4&STB=T,G2 [accessed 2.9.2010].

Chanan, G. 1997. *Active citizenship and community involvement: getting to the roots*. Luxembourg: Office for Official Publications of the European Union.

CPB, Centraal Plan Bureau, 2007. *Verdubbeling van de instroom in de Wajong: oorzaken en beleidsopties*. Den Haag.

Cross, P. 1977. Not can but will college teaching be improved? *New directions for Higher Education*, Spring, 17.1-15.

DfES, Department for Education and Skills, 2005. *Every child matters*. London: Stationery Office.

Dominelli, L. 2002. *Anti-oppressive social work: theory and practice*. Bassingstokes: Palgrave Mc. Millan.

European Commission, 2004. *Facing the challenge: the Lisbon Strategy for growth and employment*, ISBN 92-894-7054-2 (High Level Group chaired by Wim Kok).

Europe Commission, 2010. *Europe 2020. A European strategy for smart, sustainable and inclusive growth*. Brussels. COM 3.3.2010.

Eurostat 2010a. http://appsso.eurostat.ec.europa.eu/nui/submitViewTableAction.do. [Accessed 15.7. 2010].

Eurostat 2010b.
http://epp.eurostat.ec.europa.eu/portal/page/portal/crime/documents/prison.pdf.
[accessed 15.7.2010].

Ewijk, H. van, 2007. Georganiseerde discontinuïteit in de buurt, *Tijdschrift voor Sociale Interventie*. 16.4.31-37.

Ewijk, H. van, 2010. *European social policy and social work. Citizenship based social work*. Abingdon: Routledge.

Fcb, 2009a. *Meerjarencijfers 2002-2008 jeugdzorg*. Utrecht.

Fcb, 2009b. *Jaarbericht Jeugdzorg*. Utrecht.

FCB 2009c. *Brancherapport Arbeid in zorg & welzijn 2008*. Utrecht.

Gezondheidsraad, 2009. *Autismespectrumstoornissen: een leven lang anders.* (2009/9). Den Haag.

GGZ Nederland, 2009. *Zorg op waarde geschat. Sectorrapport GGZ.* Amersfoort.

Hermanns, J. 2009. *Het opvoeden verleerd.* Amsterdam: UvA.

Kiik, R. 2006. *Key themes and Settings of Social Work in Estonia.* Tartu: Tartu University.

Kunneman, H. 2009. *Voorbij het dikke-ik. Bouwstenen voor een kritisch humanisme. Deel 1.* Amsterdam: SWP/University for Humanistics.

Kwartel, A.J.J. van der, 2010. *Brancherapport Gehandicaptenzorg.* Utrecht: Prismant.

Kyzlinková, R., Dokulilová, L. and Kroupa, A. 2007. *Team work and high performance work organization.* Eurofound. http://www.eurofound.europa.eu/publications/htmlfiles/-ef0693.htm [accessed 10.7.2010].

Laan, G. van der, 1999. *Legitimatieproblemen in het maatschappelijk werk.* Utrecht: SWP. (1ste ed. 1990).

Lawy, R. and Biesta, G. 2006. Citizenship-as-practice: the educational implication of an inclusive and relational understanding of citizenship. *British Journal of Educational Studies,* 54.1. 34-50.

Lister, R. 2007. Inclusive citizenship: realizing the potential. *Citizenship Studies,* 11, 49-61.

MO-groep, 2009. *Brancherapportage Jeugdzorg 2008.* Utrecht.

Morin, E. 2008. *On complexity.* Cresskill New Jersey: Hampton Press.

NVMW, Nederlandse vereniging van maatschappelijke werkers, 1987. *Beroepsprofiel van de maatschappelijk werker.* Utrecht: NVMW.

NVMW, Nederlandse vereniging van maatschappelijke werkers, 2006. *Beroepsprofiel van de maatschappelijk werker.* Utrecht: NVMW.

Polanyi, M. 2009. *The tacit dimension.* University of Chicago (or. 1966).

Putnam, R.D. 1993. *Making democracy work: civic traditions in modern Italy.* Princeton: Princeton University Press.

Putnam, R.D. 2000. *Bowling alone: the collapse and revival of American community.* New York: Simon & Schuster.

Regenmortel, T. van, 2008. *Zwanger van empowerment. Een uitdagend kader voor sociale inclusie en moderne zorg.* Eindhoven: Fontys hogeschool.

RMO, Raad voor Maatschappelijke Ontwikkeling, 2003. *De handicap van de samenleving.* (advies 25). Den Haag: RMO.

Schinkel W. 2007. *Denken in een tijd van sociale hypochondrie. Aanzet tot een theorie voorbij de maatschappij.* Kampen: Klement.

Scholte, M. 2010. *Oude waarden in nieuwe tijden. Over de kracht van maatschappelijk werk in de 21ᵉ eeuw.* Haarlem: Inholland.

Schön, D.A. 1983. *The reflective practitioner. How professionals think in action.* New York: Basic Books.

Seligman, M.E.P. 2003. *Authentic happiness. Using the new positive psychology to realize your potential for deep fulfillment.* London: Nicholas Brealy Publishing

Taylor, Ch. 1989. *Sources of the self. The making of the Modern Identity.* Cambridge, Massachusetts: Harvard University Press.

UWV, 2010.
http://www.uwvjaarverslag.nl/jaarverslag-2009/aDU1006_Ontwikkeling-aantal-Wajong-uitkeringen-2009-.aspx. [accessed 15.7. 2010].

WHO,World Health Organization, 2010
http://www.euro.who.int/mentalhealth/CtryInfo/CtryInfo.
[accessed 15.7. 2010].

3. Concertation in the social zone

Hans van Ewijk

3.1 Introduction

In the previous chapter we discussed the relation between active citizenship and social work. In this chapter we will try to find an answer to the question of how the complexity of care for vulnerable citizens can be reduced. This can be done by setting up a flexible social zone at the local level in such a fashion that fragmentation and institutionalization are avoided as much as possible, and an appeal made to/for the power of immediate surroundings and citizens supported by generic social workers. The chapter is mainly based on a series of research executed by our research centre.

3.2 Plea for a social zone

The Ondiep case

A local welfare organization in the city of Utrecht counted the number of 'rehabilitants' living in the small industrial residential area of Ondiep.[4] A rehabilitant in this case refers to someone who was previously living in a special institution and is now placed in a unit in the neighbourhood in order to integrate into daily life. WHO refers to this programme more specifically as community-based rehabilitation (CBR). This placement can be an action in the context of mental healthcare, youth care, care for the physically impaired, crisis shelters, care of the elderly or probation and after-care. In this neighbourhood with a few thousand inhabitants, they counted hundreds of these rehabilitants, whereby more than 160 placing organizations were involved. I imagine that these rehabilitants are visited more or less regularly by a supervisor, perhaps a carer, and a few other professionals helping them out with fighting debts, raising children, relationship issues and behavioural problems. That means Ondiep is visited by few hundreds of these professionals, driving their cars, scooters or cycles, on their way to meet their clients. Both the

---

[4] No report of this research has been published yet, but it was reported by Portes in the WMO-kenniskring 'Samenspel' (transl. concertation), which is a discussion group consisting of several care and welfare organizations, the city and our research centre, which discusses good practices concerning cooperation in neighbourhoods. (Kenniskring Samenspel, 2010)

rehabilitants and the professionals are not from around this area they don't know the neighbourhood and the professionals come only, probably, to visit their own clients, the rehabilitants.

What goes wrong?

The Ondiep case is but one of the many examples of a questionable organizing of care and welfare work. The idea of community-based rehabilitation is not to put people in institutions but to integrate them into their neighbourhoods. But why then are we placing people into neighbourhoods that are not their own? And why are they supported by professionals that are not from the neighbourhood and not neighbourhood-oriented in their approach?

This case shows first and foremost, a fundamental misfit in the de-institutionalization of The Netherlands. What we have been doing for fifty years now, is starting at the wrong end. First we put people in institutions, and then we rehabilitate them into neighbourhoods. That's how we keep ourselves busy. The availability of affordable housing seems to be the norm that decides where the rehabilitants are placed. Municipalities haven't the faintest idea how many rehabilitants are living in their city and in which specific areas they are placed. Countries that are de-institutionalizing more effectively have started at the front end, i.e. by first ensuring that people can keep living in their own environment by creating an integrated local care structure, ranging from mild to intensive care, as in the Nordic countries..

Secondly, this case makes us once again aware of how many people are living in institutions or are treated by institutions (see previous chapter).

The third lesson we can draw from this case concerns the fragmentation of our care and welfare system. And obviously, it's not only the rehabilitants in Ondiep that receive care and support at home. Besides the 160 placing organizations, dozens of other organizations are working for the inhabitants of the neighbourhood as well.

Lastly, we need to ask ourselves from which dominant perspective and at which scale (neighbourhood, municipality, province, country) we try to tackle the life problems of citizens. All we know is that in Ondiep, countless perspectives and scales are seriously overlapping.

Reducing complexity

It is an obvious move to bet on reducing the complexity of care. When it comes to the engagement and integration of rehabilitants into their own environment, we need to work from that point and/or at that scale towards an improved social functioning of citizens and neighbourhoods. If we take community involvement serious, do we really need 160 placing organizations and hundreds of visiting professionals who are strangers to the neighbourhood? Institutions are breeding grounds for professionals, where citizens hardly have a role to play, as co-creators and as co-workers. Once a child enters the youth welfare or mental health care system, he/she becomes an object of treatment by professionals. In local welfare work however, we see hundreds of active residents. The current system of mental health care and youth welfare needs to therefore be overturned; and that is exactly the change we are facing at the moment. Characteristic of this change is foremost the creation of a social zone in which citizens take/play the lead, and where professionals provide support. In this local social zone, three things matter:

1. promoting and maintaining active citizenship;

2. taking care of, often long-lasting, support of the most vulnerable citizens;

3. responding adequately to critical situations in and around the private sphere.

In such a social zone we combine civilian and professional strength, in order to enable people to participate and to take control of their own lives. If that is done well, we will need institutions less as treatment centres, but more as places of expertise, that we consult if and when needed. The mention of this social zone is present in all sorts of terminology, such as 'pedagogic civil society', the 'housing-welfare-care zone', and of course in welfare work, where the neighbourhood-oriented approach has always been the point of departure, but which has often been understood in a narrow way and executed in much too fragmented a manner. An essential feature of this social zone is that the care and support is not sought with the focus lying on the disorder, the handicap, the arrears, or the cultural background, but on the social functioning of the individual in his/her direct environment; of central importance here is the social perspective within the context and complexity of life.

The metaphor of the professional friend

'Professional friend' refers to people with temporary or long-term problems, but self-reliant, who are best served by a fixed person giving them non-material support (Berggren, 2010). We can further explain this metaphor by identifying different phases or gradations of the support process. In by far the most cases, it is the partner, the parent, the child, a near relative or a friend that fulfils such a role. When the inhibition to act gets too strong, self-reliance has been seriously damaged, or the complexity of matters becomes overwhelming for the ones involved, then a firmer support is needed. In principle, we should then try to find someone from the network – with a certain mandate of the network – who can take up this role. This is a strategy we witness more and more, for example in the Family Group Conferences. When significant members of a person's network come together as soon as possible, and discuss, together with this person, what needs to be done, a very effective form of support can be organized. Only when this has no effect or cannot be practically arranged, the need for a skilled professional assuming the role of the professional friend arises. The emphasis shifts from an expert and reliable supporter from one's own network, to a professional –or skilled and educated volunteer –, equally reliable but with more expertise. This professional or skilled volunteer supports the citizen and his network, in order to help the citizen to maintain or reclaim his self-reliance and participation. This professional acts as the supervisor, and as the one who, together with the person concerned, aligns the formal and the informal environment with the person's needs. This might be the school, work place or sports club, which are supported with making the person function adequately by removing obstacles and empowering the person. It might also involve calling in specific expertise, such as a diagnosis, therapy, a work preparation or debt settlement program. It is very essential that the citizen and professional work in a partnership, and are not related to each other as client and treatment officer. Besides, the professional mainly stimulates the informal environment to keep participating, and not to let the expert unnecessarily take over or 'give solo performances'. This image of the professional is close to that of *lead professional* proposed by the British government a few years ago (DfES, 2005).

Gradations of professional friendship	
C + C	Citizen and citizen. The person involved (e.g. the rehabilitant) plus someone from the informal network.
C + V + C	Citizen and skilled volunteer (as coach, mentor, mediator) and informal network.
C + P + C	Citizen and professional and citizen. The difficulty or inhibition to act is too strong, or the network is too weak. The help of a professional is needed, but mostly in order for the C + C connection to function.
C + P + E + C	Citizen and professional and expert and citizen. In this case experts are called in, but only if consistent with the line citizen – professional – citizen.
C + I + C	Citizen in institutional setting. This is the last resort when all the previous phases don't work, or sometimes in crisis situations where immediate action is needed. However, even then, the institutions need to incorporate the citizens' environment more actively than is done presently.

The role of social work

Our studies revealed that the respondents from the social work sector think that with themes such as active citizenship, the social zone and the professional friend, social workers are eligible par excellence. They have the most knowledge of the neighbourhoods, the context, and the residents with whom they also have connections. The strength of social work would lie in the link at the level of the direct living environment. The work, however, will have to profile itself better and gain more authority. Behind this need for legitimation lies a perplexing dilemma for social work. Originally, the orientation of welfare organizations has been on engagement of the rehabilitants through collective activities and approaches. My estimation is that, with the transfer of everything related to engagement and support to a more individualized approach aimed at the most vulnerable, social work will focus even more on individuals. The central question for local policy makers seems to be: How can I support people that barely make it in society, and how can I engage their environment in such a way that these people can maintain their daily lives? It is the shift from thinking in terms of a cure to the ability to live as normal and social a life as possible. Social and socio-psychological impairments are only moderately curable; instead we should try to keep the situation of the rehabilitants stable and engage them in society. The government has bestowed the responsibility for the more collective arrangements of activation upon civil society: voluntary work, the world of sports and culture, spontaneous initiatives. For professional welfare workers I think this means less will be left to take care of. The 'perplexity' is however not only caused by this push towards care and individualization, but also by the fact that the more collective engagement in socio-cultural work and community work has ensured that professionals are surrounded by dozens of volunteers and that they get to know their clients, the rehabilitants in their neighbourhood, fairly well. In that sense it is correct to say that social workers of all professionals are surrounded most by citizens, and are most connected to the self-organization of citizens. This means that with further individualization, these networks of citizens around professionals could also come under pressure. Welfare organizations and their professionals will have to develop new strategies and methods to maintain their strong ties with neighbourhoods and citizens, and simultaneously work in a more care- and aid-oriented manner.

3.3 Cooperation between citizens and professionals

Professionals in social work identify themselves as team workers par excellence, they can't seem to get enough of it; that's the image that keeps revealing itself in our studies. At the same time we see how the spirit of cooperation is hampered by fragmentation, competition and power relations. Social workers are on the whole not very good at competing and playing power games. As a lectorate, we previously reported on the complexity of cooperation and looked for possible solutions to solve it (De Waal, 2007). In an ongoing research within the framework of the WMO-workshop[5] 'Samenspel' [transl. concertation] we are meanwhile focusing on three core issues. The first is the diffused and modest role that citizens are being given and are themselves taking up in this teamwork. The second is the lack of an explicit expression and operationalization of a common, shared guiding vision. The third concerns the precarious position of leadership in the envisioned renewal

---

[5]   WMO/Wmo: 'Wet Maatschappelijke Ondersteuning', which translates as 'Social Support Law'. This law, implemented/installed on January 1st 2007, focuses more on active citizenship, self-reliance and the support of immediate surroundings, rather than taking professional support as the starting point.

processes. The analyses and visions of the future that we outlined in the first part of this chapter, are in opposition to the unruly reality.

Different roles and relationships between citizens and social workers

In our studies we see the citizens not just as those demanding help, i.e. the target audience, the help givers, informal carers and volunteers, but also, hopefully, as team players, co-developers and co-decision makers. In our study in the neighbourhood 'Zuilen'(Van Ewijk, Scheijmans & Van de Maas, 2008), residents identified welfare workers as 'passers by', who came in their time to do their thing. This observation served as a shock to the welfare organization and the professionals. For aren't welfare workers supposed to be the natural allies of the residents? Well, it appears not.

In today's times of products and projects, the work had degenerated to services of a number of hours per area per activity. The results of the study contributed in making a shift towards a broad neighbourhood-oriented worker. Not only in the Zwanenvechtplein area in Zuilen, but also in our knowledge centre, we became increasingly aware that welfare work should be characterized by proximity, familiarity and loyalty. Fundamentally, primary social professionals should be mere extensions and accessories of the social organization of citizens. The core problem of our times is not so much a lack of commitment on the part of citizens, but the threat of a decline of civilian power, because of progressive mobilization, differentiation and greater complexity of daily life. The question is thus how can professionals support citizens in their role of (co-)responsible participants, and maintain the social fabric/network? Based on everything we have seen in our studies, I also get the impression that social workers too have little regard for and make too little use of this social fabric themselves (cf. Blokland, 2006; Linders, 2009.).

What also strikes us in all our studies, whether it is on child welfare, health care, neighbourhood or education matters, is how we fail to see citizens as co-creators of what needs to happen in the social zone (see also Metz, 2011). We can certainly speak of a gap between the professional world and the civilian world, or between civilian power and the power of the system. We will have to give a much clearer role to civilians in describing the core issues, in investigating what's going on in their context (such as area or family), and in making plans, for themselves. We have gained experience with this in our WOK-projects[6], but not nearly enough (Van Ewijk, Scheijmans & Van der Maas, 2009). We also need to be wary here of the 'participation paradox.' This means that, the more we arrive at policy and services through participation, the greater the danger of certain citizens being excluded, and the greater the risk of professionals mainly entertaining each other. Engaging citizens in decision making asks for methods other than participation meetings and community councils, such as Family Group Conferences, communities of practice, and working with degrees of professional friendship.

View on cooperation

It is striking that in all our studies and discussions, a reasonably clear picture emerges, of what is good for citizens and what needs to change in practice. Everything and everyone nowadays is focused on active citizenship, self-reliance and the support of immediate surroundings. The Wmo (social support law) and the innovated welfare agenda are leading examples of this focus (De Waal, 2007). The danger of being in such a joint seventh heaven, is that parties enthusiastically start working together without questioning if it will really yield better results for citizens. It has been studied that with many innovations, a shared vision is assumed from the start, barely thought out and elaborated upon by the parties involved (Scheijmans, 2011). As a result we often see objectives somewhere between being strategic and operational, which may contribute to (apparent) consent yet ambiguity of targets in the long and short terms. Perhaps the biggest flaw in innovation projects is the lack of a well thought out cooperation strategy. Parties do not speak of a development in which the cooperation is built up incrementally (Van Delden, 2009). Broadly speaking, partners choose for a 'process approach', expecting the cooperation and objective realization to happen in the process of doing the work, or for a design approach in which tasks, responsibilities and concrete targets are set in advance (Van Delden, 2009). In the 'process approach', partners often omit gradually explicating the steps and forms of cooperation, while in the design approach they forget to regularly examine and update the design. An essential element of the vision is a perspective on implementation and realization of the proposed innovation. An interesting shift can be seen in this context. Ten years ago, innovation meant developing and

---

[6]   WOK: 'Wijk, Onderzoek en Kennisontwikkeling', which can be translated as 'Neighbourhood, Research and Knowledge Development'.

implementing a completely new, concrete way of working. These innovations were product-oriented and project-driven. The problem though, was that in welfare organizations more people were working on these innovations than doing their regular work (Scheijmans & Van Ewijk, 2006). Understandably, implementation and realization didn't amount to very much. Meanwhile, the world of welfare has grown tired of this 'innovation diarrhoea', and we have started looking for durable changes, that we preferably wish to express in terms of 'tilt', 'breakthrough', 'renewed welfare' or 'new style welfare'. From accountable project- and product thinking, we have made a shift to achieving social tasks by means of mandate. We also see this shift reflected in the innovations that are the topic of research in our regional Wmo-workshop, such as the realization of youth and family agencies, social brokerage, and breaking social isolation. It is not so much about new methodologies, but more about a fundamental repositioning of actors (professionals, citizens) and developing integrated approaches.

Another shift that we observe is that we have evolved from chains to networks, and from networks to 'flowers' (Admiraal et al., 2011). Agreements between organizations are central in the chain approach. In this approach, we often see agreements at steps and links in the chain, such as a common diagnosis, referral criteria and integrated approaches. A network approach focuses on collaboration between professionals of different institutions. A 'flower approach' focuses on key professionals arranging care and expertise together with clients, by addressing and, if necessary, committing to different parties. These three modes of cooperation are of course to some extent interdependent; indeed, a 'flower approach' needs agreements between parties and professionals, and the chains will remain cold metal if they are not augmented by warm-blooded professionals with hearts.

View on leadership

For any company, project or collaboration to succeed, leadership is indispensible. In cooperation between different parties – probably the most difficult form of work – this leadership is especially a complex challenge, and it takes place at different levels. The most common form is for a form of collaboration to be provided with a steering committee, a project manager and a covenant in which cooperating parties capture their goals, commitments and obligations. The collaborative is accountable to the sponsor, mostly the local government, with sometimes, a combination of parties having a chair in the steering committee as well. By now we have extensive experience with steering committees, however, this information is not yet systematized. I will give some preliminary reflections.

A pressing question is whether the steering committee also has and takes up the responsibility of realizing the proposed renewal. Is it the addressee of the proposed renewal of the project group? Many steering committees act primarily as supervisors and heads of the collaborative, but are much less accountable as being the ones who stand for the realization of the goals. The realization is left to the collaborative, with the project manager as scapegoat. If the steering committee doesn't see itself as the addressee of the project group, innovations will be highly vulnerable. Another weakness of many steering committees is that, although members do come from important parties, these members hardly involve their own base. They join committee meetings a few times a year, just like any other meeting. The following link is the project manager. In our ongoing study on concertation within the Wmo, it emerges that the pitfall for these project managers is that they strongly take up the responsibility for themselves (Scheijmans, 2011). They take the objectives of the collaborative as a highly personal responsibility. This is exacerbated by the problem of steering groups being difficult to address. Even the cooperating professionals are happy to have the final responsibility for success resting in the hands of the project manager. Both the vertical line (steering committee and management) and horizontal line (team members and organizations involved) tend to hold the project manager responsible; however, the main aim of the project was more cooperation. Such an aim asks for distributing the responsibility over the vertical and horizontal line. We need a model of cooperative or coordinated leadership. I am however, under the impression that there is very little reflection on the type of leadership in such collaborative projects. All parties benefit in some sense from the unspoken idea that the project manager is 'normally' responsible. Adding to all this, is also the misconception that innovation can be 'put away' into a project.

The last link is that between the collaborating professionals and the collaborating organizations. The first thing that strikes here, is that in many covenants many more parties are listed than are actually partaking in the project. The role and responsibility of these parties is obscure. Their role is, presumably, mainly symbolic, both in their own interest and in the interest of the project. If we then limit ourselves to the parties actually spending time and money on the innovation, we can question how seriously these parties really want and will execute the intended innovation. Innovations are, usually and to a large extent, driven on external and temporary money, which doesn't make them stronger. Most actors work a limited number of hours on the innovation. Our experience and initial survey data also indicate that project team members are generally enthusiastic about the project work, but slow in fulfilling the project ambassador role. They do not feel very responsible for towing along the organization to participate in the 'reform movement', and their management encourages either. Steering committees, project groups, project managers and collaborating parties as a whole, should engage in a much stronger joint effort for innovations. In the majority of projects, this game is still played badly by far. The power of collaboration is usually restricted within the project team.

3.4 Working on local innovation through research

The Research Centre for Social Innovation has from the very start, based its research tradition on contribution to innovation and improvement, by research, in local contexts and practices. This applied research is not a stand alone activity, but part of innovation processes and knowledge development (Nowotny, et al., 1991). In both aspects, it is no more and no less than a part of the whole. In our view, this also means that the corresponding theory of science and research strategy have to relate to innovation on the one hand, and knowledge development on the other. The core of applied research is the art of defining the problem: *contextualist* research (Schön, 1983). The provision of the problem is the beginning of the answer. This also means that a poor or faulty problem definition will lead to a wrong or dubious solution. I already showed how in our sector, much of the 'problem defining' starts with the professionals' problems instead of those of the citizens. When researchers investigate contexts of citizens (neighbourhood, family, network, etc.), they decide the perspective (what is important?) and define the problem. This danger is even greater in applied research, since it is part of an innovation, and many innovations have their origin in the offices of the government or large institutions.

Contextual validity

In many theories of science, research is given the role of searching for universal validity, like in the case of Newton's apple, which is guaranteed to fall down. The reliability of this type of research is eventually defined by the possibility of its repetition, and the obtained assurance that the same law holds in other cases. Applied research, especially in the social sphere, cannot realize this kind of validity. Individual and collective social behaviour are subject to spontaneity, creativity, and the ability to undertake autonomous actions. The social domain is characterized by complexity and uniqueness, rather than replication and consistency. Therefore, applied social research finds its legitimacy in contextual validity. In our research centre, we have fleshed out this concept by seeing contextual validity of research findings as the recognition and acceptance of these findings by actors relevant to the context (Van Ewijk & Wilken, 2005). Furthermore, these findings have to be obtained through sound scientific method. In other words, whether your research has been good depends, on the one hand, on the question of whether most of the actors were benefited, i.e. if the research helps them to improve and innovate. Validity is not only inter-subjective within the community of researchers, but also inter-subjective between researchers, professionals, policy makers and citizens (cf. McLaughlin, 2007; Marsh, 2007). On the other hand, applied research has to be done according to the rules of the game. In contextual and applied research, we usually work with a set of studies that are carried out both simultaneously and sequentially. An important criteria is the match between research strategy and methodology, and the question and problem definition.

Communities of research practice

Communities of practice are popular, and often refer to Wenger (2008). Wenger was mainly concerned with teams working together in the long term, and by working, learning from each other. These days, we also use the term communities of practice as a working method for research; to distinguish between the two concepts, I will speak of communities of research practice. Typical of such a community is its mixed composition. It consists of researchers and professionals at the least, but if possible, also residents, clients or students. It's very fascinating to see the interaction that arises within such a team, when the members ask what is going on in their context and what needs to be addressed. Citizens and professionals are drawn into a more open approach, and the researchers get to work in a very different environment, one that continuously challenges them to see through the eyes of residents, clients and operating professionals. Experience also teaches to better appreciate the different roles and qualities of the different parties, instead of suggesting that everyone can do everything. It is especially advisable to articulate the role of residents or clients. A critical question is whether these few citizens are representative of the whole. Obviously they are not, in relation to their views and opinions representing those of all the residents and clients. Their representation is rather in their *position* as resident of that particular neighbourhood, or client of that particular institution. The objective representation of the research depends on the research method, not on the composition of the research team. However, our experience is that a diverse research team with residents and professionals, has a clear added value (Van Ewijk et al., 2009). The problem of the power of problem definition or the process of problem defining is shared, and approached through the different perspectives of the researcher, the professional and the resident/rehabilitant. The idea is that a researcher gains much understanding from collaboration with professionals and citizens in the context of research. The value of a community of research practice is even more evident in the development of an innovation. In a dialogue between the citizen, professional, and the researcher, the innovations gain greater realism and give implementation and assurance a greater chance of success.

The specific role of the researcher

The practice-oriented researcher is a unification of different roles. Of course he is primarily a skilled and competent researcher. He is well-versed in scientific theory and research strategies, knows the methods and the craft. An important quality is his experience with and knowledge of researching contexts and professional practices. This asks for the capability of combining several methods simultaneously and sequentially, and connecting the different results. The process of interpreting the data, always one of the hardest and most precarious parts of research, is essential as well. This brings us to the next role and quality of a practice-oriented researcher. He doesn't interpret his data in his study, but in an interactive process with his team, using the knowledge and perspective of the members in the best possible way. And of course, this does not only apply just to the process of interpretation. In obtaining the data and the dissemination of the results, it is essential to involve the whole team as well. Related to this role of utilizing the available expertise is the role of the research leader. It is our experience that the researcher is almost always the driving force of the research, which also asks for team management as a specific skill. Besides the management, the research leader also has to take care of a productive relationship with the steering committee (the addressees), keeping the partners involved (the horizontal line), and realizing the contextual validity (the recognition and acknowledgment of the findings by residents, professionals and clients). Finally, according to our experiences and those of many other researchers, the researcher cannot make do with the roles of researcher and research leader alone, but also has the role of an expert (Van Ewijk, 2011). Both, his knowledge of good research, as well as his knowledge of the subject, of social issues and of implementation and policy, are of importance.

3.5   In conclusion

This chapter is a personal translation and selection of nearly ten years of work as a researcher in a series of studies with many, many teachers, students, professionals and residents. I have learned so much from them. Doing research together with others contributes to more insight, more involvement and more knowledge. I also dare to say that we as a research centre, have further trained and profiled ourselves rather consistently in a certain direction. This must definitely continue. The Research Centre for Social Innovation will itself have to be a community of research practice, of researchers, teachers, and students in direct interaction with professionals, residents and clients.

Bibliography

Admiraal, L., Wopereis, M., Oosterink, M. & Ewijk, H. van (2011). *Geen Kind over Boord. Een onderzoek naar zorgarrangementen voor overbelaste kinderen en jongeren in het kader van het Regionaal Innovatieprogramma 'Regionaal Jeugdcentrum'. Eindrapport.* Utrecht: Hogeschool Utrecht.

Berggren, U.J. (2010). *Personligt ombud och förändringsprocesser på det socialpsykiatriska fältet.* Götenborg: Linnaeus University Press.

Blokland, T.V. (2006). *Het sociaal weefsel van de stad.* Den Haag: Gradus Hendriks Stichting.

Delden, P. van (2009). *Sterke netwerken. Ketensamenwerking in de publieke dienstverlening.* Amsterdam: Van Gennep.

Ewijk, H. van (2007). Georganiseerde discontinuïteit in de buurt. *Tijdschrift voor Sociale Interventie, 12*(4), 31-37.

Ewijk, H. van (2010a). *Maatschappelijk werk in een sociaal gevoelige tijd.* Amsterdam: SWP/Humanistics Univerity Press.

Ewijk, H. van (2010b). Positioning Social Work in a Socially Sensitive Society.*Social Work & Society*, 8. urn:nbn:de:0009-11-26969. www.socwork.net/2010/1/vanewijk.

Ewijk, H. van (2011). Collaboration in community research. *European Journal of Social Work, 14*(1), 41-53.

Ewijk, H. van & Wilken, J.P. (2005). Developing research practices in social work: a challenging endeavour for the Centre of Expertise for Social Policy and Social Care. In J. van Eijken & H. van Ewijk, *Re-inventing Social Work* (pp. 115-123). Utrecht: Hogeschool Utrecht.

Ewijk, H. van, Scheijmans, I. & Maas, A. van der (2008). *Rapportage Zwanenvechtpleinbuurt.* Utrecht: Hogeschool Utrecht.

Ewijk, H. van, Scheijmans, I. & Maas, A. van der (2009). *Kennis van de wijk. Werken met wok.* Utrecht: Hogeschool Utrecht.

Kenniskring Samenspel (2010). *Verslag van de kenniskring samenspel op 16 juni.* Utrecht: Hogeschool Utrecht.

Linders, L. (2009). *De betekenis van nabijheid. Een onderzoek naar informele zorg in een volksbuurt.* Den Haag: Sdu.

Marsh, P., 2007. *Developing an enquiring social work practice: practitioners, researchers and users as scientific partners.* Houten: Bohn Stafleu van Loghum, and Marie Kamphuis Stichting

Metz, J. (2011). *Welzijn in de 21ste eeuw. Van sociale vernieuwing naar Welzijn Nieuwe Stijl.* Amsterdam: SWP.

Nowotny, H., Scott, P., and Gibbons, M. (1991). *Re-Thinking science: knowledge and the public in an Age of uncertainty.* Cambridge: Polity Press.

Scheijmans, I. (2011). *Samenspel binnen de WMO. Verschillende vormen van samenwerken in beeld* (een tussenrapport en interne publicatie). Utrecht: Hogeschool Utrecht.

Scheijmans, I. & Ewijk, H. van (2006). *Advies Projectengarage Utrecht.* Utrecht: Hogeschool Utrecht.

Waal, V. de (2007). *Samenspel in de buurt: burgers, professionals en beleidmakers aan zet.* Amsterdam: SWP.

Wenger, E. (2008). *Communities of practice. Learning, meaning and identity.* New York: Cambridge University Press.

Wilken, J.P. (2010). *Recovering Care. A contribution to a theory and practice of good care.* Amsterdam: SWP

4. Returning to the basics

Social work and citizens with complex problems

Lia van Doorn

4.1 Introduction

With the 2005 riots in the Parisian banlieues still fresh in mind, in the summer of 2011 Great-Britain was startled by troublemaking youths in London. These riots lasted for several weeks and spread to other cities. British politicians were shocked, riots of this magnitude cause social unrest and disrupt the social order.

In the Netherlands, there have hardly been any urban riots of such scale till date. Collective action by deprived citizens – organized or spontaneous – is scarce. At most, there are sometimes relatively small skirmishes in deprived neighbourhoods. The Dutch 'underclass' does not really cause riots, but withdraws and becomes introvert. (Engbersen and Van der Veen, 1987). Social problems mostly happen at the individual level, or in the privacy of families, neighbourhoods, or subgroups. Problems smoulder beneath the surface: they remain hidden behind the front door and only become visible when they accumulate and escalate. We see them for example, when family dramas take place where children lose their lives, when a lonely elderly person passes away and is found only after some time, or through complaints of neighbours experiencing nuisance.

It is undesirable when citizens lose touch with common social institutions such as work, education, and authorities; when they do not participate there anymore, and withdraw and seclude themselves, or isolate as a group and create their own parallel antisocial communities with different rules and patterns of behaviour. This leads to personal tragedies for those directly involved as well as the neighbours, and in society at general, it leads to social unrest. For (local) politicians these are tough and stubborn issues which are difficult to grasp through the common channels for influencing social policy. The efforts of social work also do not always bring solace. De Boer and Van der Lans (2011b) formulated the following problem: 'The tragedy of the rich Dutch welfare state might be that it functions better for people with fewer problems (or those who are less vulnerable, you could say). Where problems accumulate, in cases of persons, networks, neighbourhoods or districts, institutional care functions the worst. If you have only one problem in this country, then there is always someone to help you. If you have more than one problem however, you end up in a labyrinth of institutions and professionals, each extending there own professional hand, but having lost the view of the whole, or having it left to the 'chain collaboration.'

In this chapter I will argue that it is an important task for social work to contribute to exactly these tough social issues. Social work needs to focus (again) on clients with complex problems, such as multi-problem families, marginal youth, people living on subsistence for a long time, homeless, home polluters, nuisance-makers, and care avoiders.

This chapter is structured as follows. First I will discuss the extent and characteristics of citizens with complex problems. Then I will outline how over the past decades, social work – in particular the social work that is rooted in the fight against poverty and antisocial behaviour – has turned away from the group with complex problems. This is followed by the statement that the current social developments compel social workers to return to clients with complex problems. Lastly, I will indicate how the research group Innovative Social Service Provision tries, through its research and development programme, to contribute to the strengthening of professional help and service to citizens with complex problems.

4.2 Citizens with complex problems

Within the field of social work, there are various terms to describe citizens with complex problems; those missing the connection with the major institutions in society, being insufficiently capable of providing their own means of living, and running the risk of being marginalized. Varying from multi-problem clients, marginal youth, social misfits, and socially disadvantaged, to populations with low socio-economic status, the target of public mental health care (Wolf, Bransen & Nicholas, 2001), people in poverty (Driessens & Regenmortel, 2006), the social underclass (Engbersen, 2006), alarming and nuisance causing care avoiders (Ministries of Public Health, Welfare and Sports and of Internal Affairs, 2011), languished and derelicts (Research voor Beleid, 2002), and 'unprofitables' (Van Dam, 2009, transl. eds.). An aspect that many people falling under such categories have in common is that they suffer from problems in different areas of life: housing, finances, physical and mental health, social contacts and relations, and sometimes problems with drug or alcohol addiction as well.

In this paper we refer to the diffuse, dynamic population of people who find themselves 'at the margin' of society and who are faced with a multitude of problems, with the generic term 'clients with complex problems'. This category is not easy to define. There is no clear and well-defined definition or description of people with complex problems. It is unclear who precisely belongs to this category; how broadly or narrowly it has to be viewed. Partly due to this, we can only say by approximation how many people with complex problems live in our country. The general estimate is that between 15 to 20% of our citizens are socially vulnerable and need support once in a while to keep their heads above water, socially and economically (Heineke, Van der Veen & Kornalijnslijper, 2005; Sprinkhuizen, Scholte, Penninx, Heineke & Van Doorn, 2011). Of some subcategories we have more detailed figures. For example, the number of 'derelicts' – including people who pollute their homes and are socially isolated – is estimated at a 110,000. Of those, 33,000 are registered with official institutions and the other 77,000 are not (Research voor Beleid, 2002). Furthermore, we know that 6% of the total Dutch population is living below the poverty line, some hundred thousands are dealing with problematic debts, and 1.5 million Dutch people are illiterate or very low educated. And there is an undocumented underclass of around 150,000 to 200,000 illegal aliens who are excluded from public services and stay in illegality (Engbersen, 2006).

Characteristics

One way to characterize the target group 'citizens with complex problems' is by using the definition of this target group used by policymakers of Public Mental Health Care (*OGGZ*) (Wolf et.al., 2001). *OGGZ* focuses on people who are struggling with problems in several areas, or who are insufficiently capable of providing their own livelihood (housing, food, income, social contacts, self-care). They often live in marginal areas, where problems such as nuisance, criminality, and unemployment pile up. They often lead a marginal existence, and thereby bring themselves, and sometimes others, in danger. Some stay invisible to professional care: they defy authorities and avoid organized support (care avoiders). Others are highly visible though, since they keep getting into trouble (regressives, revolving door clients), or because they cause nuisance. The target group, in general, concerns people who do not receive any help (anymore), although according to common public views they need this help. They do not pose a demand for care which regular welfare services can answer. Sometimes concerned family members, neighbours, and bystanders ask for help, which calls for unsolicited interference or support (outreach care). And if social work does reach these people, there is a high drop-out rate: they pull themselves out of the reach of care prematurely or keep reverting to their old behaviour (recidivism). Besides, they usually do not make use of social provisions – such as special assistance, rental subsidies, or other tax reductions or financial supplements – for which they do qualify. To make matters worse, society demands more of citizens' self-reliance and independence. They are expected to take more initiative themselves and do things more by themselves. But at the same time society is becoming increasingly complex and the supporting social networks are subject to erosion. For many vulnerable people it is a growing challenge to maintain themselves socially and deal with the complexity, says Van Ewijk (2010).

Citizens with complex problems who do come into view of professional support, are often confronted with different professionals who are specialized in a particular topic and focus on sub-problems, whereby the cooperation and coordination between the professionals involved is hardly ever optimal (Hijzen, Kruiter, De Jong & Van Niel, 2008). It is exactly for these clients that we need wide-oriented professionals who can analyze from a broader and more integral perspective, who are mandated to 'do what needs to be done', and who can manage the care process in direct cooperation with the client (Scholte, 2010; Van Ewijk, 2010). Professionals who went through a socio-pedagogical training, are theoretically very well suited to carry out the care and support process of clients with complex problems. They are broadly educated, and have an integral approach and practical style needed to identify and counsel these groups (Gezondheidsraad / Health Council of the Netherlands, 2004).

4.3   Social work and citizens with complex problems

Within social work in the Netherlands, these target groups at the margins of society have received oscillating attention over the years; sometimes more, sometimes a lot less than was needed. I will now discuss the shifts in these pendulum-like movements.

Social work in the Netherlands came about around a century ago. Its roots lie in the care and support for the underclass and poor relief. Social workers and housing supervisors – mostly well-to-do ladies – visited the 'antisocial families' who were under supervision in residential schools in order to be re-educated to become respectable citizens. For these pioneers of social work, the usual approach was to visit the families in their homes; they went to the families themselves, solicited or unsolicited (Van der Linde, 2010, 2011).

In the sixties came the fight against antisocial behaviour, whereby social workers who went to visit the 'antisocial' came under fire. Social workers were accused of being patronizing in their treatment of clients (Milikowski, 1967).

At that time, other voices were also heard. In 1963 Marie Kamphuis, one of the founders of Dutch social work, published the book *New ways in working with problem families: the casework-experiment in the Family Centred Project in St Paul* [transl. eds.]. In this – still very readable book – Kamphuis reports on a new approach in the United States in working with problem families. She argues that in the field of combating antisocial behaviour, much more is possible than was assumed in the Netherlands till then, that making house visits could methodically be substantiated, and she gave practical advice on how to avoid paternalism and patronization of clients. Kamphuis' plea however, was of no avail.

In the seventies there was growing criticism of paternalism in residential schools. Both policymakers and practitioners embarrassedly distanced themselves from these paternalistic civilization attempts. In response to this, social workers developed what was also called the 'paternalism syndrome': they withdrew themselves further from the social environments of their clients (Kuypers & Van der Lans, 1994). Clients had to come to the institutions themselves, with a clear question and the correct motivation. In the seventies the last residential schools were closed. The baby was thrown out with the bath water.

From the seventies and eighties, social workers rarely ventured into forms of care and support that were even vaguely paternalistic. They developed an ever increasing supply of programmes for motivated clients with a well-articulated demand, an understanding of their own situation and motivation to accept support. Social work developed more into a kind of psychotherapy. Indeed, many social workers followed courses in psychotherapy or coaching. This was a great career option as well, and provided them with more status. The conversation with clients were almost exclusively carried out in the offices of the social workers. The assistance offered turned out to be mostly to clients with a YAVIS profile: young, attractive, verbal, intelligent, and successful. Thus, other clients who did not meet this profile, were less well served. They did not come to consultations, or quit after a few meetings with the social worker: disappointed, disheartened, or frustrated. Care workers identified this as 'the client is unmotivated' or 'doesn't meet the agreements'. This placed the responsibility of the failure unilaterally on the client. The office became the standard workplace for many social workers, to which only the already motivated and reasonably self-supporting could find their way.

The right to self-determination and self-fulfilment gained more importance. Setting boundaries to clients' behaviour and getting in touch with clients unsolicitedly, was frowned upon more and more (Jagt, 2001). These outreaching and other forms of conditional and involuntary support became a taboo (Menger, 1997). Fewer home visits were made. The private domain of citizens, the terrain behind the front door, became a no go area to social workers (Van der Lans, 2010; Van Doorn, Van Etten & Gademann, 2008). The socially vulnerable were increasingly less reached and supported. This development was later on described as the largest error of social work in the Netherlands (Jagt, 2001).

Because of this movement of withdrawing from people's private domains, the problems of residents were kept hidden from the outside world. They only surfaced when the dam burst; problems within the home escalated or neighbours complained about nuisance. Realization began to dawn that it was precisely these people we needed to keep an eye on, but that we could not do this with the usual approach of conversations in the office and the precondition of a motivated client (Van der Lans, 2010).

In the mid-nineties, social workers came under fire again. Now they were blamed for not helping clients who needed the help, but didn't ask for it themselves. Now the social workers were not charged for wrongly interfering (paternalism), but for wrongly *not* interfering (Van der Laan, 1990). Henselmans (1993) argued for *interference care*, and Kuypers and Van der Lans (1994) for *modern paternalism*. The plea for an outreaching approach had increasingly more support, also in political and administrative circles. What was lacking in the approach of care and welfare institutions was put into words by an employee of a housing corporation who attempted, together with a social worker, to reduce the problems in a deprived area. "I think we don't reach the right people with what we are doing here. We have a completely degenerated block of 260 houses where only five families are the cause of all the trouble, and with these families I mean five single mothers with children. We greatly worry about them, but we can hardly reach them. You can offer parenting support or after school care, but they won't come. With all those beautiful programmes you only reach the people who are already of goodwill."

From the late nineties onwards, the need grew to go and 'look behind the front doors' of citizens with complex problems who could not find their way to the institutions or who avoid care, and give them unsolicited assistance if needed. Now, instead of waiting for them to come, they are identified and visited at home. The 'behind-the-front-door'-policy is mostly used in districts and neighbourhoods where social problems such as unemployment, school dropout, crime and nuisance accumulate. Local social work gives shape to this through methodical approaches such as 'interference care', 'towards it/*eropaf!*' or 'outreach work'. The professional attitude has shifted from waiting to taking initiative, from being reactive to confronting. While the 'behind-the-front-door'-approach was just merely tolerated in the nineties and used only occasionally, nowadays it has become more widespread and accepted (Hoijtink, 2008).

The revival of working behind-the-front-door with clients not asking for help themselves, was partly encouraged by the introduction of the Social Support Act (Dutch: *Wmo*, 2007). This Act, which changed several old welfare laws, meant a real break from the prevailing trend. This legal framework set out contours in which the old concept of 'welfare state' was let go of in favour of the new concept of the 'participation state'. According to progressive insights, citizens should no more be pampered with all kinds of professional support from the cradle to the grave. Instead they need to be made aware of their own responsibility. The legal framework of the *Wmo* also stimulated professionals to get away from their desks and actively approach citizens with stubborn problems. On the other hand, the more self-reliant citizens who need support are stimulated to tap into their own network and call in the help of family, neighbours, volunteers, and others. Only when the citizens do not have resources in their own networks, and do not have the financial means to hire private help, can they can call upon professional support that is financed by the government.

Currently, the ideas of the *Wmo* are being developed further in the programme 'Welfare New Style' (Duch: *Welzijn Nieuwe Stijl*). In the report 'Citizen strength. The future of social work in the Netherlands' (Dutch: *Burgerkracht. De toekomst van sociaal werk in Nederland*, De Boer & Van der Lans, 2011a), the future of social work is outlined in accordance with the previously mentioned developments. According to this report, social work will make more space for initiatives where citizens support themselves and others – for example with family conferences. It is expected that support will only be given to clients who are not able to find solutions for their problems on their own, and who are deprived of support in their own circles. Sharply formulated: the client base of social work will change dramatically in the future. It will increasingly consist of citizens with complex problems, with limited support from social networks and low financial standing. Correspondingly, the proportion of clients who avoid care or cause nuisance will increase.

The trend of the last decennia, where the profession of social work increasingly moved in the direction of therapeutic care, and where it mostly focused on self-reliant clients with a clearly defined need for care, has been turning. The image of the social worker working from his office and only serving motivated clients, is currently outdated. This is now an old-fashioned professional profile which less and less matches the current social challenges.

The task for social work today is to return to the basics; to working with the socially vulnerable, and strengthening the professional equipment to be able to reach and guide these clients, thereby making the profession future-proof. There are also pragmatic reasons for focusing on clients with complex problems and thereby on potential flashpoints in society. Social work is currently under fire yet again, there are substantial cutbacks in the sector. In order to survive, social work will have to focus, out of enlightened self-interest, on social issues and target groups in society that have high priority. In this way it can prove its value and need to society as well.

4.4 Tasks for social work and education

In the previous paragraphs I argued that it is an important task for social work today to focus itself explicitly (again) on clients with complex problems. Therefore, social work needs to develop new approaches and methods (or revalue old approaches, such as the 'Towards it!'- approach (*Eropaf!*) to strengthen the connection with this target group. To get to this point, social work needs to professionalize further.

In line with this, there are also major challenges for the socio-pedagogic training programmes. The innovation in the curriculum needs to keep up with the innovations taking place in the work field. It is rather useless to train new batches of students on the basis of an outdated professional profile of the social worker who worked mostly in the office. In their current social work training, students need to be adequately encouraged and equipped to work with citizens with complex problems.

The research group Innovative Social Service Provision wants to contribute to this development by strengthening the knowledge base for the professional supply of assistance to citizens with multitudinous problems, and to enhance the education of these professionals in the socio-pedagogical training programmes. We do this, among other ways, by carrying out practical research. We carry out this research in close cooperation with students, teachers, and fellow professors of the Research Centre for Social Innovation. The research must conform to common quality standards of scientific research. The external assessment lies, in part, with the doctoral students who will graduate within the research group, and with papers we offer for publication to scientific journals. Besides carrying out research, the research group focuses on translating research results into practical applicable knowledge for the professional practice, and for educational material. I will now give some examples of these (research) projects.

In 2008 we published *Outreachend werken, Handboek voor werkers in de eerste lijn* ('Outreaching work, Handbook for professionals in primary care'[transl. eds.], Van Doorn et al., 2008). This book, which is meant for university students and social workers, gives an impression of the different aspects, possibilities, and limitations of outreach work. The publication is illustrated with practical experiences and offers pointers to apply this way of working. The reason for writing this book was our observation of the lack of a handbook on this theme. The handbook is mainly popular in the pedagogical training programmes of universities.

A second book, for students training for socio-legal service provision, is currently in development. This book offers students pointers on dealing with clients with complex problems, such as people with psychiatric backgrounds, marginal youth, care avoiders, etc. Parallel to the development of this book, the curriculum of the training programme is also being renewed, based on the principles in this book.

Another example is a project in which research is combined with mutual learning for students as well as homeless youth working together. In this project, the residents of a hostel for homeless youth and the students of the socio-pedagogical programmes of the HU University for Applied Sciences in Utrecht are grouped together in pairs. Both, the former homeless youth (in their roles as co-researchers) and the students, are offered a training on research and interview skills. The pairs then go out together to interview former residents of the hostel on their satisfaction with the (after)care they received from the hostel. This project cuts both ways. Homeless youth gain experience as interviewers, they learn from the experiences of former hostel residents, and they learn to cooperate with students. The students conversely, are introduced to the world of homeless youth in the intense setting of working together with them. And the hostel for homeless youth gains valuable policy information on their former residents (Deth & Van Doorn, 2010; Deth, Van Doorn & Rensen, 2009).

An example of practical research with its consequent effect in the professional practice is the study carried out on clients who received debt counselling, reviewing specifically the dropouts from the debt counselling programme. Around thirty dropouts were interviewed in Utrecht, to discover the reasons of their 'failure'. This resulted in recommendations to the debt counselling professionals to help them reduce the failure and relapse rates among clients, and in a training programme for debt counsellors and social workers (Akkermans, 2011).

Another study, one that in particular had spin-off effects in the media, politics, and science is a national study on the prevention of home foreclosures. We carried out this research on assignment by the Ministry of Housing, Welfare and Sports, and in cooperation with Utrecht University. The research got wide coverage in the media (Van Doorn, De Graaf, Akkermans & Kloppenburg, 2011), and led to parliamentary questions and publications in scientific journals (Stenberg, Van Doorn & Gerull, 2011; De Graaf, Van Doorn, Kloppenburg & Akkermans, 2011; Van Doorn, 2010).

As a last point, the research group also tries to increase historical awareness through close cooperation with the extraordinary research group History of Social Work, of Maarten van der Linde (2011). By looking back at a long and rich history of social work, and keeping an eye on long-term developments and the oscillations observed therein – or, as Kamphuis (1963) stated, 'by looking in the mirror of the past' – and by building on old values in today's innovations of social work, we attempt to achieve sustainable development. Looking back at the history of social work shows us that the contemporary task of social work to focus more on clients with complex problems is not new, but a return to the basics; the original foundation of social work.

Bibliography

Akkermans, C. (2011). *Schuldhulpverlening en dreigende huisuitzetting*. Lectoraat Innovatieve maatschappelijke dienstverlening, Kenniscentrum Sociale Innovatie. Utrecht: Hogeschool Utrecht.

Beck, U. (1992). *Risk Society: Towards a New Modernity*. New Delhi: Sage.

Boer, N. de & Lans, J. van der (2011a). *Burgerkracht. De toekomst van het sociaal werk in Nederland*. Den Haag: Raad voor Maatschappelijke Ontwikkeling.

Boer, N. de & Lans, J. van der (2011b). Laat meer over aan de zelfredzame burger. *Tijdschrift voor sociale vraagstukken*, *9*, 20-25.

Boutellier, H. (2002). *De Veiligheidsutopie. Hedendaags onbehagen en verlangen rond misdaad en straf*. Den Haag: Boom Juridische uitgevers.

Brandsen, T. et al. (2010). *Achter de voordeur. Professionals in de frontlijn tussen burgers en instanties. Internationale vergelijking*. Rotterdam: Stuurgroep Experimenten Volkshuisvesting.

Bransen, E., Hulsbosch, L. & Wolf, J. (2003). *Samenwerkingsprojecten Openbare Geestelijke Gezondheidszorg voor sociaal kwetsbare mensen* (Trimbos-instituut). Houten: Bohn Stafleu Van Loghum.

Cornelissen, E. & Brandsen, T. (2008). Kritiek op huisbezoeken is vrijblijvend. *Tijdschrift voor Sociale Vraagstukken*, *5*, 18-21.

Dalrymple, Th. (2004). *Leven aan de onderkant*. Amsterdam: Het Spectrum.

Dam, M. van (2009). *Niemandsland. Biografie van een ideaal*. Amsterdam: De Bezige Bij.

Deth, A. van (m.m.v. L. van Doorn, A.M. van Bergen, P. Rensen et al.) (2010). *Van zwerfjongere tot medeonderzoeker. Combating Youth Homelessness*. Utrecht: Movisie.

Deth, A. van & Doorn, L. van (2010). Zwerfjongeren als mede-onderzoeker. In M. Huber & T. Bouwens, *Samensturing in maatschappelijke opvang. De tegenstelling voorbij* (pp. 118-125). Wmo Werkplaatsen reeks. Utrecht: Movisie.

Deth, A. van, Doorn, L. van & Rensen, P. (2009). *Social exclusion of young homeless people:The State of Affairs in the Netherlands. A preliminary study for the European research project 'Combating Youth Homelessness'*. Utrecht: Movisie.

Doorn, L. van (2004). *Outreachende hulpverlening. Praktijkervaringen van 10 experimentele projecten*. Oranje Fonds. Arnhem: Uitgeverij Hoogland en Zoon.

Doorn, L. van (2009a). Dringen achter de voordeur. In E. Tonkens, *Tussen onderschatten en overvragen. Actief burgerschap en activerende organisaties in de wijk* (pp. 114-123) SUN Trancity – de STADSWIJKstudies. Amsterdam.

Doorn, L. van (2009b). *Maatschappelijk dienstverlenen in een veranderende omgeving.* Co-referaat Lou Jagt. Marie Kamphuis-lezing. Houten: Bohn Stafleu van Loghum.

Doorn, L. van (2010). Perceptions of Time and Space of (Formerly) Homeless People. *Journal of Human Behavior in the Social Environment, 20*(2), 218.

Doorn, L. van, Etten, Y. van & Gademan, M. (2008). *Outreachend werken. Handboek voorwerkers in de eerste lijn.* Bussum: Coutinho.

Doorn, L. van, Graaf, W. de, Akkermans, C. & Kloppenburg, R. (2011). Alarm over daklozegezinnen. Reconstructie van een mediahype. *Journal of Social Intervention: Theory and Practice, 20*(4), 5-20.

Driessens, K. & Regenmortel, T. (2006). *Bindkracht in armoede. Leefwereld en hulpverlening* (boek 1). Leuven: Uitgeverij LannooCampus.

Engbersen, G. & R. Van der Veer (1987). *Moderne armoede.* Leiden/Antwerpen: Stenfert Kroese.

Engbersen, G. (2006). Sluit je ogen niet voor de onderklasse van de 21e eeuw. *NRC Handelsblad*, 17th June 2006

Ewijk, H. van (2010). *Maatschappelijk werk in een sociaal gevoelige tijd.* Oratie. Utrecht: Humanistic University Press.

Garland, D. (2001). *The culture of control. Crime and social order in contemporary society.* Oxford: Oxford University Press.

Gezondheidsraad (2004). *Noodgedwongen.* Publicatie nr. 2004/10. Den Haag: Gezondheidsraad.

Graaf, W. de, Doorn, L. van, Kloppenburg, R. & Akkermans, C. (2011). Homeless families in the Netherlands: Intervention, Policies and Practices. *Journal of Social Research & Policy, 2*(1), 5-18.

Heineke, D., Veen, R. van der & Kornalijnslijper, N. (2005). *Handreiking ketensamenwerking in de Wmo. Maatschappelijke ondersteuning in samenhang.* Utrecht/Den Haag: NIZW/SGBO.

Henselmans, H. (1993). *Bemoeizorg, ongevraagde hulp voor psychotische patiënten.* Delft: Eburon.

Hermanns, J. (2009). Het wraparound care model en de vraag naar nieuwe jeugdzorgprofessionals. In: J. Gerris & R. Engels (red.), *Professionele kwaliteit in jeugdzorg en jeugdonderzoek* (pp. 85-98). Assen: Van Gorcum.

Hijzen, C., Kruiter, A.J., Jong, J. de & Niel, J. van (2008). *De Rotonde van Hamed. Maatwerk voor mensen met meerdere problemen.* Den Haag: NICIS.

Hoijtink. M. (2008). Bemoeizorg: de gedoogstatus voorbij. *Maatwerk, vakblad voor maatschappelijk werk, 15*(2), 4-9.

Inspectie voor de Gezondheidszorg. (2003). *Deelrapport staat van de gezondheidszorg 2003: Van overlastbestrijding naar bemoeizorg. Een onderzoek naar de kwaliteit van de ketenzorg voor zorgwekkende zorgmijders.*

Jagt, L. (2001). *Moet dat nou? Hulpverlening aan onvrijwillige cliënten*. Houten: Bohn Stafleu van Loghum.

Jagt, L. (2008). *Van Richmond naar Reid. Bronnen en ontwikkeling van taakgerichte hulpverlening in het maatschappelijk werk*. Proefschrift Universiteit Utrecht. Houten: Bohn

Stafleu van Loghum, Kamphuis, M. (1963). *Nieuwe wegen in het werk met probleemgezinnen: het casework-experiment in het Family Centered Project in St Paul*. Alphen aan den Rijn: Samsom.

Kuypers, P. & Lans, J. van der (1994). *Naar een modern paternalisme*. Amsterdam: De Balie.

Laan, G. van der (1990). *Legitimatieproblemen in het maatschappelijk werk*. Utrecht: SWP.

Lans, J. van der (2010). *Eropaf! De nieuwe start van het sociaal werk*. Amsterdam: Augustus.

Linde, M. van der (2010), *Basisboek Geschiedenis sociaal werk in Nederland* (4de druk). Amsterdam: SWP.

Linde, M. van der (2011). *Doe wel, maar... zie om. Een pleidooi voor historisch besef in het sociaal werk*. Utrecht: Hogeschool Utrecht.

Lindt, S.M. van der, Bokkem, J.S. van & Rooijen, S. van (2004). *Samenwerkingsmodel OGGZ. Rapportage van een studie naar OGGZ-samenwerking ten behoeve van 'zorgwekkende zorgmijders'*. Utrecht: Trimbos-instituut.

Lourens, J., Scholten, C., Werf, C. van der & Ziegelaar, A. (2002). *Verkommerden en verloederden. Een onderzoek naar de omvang en aard van de groep in Nederland*. Amsterdam: Research voor Beleid.

Menger, A. & Bouwens, J. (1995). *Activerende hulpverlening. Rapport methodiekontwikkeling*. Rotterdam: Hogeschool Rotterdam en Omstreken.

Menger, A. (1997). Voorwaardelijke, gedwongen, outreachend, bemoeizorg of gewoon AMW? *Tijdschrift voor de Sociale Sector*, 6, 10-13.

Milikowski, H.Ph. (1967). *Lof der onaangepastheid. Een studie in sociale aanpassing, niet aanpassing, onmaatschappelijkheid*. Meppel: Boom.

Ministeries van VWS en BZK (2011). *Aan de slag achter de voordeur. Van signaleren naar samenwerken*. Den Haag.

Raad voor Maatschappelijke Ontwikkeling (2001). *Kwetsbaarheid in kwadraat. Krachtige steun aan kwetsbare mensen. Advies 16*. Den Haag: Sdu Uitgevers.

Raad voor Maatschappelijke Ontwikkeling (2008). *De ontkokering voorbij. Slim organiseren voor meer regelruimte*. Den Haag: Raad voor Maatschappelijke Ontwikkeling.

Rakers, M. & Jong, C. de (red.) (2006). *Eopaf. Outreachend werken in welzijn en wonen*. Amsterdam: Van Gennep/de Balie.

Research voor Beleid (2002). *Verkommerden en verloederden. Een onderzoek naar de omvang en aard van de groep in Nederland.* Houten: Trimbos-instituut i.s.m. uitgeverij Bohn Stafleu Van Loghum.

Riet, N. van (2010). *Social Work. Mensen helpen tot hun recht laten komen.* Assen: Van Gorcum.

Rutte, M. (2009, 20 april). Mensen krijgen kans op kans maar kiezen een plek aan de zijlijn. Essay. *NRC Handelsblad.*

Scholte, M. (2010). *Oude waarden in nieuwe tijden,* Amsterdam: Hogeschool Inholland.

Schuyt, C.J.M. (1995). *Kwetsbare jongeren en hun toekomst. Een beleidsadvies gebaseerd op een literatuurverkenning.* Amsterdam: Centrale Directie Voorlichting, Documentatie en Bibliotheek van het ministerie van Volksgezondheid, Welzijn en Sport.

Spierings, F. (1998). Dak- en thuislozen in Rotterdam. Hulpverlening en overlastbestrijding. *Justitiële Verkenningen,* (24)1, 82-92.

Sprinkhuizen, A., M. Scholte, K. Penninx, D. Heineke en L. van Doorn. Burgerkracht of spierballentaal. *Tijdschrift voor Sociale Vraagstukken.* No 7-8 / juli-augustus 2011, 20-25.

Stenberg, S.A., Doorn, L. van & Gerull, S. (2011). Locked out in Europe. A comparative Analysis of Evictions due to Rent Arrears in Germany, the Netherlands and Sweden. *European Journal of Homelessness.* Volume 5, no. 2, December 2011, 39-62.

Stichting Eropaf! (2009). *Manifest Eropaf! 2.0.*

Tonkens, E. (2009). *Tussen onderschatten en overvragen. Actief burgerschap en activerende organisaties in de wijk.* Amsterdam: SUN.

Wetenschappelijke Raad voor het Regeringsbeleid (2004). *Bewijzen van goede dienstverlening.* Amsterdam: Amsterdam University Press.

Wolf, J., Bransen, E. & Nicholas, S. (2001). Mensen in de marge. Kenmerken van sociale kwetsbaarheid. *Justitiële verkenningen, 27*(6), 19-38.

Wolf, J., Zwikker, M., Nicholas, S., Bakel, H. van, Reinking, D. & Leiden, I. van (2002). *Op achterstand. Een onderzoek naar mensen in de marge van Den Haag.* Trimbos-instituut in cooperation with Bohn Stafleu van Loghum.

5. Looking for the forgotten *Eropaf!*-pioneers[7]

A plea for historical awareness in social work

Maarten van der Linde

In this contribution, my thesis is: the outreach- or *Eropaf!*-method, which was discovered by the end of the twentieth century as being the core business of general social work, is placed in a century old tradition.[8] In order to prove this, I will put the spotlight on five largely forgotten *Eropaf!*-pioneers from the nineteenth and early twentieth century: Elizabeth Fry, Thomas Chalmers, Daniel von der Heydt, Octavia Hill and Johanna ter Meulen.[9]

5.1 Getting started at the front line

After the eighties of the last century, years of spending cuts and social breakdown, a new impetus arose in the Netherlands – partly inspired by the motto of 'Social renewal' of the confessional social-democratic Lubbers/Kok administration – with which, in a new self-conscious tone, positive spirit was given to confounded concepts such as 'interference' and 'paternalism'.[10] The town of Bergen op Zoom had already broken a taboo by forcing to relocate families causing serious disturbance.[11] Publications on education, civilization and guidance of problem families, drew attention to traditional and modern solutions and methods.[12] Historian and publicist Geert Mak has written about neigbourhoods that had fallen into decline, such as the Indonesian neighbourhood (*Indische buurt*), or people who were left to their fate, completely dirty and isolated.[13] In 1995 he observed the 'dissolution of the home visit': 'the labour-intensive handwork of the welfare state, that has gone completely

---

[7] *Eropaf!* translates roughly as 'Go for it!'. It stands for a professional orientation in social work that favours an outreaching approach of actually visiting clients, even when there is no official demand or question on their behalf.

[8] Especially: Räkers & Huber, 2010; Van der Lans, 2011b; Van Doorn, Van Etten & Gademan, 2008; Van Doorn, 2004; Räkers & De Jong, 2006; Van der Lans, Medema & Räkers, 2003; Kuypers & Van der Lans, 1994; Henselmans, 1993.

[9] This article is an adjusted version of the second part of my public lecture of 11 November 2011; see Van der Linde, 2011b.

[10] For a description of this development see Van der Linde, 2010, p. 239-244

[11] *Woonschool voor asocialen* ('Boarding school for anti-socials'), NRC Handelsblad, 18 March 1989

[12] De Regt, 1986; Dercksen & Verplanke, 1987.

[13] Mak, 1991, 1992

out of sight at certain official care institutions'. Mak wrote about the budget cuts on the infant and toddler care of the Amsterdam Municipal Health Service, where he cited Wil Ottens, district nurse in the *Bos en Lommer* neighbourhood: 'But what if a mother fails to visit us, and we know the situation is worrisome? Now we pay her a visit, and we keep doing so. Such additional activity will soon be no option for us anymore.' Maks conclusion: 'The Dutch administrators are far too decent for blunt cost-benefit estimates as is done today in America with comparable programs. Like, every hundred dollars spent now in toddler care will save us seven hundred dollars on education, health care and police. Still we can wish they did. Some cuts and privatizations have gradually transcended all rationality. It has become an ideology, of which the dogmatism exceeds that of the old Marxists.'[14]

Nico van Velzen, director of the National Housing Council, argued in 1990 for a revaluation of functional monitoring, for example to be carried out by the landlord, and a stricter approach of the police in cases of trouble. In his doctorate thesis in1993, social nurse Henri Henselmans launched the concept *bemoeizorg*, which translates roughly as 'interference care' or 'outreach care'.[15] With this new word he combined the concepts 'interference' and 'caring', and in doing so opposed to the commoditization of the social sector and to the culture of 'wait and see' and detachment. It had to be about providing support to people who did not ask for it, but of whom you, as a professional, know that they need it.

In 1994, community work veteran Paul Kuypers and social work expert Jos van der Lans published the pamphlet 'Towards a modern paternalism' (*Naar een modern paternalisme*): 'What we need is a new blend of commitment and effectiveness (...) for professionals doing their work in the broad field of welfare. One example of this is the emergence of the term 'interference care' in the mental health care sector. The essence of that approach is: not waiting till they come to the institutions, but to keep coming after them, keep looking for them, correcting them if necessary, and most of all, offer a lot of practical help. (...) We argue for a new professional interpretation of what we still see as belonging to the heart of the Dutch welfare state – the principle that no one should be left to their own fate. This indeed does involve interfering, visiting, ringing the door, arranging and directing, instead of (professionally) waiting till it's too late. This is an attitude that will soon be seen as a new form of

---

[14]   Mak, 1995 [transl. eds.]
[15]   Henselmans, 1993

paternalism – so be it. In our eyes, it is a kind of paternalism we seriously lacked during the past decennium.' [transl. eds.]

In that same year, 8 years before the success of Pim Fortuyn's popular revolt, Van der Lans wrote in an essay in the left-liberal weekly De Groene Amsterdammer: 'What happened to the old-fashioned craftsmanship in the institutions of the welfare state? Professionals prefer to sit behind their desks being specialists, rather then exercising their crafts in the front lines on the streets.' He argued thus for a new professional élan and for 'reaching out'.[16] More or less simultaneously, social work professor and –manager Anneke Menger developed, together with her colleagues at the Social Work department of Hogeschool Rotterdam, a new methodology called 'activating care' (activerende hulpverlening). This methodology was based on a social work project in The Hague for the long-term unemployed.[17] Since coercion and pressure quickly came high on the agenda of the care sector in the nineties, Menger explained the different meanings of care methods: 'Conditional, forced, outreaching, interfering or just social casework?'[18] At the 1997 conference Ongevraagd bijgestuurd [transl.: 'Uninvitedly corrected'], organized by the Dutch Society of Social Workers (NVMW), it became clear how much resistance these new approaches evoked. But the development towards more interference and more outreaching work continued. Successful projects were set up. In Rotterdam it was the project 'Curb' (Stoeprand), which was aimed at tenants with debts, who were threatened to be put out of their homes. Study of the individual situation of clients seemed to be indispensable here: sometimes intensive supervision was needed, in other cases just keeping an eye was enough. Clients were given supervision contracts, although such an intense form of support often turned out to be unnecessary. In Amsterdam in the mid nineties, 'The Flying Dutchman' (De Vliegende Hollander) became active, a team for urgent needs. It originated from the mobile service centre of HVO-Querido, the municipal organization for shelter and care for the homeless. Marc Räkers remembers the occasion: the house of a woman with substantial rent arrears was almost evicted, although no one had come to see her, no one had tried to get in touch with her. Social work was out of the picture, the housing corporation only communicated in writing. How was it possible that social work had not shown up, and how could the housing corporation have let it come this far? Together

---

[16]   Van der Lans, 1994 [transl. eds.]
[17]   Menger & Bouwes, 1995
[18]   Menger, 1997 [transl. eds.]

with the Salvation Army, HVO-Querido founded the The Flying Dutchman-team, which managed to prevent around six hundred evictions in the following years.[19]

These innovative experiments were not only conceived of and executed in the Randstad region, but all over the country; albeit often on a small scale. One example from the east of the country: community worker Joop Schinkel formed in 1994 the Neighbourhood Innovation Team Zwolle (*Buurt Innovatie Team Zwolle (BITZ)*), in the Indonesian neighbourhood[20], together with the local police officer and a social employee of the housing corporation. They had a contract with the city for fifteen years (!), worked integrally, with broad mandate, outreaching and went 'towards it' par excellence.[21]

In 1997, the ministry of Health, Welfare and Sport (*VWS*) made interfering/outreaching care spearhead of its policy. Within the social work profession, the vision and corresponding methods of work were discussed and elaborated. From 2001 to 2003, the *Oranje Fonds* financed a program called 'Outreaching Care' (*Outreachende hulpverlening*), in which twenty-four organizations in the broad field of welfare work were offered the opportunity to develop outreaching care in their own situation. Requested by the Oranje Fonds, Anneke Menger and her colleagues travelled through the country to train social workers in this new method. Afterwards, the practical experiences gained from ten of these projects were described by pedagogue Lia van Doorn, who herself had done a multi-year study of the homeless in Utrecht city.[22] That's how a caring paternalism reappeared on the scene during the nineties.[23]

If she would have been able to witness it, this would have brought a grateful smile to social work veteran Marie Muller-Lulofs, who passed away in 1954, almost hundred years of age. For more than half a century she had been the epitome of that same caring and social-liberal kind of paternalism. She was known for her people skills and extensive practical work in the city of Utrecht, and already by the year 1900 she laid the foundations of the then modern methodological individual welfare work in the Netherlands.[24] She was also initiator of the establishment of the

[19] Räkers, 2008; S. Spinder et al., 2008, p. 63-74; De Koning, 2003.
[20] The name refers to the streetnames, which are inspired by the Indonesian colonial heritage. It has nothing to do with the ethnicity of the residents.
[21] The approach has been described by Hes, 2000.
[22] Van Doorn, 2004; Van Doorn, 2002
[23] Tonkens & Duyvendak, 2001
[24] Muller-Lulofs, 1906. On the meaning of Muller-Lulofs as founding member of

School for Social Work in Amsterdam (1899). She was a spirited speaker and she acted in a similar spirited fashion. In 1916 she wrote:

'Every care for the poor, which does not penetrate to the deepest sources, from which the poverty arises, and lets the core of poverty remain unchallenged; every care for the poor which only works alleviatory and not preventive, i.e. not to be found in the forefront of those actually participating in the work of social reform: the improvement of housing, control of tuberculosis, curbing of alcohol abuse, child protection, expansion of insurance options, promoting of the trade union life, increase the level of our public education, combating usury, educating housewives and mothers, improving the health care for the poor, every such care is partly to blame for the contempt, to which the care for the poor, despite the significant evolution it has undergone over the pas thirty years, is still exposed. Care for the poor without a social politics will never achieve its highest goal: rehabilitation, the elimination of poverty in the most comprehensive manner.'[25]

5.2 *Eropaf!*-moment 1: Inmates are humans too. London, 1813: Elizabeth Fry

Image 5.1 Elizabeth Fry, around 1815

---

modern social work: Bervoets, 1999; Geertsema, 2004, p. 67-71; Jagt, 2008, p. 95-105; Simpelaar, 2011. Jan Adriani (1874-1948) and Hans Everts (1882-1954), two social work cracks of the first half of the twentieth century, learned the craft with her.
[25] Muller-Lulofs, 1916, p. X [transl. eds.]

On January 13th, 1813, Elizabeth Fry rang the doorbell of the infamous Newgate prison in London. She had founded a women's committee, and asked permission to speak with the female inmates and their children. She wanted to know what these women needed, whether they would appreciate being read from the Bible for an hour, whether they would like to work and earn some money, and whether they wanted their children to receive education. The warden didn't like the idea, and moreover thought it would be dangerous. He feared for the safety of Fry and her friends. Elizabeth was not put off, and managed to get inside. Her visit was a milestone in the reform of the prison system, and a starting point for the concept of rehabilitation.

Elizabeth Fry (1780-1845) grew up in a Quaker family. The Quakers harnessed strong ideals of equality and pacifism. Quakers were early opponents of slavery and active in philanthropic projects. Her faith inspired Elizabeth to care for people being less fortunate then herself. 'Faith without action is mockery', was her motto. In her hometown she would visit families and offer practical help. At young age already she started a girls school and later she was admitted to the ministry – Quakers could also have women ministers. In the Irish colony of her hometown she did work that we would now call district nursing or home care.

From 1813 onwards she continued her visits to the women in Newgate. She brought food, clean sheets and medicines. Friday became Newgate-day; year after year she would visit the women and their children. With other women she started a prison school for the children. The female inmates called her 'the Angel of Newgate'. Her work was noticed and had influence on politics. Her method had three basic rules:

1. Male and female inmates need to be separated from each other. Surveillance of women by women, surveillance of men by men.

2. Inmates should receive education and be able to do paid work.

3. For visiting female inmates, women's committees need to be set up. Volunteers take care of the education and paid work during detention. After release from the prison, they offer guidance and supervision to enable a successful return into society.

Fry was practical, but she also published on the principles, methods and goals of prison reform and rehabilitation. She visited prisons all over the United Kingdom and was involved in the creation of dozens of women's committees. She was consulted by the House of the Commons and the House of the Lords.[26] In the Netherlands, her work had already drawn attention since 1820, and she helped the impetus to the Dutch Society of the Moral Improvement of Prisoners (*Nederlands Genootschap tot Zedelijke Verbetering van Gevangenen*), in 1823.

Fry travelled to six European countries, in 1840 and 1841 she visited Dutch prisons in eight cities.[27] In Amsterdam and Zwolle, women's committees for visiting female inmates were founded in the presence of Fry. She also visited the women's prison in Gouda, and made acquaintance with Barbara van Meerten-Schilperpoort, who was one of the first to visit Dutch women in prisons, already from 1832.[28] In Gouda, Fry and her commission objected to male visitors having free access to the whole building. Fry personally complained at the Ministry of Justice of the Netherlands.[29] After a year she returned to the Netherlands to see if her advice had been followed up. She also travelled to France. After an inspection tour of the Paris prisons, she reported to the king of France. In the preface she wrote: 'When thee builds a prison, thee had better build with the thought ever in thy mind that thee and thy children may occupy the cells.'[30]

Fry was accustomed to speaking in public. She spoke with emotion, and appealed to her audience to not live for worldly affairs, but to live by faith. This moved her audience to tears. She didn't restrict herself to the urgent need for reform of the prison system, but also argued passionately for the abolition of slavery, the reform of the insane asylums, and abolition of the death penalty. The antirevolutionary Calvinist politician Groen van Prinsterer and the conservative poet Isaac da Costa were impressed, even though they were not in favour of radical reforms.[31] Their conservative friends were shocked at how they let themselves be

---

[26] Van Drenth & De Haan, 1999; De Haan, 1995; Krutzen, 2007.

[27] Betsy Groen van Prinsterer (1807-1879) guided Elizabeth Fry during her visit to the The Hague prison. She herself was active in social work, i.e. in club work and the foundation of a sewing school for girls from needy families.

[28] Krutzen, 2009.

[29] Franke, 1990, p. 85

[30] 'Report on Paris Prisons.' Addressed to the King of France, cited by Elbert Hubbard, *Little Journeys to the Homes of Famous Women*. New York, 1911.

[31] Janse, 2007, p. 55. In his *Bezwaren tegen de geest der eeuw* [transl. 'Objections to the spirit of the age'] (1823, later print 1974), Isaac da Costa (1798-1860) objected to 'hundreds of societies' rushing into 'immature and thoughtless designs of improvement, rehabilitation, or eradication of one or the other physical or moral disease'. [transl. eds.]

carried away by Fry, and pointed to the yawning gap between the Dutch Réveil and the British Quakers. The Quakers were racial-liberal and reformist, something the Réveil very much opposed to.[32]

The special thing about Fry was that she knew how to inspire both conservatives and liberals, both orthodox and liberal Protestants. She was an example for the orthodox Protestant minister Otto Gerhard Heldring, but also for the liberal merchant-philantropist Willem Hendrik Suringar. In Amsterdam she inspired the emerging educational work for the poor. Women played a big role in the forties (!) of the nineteenth century in the foundation and daily management of the Association of Assistance to Fair and Diligent Poverty (*Vereeniging Hulpbetoon aan Eerlijke en Vlijtige Armoede*). This association organized personal contact, home visits and work mediation.[33]

Elizabeth Fry became a figurehead of the humanitarian reform movement of the early nineteenth century. Because of her example of what women can accomplish, she was also at the birth of the nineteenth century women's movement.

Elizabeth Fry's enduring values:
- The power of a women's committee.
- Volunteering.
- Christian social and humanitarian values
- Faith in the values of the Gospel must lead to action: 'Faith without action is mockery.'
- Offering a new perspective by re-socialization.
- Fighting for depreciated people.
- Maintaining long-term, reliable and personal contact.
- Assistance with employment, housing and education.

---

[32] Janse, 2007, p. 55-56
[33] Janse, 2007, p. 103-1-4, Jo Egging, 2005, p. 63-64

5.3 *Eropaf!*-moment 2: To help the poor to help themselves. Glasgow, 1819, Thomas Chalmers

Figure 5.2   Thomas Chalmers, around 1820

In September 1819, Thomas Chalmers (1780-1847) took office as pastor of the St. Johns Church, a new parish in Glasgow East, a working class district with around 2000 families. All together, around 11000 people lived here, mostly weavers, day labourers, and factory workers. Chambers fought poverty, using the motto: 'to help the poor help themselves'.[34] Another expression that gained popularity was his exclamation: 'no measures but men'.[35] Chalmers arrived in Glasgow in times of great economic and social turmoil and indeed of social struggle. Glasgow around 1810 was the centre of a bitter battle of weavers for the legal regulation of the minimum wage.[36] Chalmers acknowledged the right of workers to organize in unions, and the right of unions to negotiate better working conditions.

Thomas Chalmers was gifted and ambitious and studied theology at the age of 16. When he was 19 he became pastor. He belonged to the moderate stream of evangelical Presbyterianism. Chalmers also had a

---

[34] Adriani, 1940, p. 74, footnote 1; Tjeenk Willink & Treurniet, 1958, p. 298, in their review article *Voortgang en Samenhang 1908-1958* [transl. Progress and Coherence 1908-1958) start the 'care for the poor as learning case for social work' with Thomas Chalmers work in the St. Johns Parish. For convenience they start with the year 1808, instead of 1819 (1808-1908-1958).

[35] De Bruijn, 1954; Hilton, 1988; Beutel, 2007; Melief, 1955.

[36] Thompson, 1980, p. 591-593.

great talent for mathematics, and since he was leading a small community, had had time to teach mathematics at the University of Edinburgh. But in 1809 he went through a faith crisis, due to the heavy and prolonged illness of close relatives who ultimately died shortly after each other. This faith crisis changed everything. From then on, he wanted to be an 'ambassador of Christ', and with his passionate preaching style he drew big crowds to the church. In his sermons he spoke of sin, grace and salvation: 'Christ has also died for you.' Salvation was assured for everyone. He compared the sermons of the moderate 'evangelicals' to a clear winter day: 'short, clear and cold'. He himself spoke long, soulful, in a warm tone, and effective.[37]

Chalmers convinced his colleagues that social support was only effective if it was performed in regular, personal contact. He went into the neighbourhoods, and paid dozens of visits each week, about which he said: 'a house-going minister creates a church-going people'.[38] For these home visits, he also engaged women. He divided the area into twenty-five districts of each sixty to a hundred families. In every district, the families were appointed to a couple, consisting of a church elder and a deacon, and sometimes voluntary home visitors. The elder was responsible for the spiritual support, the deacon for material needs. The deacon addressed requests for financial assistance.

Chalmers' focus on the neighbourhood as a unity where people live together and know each other, was a basic principle of his method: 'locality in truth, is the secret principle wherin our great strength lieth'.[39] Chalmers organized evening meetings per street or per district, for which he invited the people that he or the duo had visited. There he spoke of 'the faith that brings joy and confidence in the heart', about how relationships between people should be, and about the plans he wanted to achieve.

First, he brought the Sunday school back to life. Therefore he mobilized a staff of fifty teachers, and in 1819 the amount of children coming to the Sunday schools rose from almost zero to twelve hundred. Together with the church elders, deacons and school leaders, he maintained contact

---

[37] Writer and historian Thomas Carlyle (1795-1881): 'No preacher ever went so into one's heart'; William Wilberforce (1759-1833): 'All the world is wild about Dr. Chalmers'. Wilberforce was sine the eighties of the eighteenth century a prominent leader of the British movement for the abolishment of slavery and slave trade. Quotes from Hilton, 1988, p. 56-58.

[38] Quote from De Bruijr, 1975, p. 40.

[39] Quote from De Bruijr, 1975, p. 39.

with the parents, made sure the children kept coming, and founded a library where parents and children could borrow books. Then he sought for the construction of neighbourhood schools, home schools, sewing schools and character education. Thirdly, Chalmers undertook a compressive attempt to reform the care for the poor, using the principle of the community being responsible for the aid and assistance for their own poor. Just as it had been in the first Christian communities. Like many contemporaries, Chalmers was looking for alternatives to public assistance funds. His objection was, that what should spring from love and compassion, had become a regulated, legal and morally neutral affair, entirely in contrast to what the apostle Paul had written in his second letter to the Corinthians: 'I say this not as a command, but to prove by the earnestness of others that your love also is genuine. (...) For if the readiness is there, it is acceptable according to what a person has, not according to what he does not have. For I do not mean that others should be eased and you burdened, but that as a matter of fairness your abundance at the present time should supply their need, so that their abundance may supply your need, that there may be fairness.'[40] He also saw permanent assistance provision as a culprit: people got used to it, lost their self-esteem, their pursuit of self-support was undermined, and inventiveness in looking for mutual and reciprocal assistance was smothered.[41]

The church council of St. John's Parish accounted for the social assistance for all the needy and poor in the area. The church council abandoned the payments from the city treasury (in 1819 around £1400 per year), and would cover the costs themselves out of the proceeds from the donations in the church. But that meant that all the proceeds would be used for the care for the poor, and no payments were to made to the city treasury. Chalmers made arrangements for people living in municipal residential institutions and asylums.

It worked. What used to cost £1400 a year in benefits, did not exceed £400 in 1819 and after. Mutual support, job creation, job placement and strong social control had their effect. To reach the desired objective – the community taking care of its own poor – little was left to chance. He expected from the church officials, mainly the deacons and home visitors, that they lived in the districts they were responsible for. They had to earn the trust of the people, and this would only be possible if they

---

[40] *The Bible*, English Standard Version: 2 Corinthians 8: 8-14
[41] Hilton, 1988, p. 100-102; Loch (1910, p. 345-377) gives a summary of Chalmers vision.

knew the residents and regularly were in touch with the families with difficulties. Chalmers insisted that 'more than with money, a community is built with neighbour interest, friendship and good advice'.[42] Personal contact and knowledge of the situation would enable deacons and home visitors to identify possible fraud, but it would also work preventative by recognizing problems in time. In this kind of care, helping to find work had to be of central importance. Unemployment was usually the source of poverty, so offering employment was more important than financial support. Even if the person concerned was unaccustomed to working, everything had to be done to change the life habits, in order for the person to be able to work again. These days we would say this person needs to build up working rhythm again. If there was no work in the labour market, than the deacon had to find out if family and friends could in some way or another assist in finding work. Parents and children, neighbours and family, rich and poor, all were responsible for each other. But help had to be inconspicuous, instead of a selfish display of mercy. Charmers also thought random donations were wrong. If someone had to rely on the financial assistance from the church, a second deacon had to carry out an investigation and report to the church council. The personal contact between resident and deacon was important, but the deacon's use of his common sense and working with great care, even more so.

Chalmers was aware that the system was largely successful due to his personal charisma and persuasiveness. In 1823 – the year that he exchanged St. John's parish for a professorship in Edinburgh – he wrote to his kindred spirit William Wilberforce that his system would function independently before he would leave Glasgow: the people would solve the problem of care for the poor themselves.[43]

Chalmers system lasted until 1837. It was not adopted by other parishes. Already in the twenties of the nineteenth century and thereafter, criticism was heard. For example: 'The area is not as poor as thought', 'The donations in church are high, this makes help easier', 'Deacons are often wealthy and give donations from their own pockets', 'The silent poor are overlooked', 'The poor are being chased out of the area because of social control', 'With a leader like Chalmers you can do this in any neighbourhood'. Critics defended the system of municipal poverty relief, and rejected Chalmers critique as being exaggerated. If there was misuse, the system could be reformed. In contrast with parish based care for the poor, state care was stabile.

---

[42] Quote from De Bruijn, 1975, p. 63 [transl. eds.]
[43] De Bruijn, 1975, p. 63

Chalmers knew how to inspire his collaborators in the parish of St. John's, but he overestimated the power of his story and the capabilities of the modern town. His ambition was even characterized as urban feudalism.[44]

The St. John's parish experiment gained popularity in Britain, the United States and the English speaking parts of the world. But his work was also translated into Dutch and German. Chalmers also had influence in the Netherlands. The concept of 'patronage', which flourished from 1830 onwards, was partly inspired by him.

Chalmers slogans 'to help the poor to help themselves' and 'no measures but men' are after two hundred years both classic and modern, and recognizable in the modern concepts of empowerment and the debate on 'what works and who works'.[45] His appeal and practice continue to inspire the diaconal community.[46] Especially in Germany, Chalmers' influence continued, in what is known as the Elberfelder-system, to which we will turn in the next paragraph.

Thomas Chalmers enduring values:
-   Plea for solidarity and unity between the rich and poor.
-   Critical attitude to distribution policy sustaining poverty.
-   Offering education, schooling and work.
-   'To help the poor to help themselves'.
-   'No measures, but men'.
-   Neighbourhood based organization of poverty relief.
-   Investigation and personal contact through home visits.
-   Mobilising resources in the neighbourhood, such as family, neighbours and the local economy.

---

[44] In *Building Jerusalem. The Rise and Fall of the Victorian City* (p. 72, 73) Hunt (1974) typified Chalmers ambition as 'urban feudalism'. Tristram Hunt is historian and publicist, and since 2010 Labour member of the British House of Commons.

[45] Menger, 2009.

[46] Beutel, 2007, p. 146-187: 'Das Konzept der diakonischen Gemeinde'.

5.4 *Eropaß*-moment 3: Aid from person to person. Elberfeld, 1853, Daniel von der Heydt.

The Elberfelder system has had great international influence.[47] It built a bridge between old municipal and diaconal systems of neighbourhood based poverty relief and modern district based social work. The Elberfelder system provided the model for the reorganization of the British and American poor relief, which was manifested in the Charity Organization Societies in the seventies and eighties of the nineteenth century.[48] In the Netherlands the system inspired pioneers who were reforming the care for the poor since 1870.[49]

Image 5.3 Daniel von der Heydt

Daniel von der Heydt (1802-1874), banker, entrepreneur, and politician in the German city Elberfeld, was the central figure in designing the new system around 1850. What did the Elberfelder system entail?[50] The innovation lied mostly in the combination between decentralization, a

---

[47] Sachße & Tennstedt, 1998, p. 214-218; Loch, 1910, p. 344-345; Darley, 2010, p. 118 and p. 359, footnote 9; Agnew, 2004, p. 62-94; Trattner, 1999, p. 91-103.

[48] In 1877, Octavia Hill pointed at the difference between the Elberfelder-system and the approach in Marylebone, London: 'The important difference between the Elberfeld and the Maylebone systems is that, whereas in Elberfeld the volunteers themselves decide on the parochial relief, our volunteers have no such authority committed to them.' In Marylebone 'the Visitor brings information and the Guardians vote relief'. Darley, 2010, p. 359, footnote 9.

[49] Van der Linde, 2011.

[50] Sachße & Tennstedt, 1998, p. 215-218; Beutel, 2007, p. 238-241

small scale and an individual approach. The city was divided into ten districts, and every district consisted of fifteen neighbourhoods. Each neighbourhood was under the supervision of a 'visitor of the poor'; in total there were around 150 of these visitors in 1853. With a growing city, this number increased. Thus, in 1872, there were eighteen districts with each fourteen neighbourhoods and in total 252 visitors of the poor. In 1902 the number of visitors of the poor had risen to 500. These visitors thus worked in clear sections, and they accompanied two to four families. It had to be done besides regular work and social obligations. The district commissions (chairman and visitors) gathered every fortnight. The decision making on granting financial assistance was decentralised. This power was transferred to the district meeting.

'From person to person' became the slogan of the Elberfelder system. The visitor of the poor needed to carefully examine each case. For the home visits, the norm was at least one visit each fortnight. In urgent cases the visitor could grant short-term assistance without consultation. For all the requests for municipal assistance, the thumb-rule was that one had ascertained that no help could be received from family members or neighbours. Another important task for the visitor of the poor was to find work for the unemployed. Visitors of the poor often belonged to the wealthier classes of society, which meant that they either hired people themselves or inquired for vacancies with their fellow visitors of the poor. Together, the visitors of the poor formed a network-like job agency in the growing economy of Wuppertal, of which Elberfeld was part. If work was offered, then the person was required to accept. The visitors of the poor were hereby instructed to also work preventive.

The voluntary act of visiting the poor was considered a civic duty; voting citizens were asked to join. It was seen as an honourable position, which was virtually impossible to reject. During the first decades, women were not eligible for the position of visitor of the poor in Elberfeld. Hamburg formed an exception; women could join there since 1900, albeit in a subordinate position. This was a difference with the Netherlands, where at the society Charity to Capacity (*Liefdadigheid naar Vermogen*), women participated as visitors of the poor from 1884 onwards. Mrs. M.C. de Marez Oyens-Reynvaan was appointed member of the committee for home visits and became the first visitor of the poor of the modern philanthropic society Charity to Capacity.[51]

---

[51] Fuchs, 1971, p. 53-54

The Elberfelder system turned out to be a great success, also financially: in the years after its introduction, the spending on poverty relief had almost been halved. It also upheld when the population tripled to 160.000 inhabitants between 1850 and 1900. At the time of the German Empire, in 1892, the Elberfelder system had been introduced into almost all municipalities with more than 50.000 inhabitants. Also in Hamburg and Berlin, the care for the poor was organized on the basis of the Elberfelder system.[52]

However, it must be noted that the system was introduced and flourished for decades in a period of unprecedented economic growth and growing prosperity and employment in Germany, with rising wages and improved training and development of the industrial workers. Elberfeld is located in the Ruhr, which speaks for itself. In the existing literature on the system, this fact is not often given its due attention.

In the early twentieth century, in most German cities, the decision making on applications for support was again centralized. One of the arguments in favour was that expertise, overview of the entire system of urban poor relief, and an equal treatment of equal cases became increasingly important. I also appeared that the combination of home visits, research, reporting, counselling and mediation, monitoring and weekly disbursement of the assistance was a heavy task for the visitors of the poor. It was not easy to find volunteers who could do all this. Another objection was that the visitors of the poor were bound to their neighbourhoods, even when they had no good rapport with the assigned families and individuals. In bigger cities this issue was solved by forming groups of visitors of the poor, and when assigning visitors to families, taking into account the specific qualities of the visitor and the specific problems of the family. Visitor of the poor as a paid profession remained a considerably big taboo. An important argument was that because of the voluntary character, the relief of the poor was supported by the population. Yet already in the nineties of the nineteenth century, a point of discussion was the possible separation between research (intake, diagnosis) by salaried officials, and the support by volunteer visitors. There was also the eternal complaint of voluntary visitors being too generous in their aid. It required much experience and people skills to

---

[52] These major reorganizations (Hamburg 1893-1896; Berlin 1896-1901) were led by Emil Münsterberg (1855-1911). He was the leading authority in the field of poverty relief during the German Empire and a pioneer in the field of poverty statistics. On care for the poor he published a.o. *Die Armenpflege. Einführung in die praktische Pflegetätigkeit* (1897).

find the right balance between the role of confidant and the role of controller. This counted especially for the paid visitors employed by local authorities, for they could not turn down clients. Visitors of the poor working for private associations had it slightly easier, since these associations chose the families and individuals themselves. Difficult families that were impossible to work with, were expelled. The method mainly worked for families and persons who more or less wanted to contribute to the improvement of their condition.[53] Around 1900, also the more systematic training and education of the visitors of the poor started. In 1907, Alice Salomon started the *Soziale Frauenschule* (Social Women's School; transl. eds.), and in 1899 the *Opleidingsinrichting voor Socialen Arbeid* (Training Institute for Social Work; transl. eds.) was launched.

Of course, the Elberfelder system was not created out of thin air. Around 1850, the system of municipal governance of the poor dealt with massive dispensation, of which supervision became impossible, and the ecclesiastical poor relief could not keep up with the rapidly growing poverty.

Already in 1800, Elberfeld had adopted the division into districts and neighbourhoods from Hamburg.[54] Since 1788, in accordance with the latest ideas of the Enlightenment on a rational approach to social issues, Hamburg used a district system with unpaid visitors of the poor. Besides that, Elberfeld adopted the Hamburg principle that 'no one should receive a schilling as support, which he could have also earned with labour'. 'Work first' *avant la lettre*.[55] The Hamburg system included workshops, vocational training, free medical care, care during pregnancy and child birth, and also education. The costs of the system were covered

---

[53] Kok, 2000, p. 152

[54] The merchant and enlightened social reformist Caspar Voght (1752-1839) played a vital role in the 1788 reorganization of the Hamburg poor relief. He advised on the reorganizations of the poor relief systems in Vienna, Berlin, Paris, Marseille, Lyon and Portugal. (Adriani, 1940, p. 74, footnote 1; Sachße & Tennstedt, 1998, p. 125-130.) A comparable approach was taken in Bremen (1779), Lübeck (1783) and Braunschweig (1805).

[55] The Work First approach emerged in the nineties of the last century in the United States. Welfare reform was one of the achievements of the Clinton administration. It led to a dramatic decrease in the number of benefits. In the Netherlands, this approach was initially controversial, but it became the starting point for the Social Assistance Act (Dutch: Wet Werk en Bijstand) in 2004. By 2012, 'Work First' has been completely integrated.

with offerings. The Hamburg system appeared to work and became internationally known.[56]

Between 1800 and 1848, Elberfeld adapted the Hamburg system to local circumstances. The city was divided into districts and neighbourhoods, with initially one visitor per neighbourhood. Till 1853, the visitors of the poor did not decide themselves on the granting of financial support to 'their' families. That power lay with the municipal poor governance.

A commission headed by Daniel von der Heydt said in 1850 that the existing system should be strengthened with the input of the ecclesiastical poor relief; the latter would be able to take care of the support for the poor living at home. To this end, the amount of deacons had to be expended, and they would also need auxiliary staff to do the home visits. Especially the Lutheran Church of Elberfeld was charmed by this proposal. The Lutheran pastor had read Chalmers and he was inspired by the example of the care for the poor in the St. Johns parish in Glasgow.[57] In 1848 he set up activities such as home visits, soup kitchens, workshops with vocational training for men and women, and assistance with finding work. It soon became clear that these activities rose above the heads of the Lutheran community. In the 1849, they handed back the care for the poor to the city council.

Daniel von der Heydt and his commission spoke for two years with the church communities (Lutheran, Dutch Reformed, Catholics, Protestants, Jews and Mennonites). The churches were offered the possibility of taking care themselves of the poor living at home, which would be paid by the city council. They would have to take care of the home visits, the research and the granting of assistance. The opinions between the churches themselves and also between the city council were so diverse, that no agreement was reached The talks were suspended, without result. Daniel von der Heydt then lifted the initiative to the municipal level. On July 1, 1852, his commission presented its proposals to the city council, and from January 1, 1853 onwards, the *Neue Armenordnung für die Gemeinde Elberfeld* came into being.

---

[56] Sachße & Tennstedt, 1998, p. 128; Van den Eerenbeemt, 1977.
[57] Beutel, 2007, p. 235-236. Also: Gewin, 1917. De Berlin pastor Otto von Gerlach translated Chalmer's work into German: *Die kirchlichen Armenpflege. Nach dem Englischen des dr. Thomas Chalmers bearbeitet durch Otto von Gerlach* (1847).

In 1850, the impoverishment of the underclass in the Netherlands could no longer be denied. But the government here – unlike in Germany – got no room to act. With the Poverty Act (*Armenwet*) of 1854, the care for the poor was put in the position of rear guard. The city could only offer help in situations of 'utmost necessity'. The law presumed that care for the poor was primarily a task for church communities and private associations.[58] Still, a big city like Amsterdam spent a quarter of its budget on poor relief.[59]

The economist N.G. Pierson was the first in the Netherlands drawing attention to the Elberfelder system.[60] That was in 1872. Pierson, Finance Minister and later Prime Minister in the 'coalition of social justice' (1897-1901), praised the small-scale and individual oriented approach: 'Here lies the main principle of the Elberfeld System and also the secret to the excellent effects that it has brought. What can one expect from a visit to the poor, as is happening all too often in the bigger cities of our country. A single person, who has to visit a large number of poor, will impossibly be able to familiarize himself with their ups and downs, their fortunes and prospects, their characters and qualities; it will be impossible for him, to help the poor with advice and deed, being his voice with others, remarking the mistakes which caused the poverty, promoting school attendance of the children, and in general awakening a better spirit in the household. His attention divides, and his zeal fades, as the field of his work expands. Give someone twenty or thirty poor to visit: he will finally have the experience of doing useless work, so that either he will give up his task in despair, or, taking things as they are, regard his profession as a naked formality; give him three or four, and his interest in the persons, who have been entrusted to his guidance, will rise, so that his task will be closer to his heart every day.'[61]

---

[58] Melief, 1955.

[59] Calisch, 1851, p. 3-4. Calish calculates the expenses for poor relief to around 600.000 guilders.

[60] Pierson, 1870. In 1891, in the general meeting of the Institute for Statistics, Pierson again spoke about the Elberfelder System. (De Vries, 1916, p. 67). The social-liberal government Pierson-Goeman Borgesius reigned from 1897 to 1901 and established the Compulsory Education Act, the Children Acts, the Housing Act, the Health Act and the Workmen's Compensation Act.

[61] Pierson, 1872, p.66. [transl. eds.] For comparison, Pierson gave figures on the number of visitors of the poor in Amsterdam: The Amsterdam based *Huiszittenhuis*, which in 1871 supported 177 families throughout the whole year and 432 families temporarily, has *five* paid visitors; 5 on 609 = 1 on 121. The

Twenty years later, he referred to it again. He pointed out that visiting the poor was already common practice in the first Christian communities, it had become well-known again because of Chalmers' work in Glasgow, and it had been put into practice by the Vincentius Association and the Charity Organization Societies. The power of the Elberfelder system lay in the fact that 'the poor would not meet societies, parishes or boards, not something anonymous, but personalities.'[62]

In the Netherlands, the Amsterdam society Charity to Capacity, was the first to introduce the system, in 1892. The board handed over its decision power almost entirely to the 33 district commissions with around five hundred visitors. In 1901, the Societies for Improvement of the Care for the Poor (*Verenigingen tot Verbetering van de Armenzorg*) in Haarlem and Utrecht followed this example. The Civil Guardians of the Poor (*Burgerlijk Armbestuur*) of Amsterdam adopted elements of the system in 1896.[63] As a municipal system, only Leeuwarden and Lekkerkerk introduced it, in 1893.[64]

Daniel von der Heydt's enduring values:
- City council is ultimately responsible for the poor relief.
- Small-scale and decentralized implementation.
- District committees decide on allocation and extent of assistance.
- Visitors of the poor are volunteers.
- The visitor of the poor has two to four families under his care.
- A home visit every fortnight.
- Integrated help and advice: debt, education, training, work, health.
- Combination of research (Is help really needed?), care and assistance.
- Assistance is always temporary.

Dutch Reformed Parish in Amsterdam, gave support to 1044 persons throughout the whole year, to 1358 persons during winter and to 191 on temporary basis, has *thirty* visiting brothers; 30 on 2593 = 1 on 88.

[62] Cited in De Vries, 1916, p.160.

[63] Louis Blankenberg (1852-1927), since 1872 secretary and from 1900 chairman of *Liefdadigheid naar Vermogen*, was member of the *Burgerlijk Armbestuur* from 1893 to 1907. He was a major supporter of the Elberfeld system. Van der Linde, 2011a.

[64] Kok, 2000, p. 153-175

5.5 *Eropaf!*-moment 4: The right to quality of life. London, 1865, Octavia Hill

Image 5.4 Octavia Hill, around 1880

As early as in the eighties and nineties of the nineteenth century, Octavia Hill (1838-1912) seemed old-fashioned in the eyes of socialist youth. Her continuous insisting on an individual approach and personal responsibility aroused irritation.[65] She held on to a personal and small-scale approach. She did not want to believe that government intervention was necessary to tackle the large-scale problems of poverty, housing and unemployment. Octavia Hill was sceptical of, even if not opposed to, a government that had often worked against her. Government initiative could never take the place of private initiatives. With the emergence and flourishing of the welfare state (1910-1970) her star faded. Nowadays, when the welfare state also seems to have its downsides, her approach and views are revalued.

In 1864, Octavia Hill introduced a new method of working in London. It focused on active involvement with people who had gotten into reduced

---

[65] Webb, 1950, especially p. 167-180. Beatrice Webb-Potter (1858-1943) belonged to the London elite. In the 1880s she worked for some time as a volunteer in social housing management. Unlike her sister Kate, who was volunteering with Octavia Hill, she found it frustrating work. She concentrated on sociological research and socialist theory. Together with her husband Sidney Webb, she became a member of the Fabian Society and later of the Labour Party. She was financially independent by the legacy of father. Together with others, she founded the London School of Economics.

circumstances – poor, addicted, unemployed, living in slums, marginalized.[66] She based her work on the conviction that you need to support people in a way that builds their self-respect and improves their faith in their own abilities. She hated philanthropy that revels in the tragic fate of the underclass, that treats the poor condescendingly, and maintains their dependency on dispensation. The Amsterdam pioneer of social work, Hélène Mercier, described in 1895 how Octavia Hill treated her tenants: '(…) with the same politeness, the same respect for the freedom and independence, that she would comply with people of her own position. Never enter without knocking, never interfere with personal affairs if they don't ask for it themselves, never give advice if not asked for. In short, nothing but a business like relationship, until from both sides that natural interest in each others person and faith have grown, which naturally leads to a friendly relationship.'[67]

Octavia Hill knew poverty from personal experience. Her father James Hill was ruined by the financial crisis of 1840. He was an admirer of utopian socialist Robert Owen, published a progressive newspaper, and earned a living as a grain merchant and banker. As a result of this financial disaster he got into a depression and could not live with his family. Mother Caroline Hill was a teacher, and in her work she followed the innovative ideas of Swiss educator Pestalozzi. She took care of a multifaceted development of her daughters. Head, heart and hands were all three to be addressed. Besides languages, art and history, Octavia also got trained as a carpenter. They also learned to work in the vegetable garden. After the financial and personal misfortune, the Hill family was dependent on income from own work and the financial support of family and friends. Mother Caroline moved with her five daughters to London, and found work there as manager of the Co-operative Women's Guild, a volunteer organization. The Guild operated a school with a workshop where children learned a trade. At the age of fourteen, Octavia started working at this school. Her task was to supervise the children who made wooden toys, and make sure they got paid per piece. She taught the children to do their work mindfully, so the toys looked good and they could be proud of their product. Octavia organized excursions, read to the children, and took care of special activities and surprises during Christmas and other holidays. The Guild was founded out of the Christian Socialist movement. Octavia discovered here that the Christian faith can inspire involvement and social reform work. But she objected to

---

[66]   Darley, 2010; Hill, 1970; Ter Meulen, 1895; Maurice, 1913.
[67]   Mercier, 1895 [transl. eds.]

using social work to win converts. She herself became member of the Anglican Church of England. In the circle of Christian Socialists she got to know inspiring people who contributed to her development. For example the socialist minister F.D. Maurice, who founded in 1854 the Working Men's College, one of the oldest adult education institutions, which exists until today.[68] Maurice and the influential art critic John Ruskin helped her find work. Meanwhile, Octavia, now 26 years old, was pondering ways to improve the life of the poorest. There were housing associations and unions, but they were mainly for skilled workers. Not for the bottom layer in the slums in the centre of town or in the infamous East End. She took up housing as her starting point, since she saw a nice house, however small, with light, air and space – and neighbours taking care of each other – as life condition number one. With John Ruskin's money she bought her first block of houses. She renovated the houses one by one, and leased them back to the same residents, if possible for a lower rent. Every week she collected the rent herself, and discussed difficulties and problems with the tenants. Housing was the basis, but also starting point for other activities: construction of gardens, planting of trees, climbers and shrubs, a play ground for the kids. Octavia moved with her mother and sisters to the same neighbourhood, and behind her house she built classrooms where she organized weekend- and night clubs for her tenants.

Due to a careful home management, Octavia stayed fare below the usurious rent. She managed to make a return of 5% interest on the invested capital. This made her homes an attractive investment project. After ten years Octavia Hill and her collaborators managed fifteen housing projects with around 3000 tenants. She extended this work, approached funds, organized support. She trained dozens of women, who were working as social workers *avant la lettre*.

From the start, Octavia Hill organized outings for her tenants: children and adults. The heathland areas on the outskirts of London were a popular destination. She was outraged when around 1870 these natural areas were threatened by urban expansion. From 1875 – she was then 37 years old – Octavia conducted action for the conservation of nature in and around London. For the city population nature was desperately

---

[68] Under the influence of Frederic Denyson Maurice (1805-1872), Octavia had herself baptized in the Anglican church. Maurice's sermons on charity and personal responsibility made a great impression, and partly formed her principles of service, duty and responsibility which she honoured and practiced her life long. Darley, 2010, p.43-48

needed to breathe and relax. Her strategy was to raise funds and use the money to buy natural areas. She supported her sister Emily, who founded the Kyrle Society with the aim of returning the refining and uplifting influence of natural and artistic beauty back to the people. After a few unsuccessful actions, they achieved success with the purchase of parks and nature reserves. She gained support till high up in the elite and political world. Also outside London her achievements in nature preservation became famous. In 1894, Octavia Hill was one of the three founders of the National Trust. Everyone visiting nature in England, knows the National Trust, which counts 3.5 million members in the year 2012, manages 250,000 hectares of nature, and 200 castles, buildings and parks.

With the advent of self fulfilment psychology and the utopian welfare state philosophy after World War II, Octavia Hill was growingly seen as a paternalist and conservative-liberal philanthropist.[69] She would have been too strict with too much emphasis on personal responsibility. In an era of professionalization and the welfare state, it seemed obsolete to work one on one, small-scale and with volunteers. And it appeared increasingly strange to work from a religiously inspired sense of duty.

The last decade has seen a renewed interest in her ideas and method. Jane Lewis, professor Social Policy with the London School of Economics, wrote in 2005 that the importance of Octavia Hill lies mostly in the importance she attached to living with the poor, acquiring precise knowledge of their problems, earning their trust, respecting their opinions, finding out which daily problems spoil their lives, and also the fight for a liveable environment.[70]

We might add two more qualities: continuity and reliability. Octavia Hill brought continuity and reliability to her social work activities. No carrousel of projects with something new every four or five years.[71]

She also had an aye for the diversity of life. The desire for fresh air, nature and beauty. She organized exhibitions, cultural festivities,

---

[69] Illustrative of the shifting perspective between 1930 and 1949 – from praising to partly critical – are two articles on social housing management in which Octavia Hill is extensively discussed, written by Nel Hubregtse, for decades housing superintendent and later chief inspector of *Centraal Woningbeheer* in The Hague: Hubregtse, 1930, 1949.

[70] Whelan, 2005, p. XXV-XXVI.

[71] In his study *Het rendement van het zalmgedrag. De projectencarrousel ontleed,* Daniël Giltay Veth (2009) looked for explanations for the lack of durability of countless social projects.

excursions, evening schools. Whoever reads the forty volumes of her 'Letters to my Fellow-Workers', discovers that she has laid the foundations of many types of work and specializations in and outside the current professional social work. Also the by her so strongly propagated idea of social entrepreneurship has risen from the dead.[72]

Octavia Hill gained popularity, but early fellow-workers also turned away from her, especially since she did not believe in solutions via the state, and did not share their enthusiasm for socialist thought.[73] Students and interns brought her method to the United States, Australia, Germany, the Netherlands and other countries in Europe. In the Netherlands, Johanna ter Meulen and Louise Went were her promoters. They both learned the profession from her personally in London, and became the first housing superintendents in the Netherlands.[74] They laid the foundations of residential social work and social housing management.[75]

Octavia Hill's enduring values:
- Every tenant has a right to a peaceful and liveable home.
- Social and Business Entrepreneurship (not commercialized).
- Enforcing house rules for a pleasant living environment.
- Every person has the right to light, beauty and nature.
- Leisure and cultural clubs for children, women, men and elderly.
- Voluntary effort from the middle class.
- Integral method and promoting self-help: social, cultural, educational.
- Generalist practice with an eye for the individual and the detail.
- Every individual counts.
- Private initiative as a basis.
- Critical attitude towards the government.
- Critical about collective arrangements.
- Fundraiser, networker.
- Proximity: Octavia Hill lives in the neighbourhood where she works.

---

[72] Whelan, 2005.

[73] Octavia Hill stuck to her principles, and her early friends found her dogmatic and rigid, such as Samuel and Henrietta Barnett, but old friendship ties remained intact. Darley, 2010, p. 322-323.

[74] Both ladies were very influential, but due to an 'incompatibility of characters' they did not meet. (Blomberg, 1985, p.71) In the biographical description of Johanna ter Meulen, written by her friend Cornelia de Lange, Louise Went does not appear. (De Lange, 1965.)

[75] About the housing superintendents in the Netherlands: Deben, 1988; Van Drenth, 1995; Fentener van Vlissingen, 1953; Ottens et al., 2000; De Regt, 1986.

5.6   *Eropaf!*-moment 5: Into the breach for social housing management. Amsterdam, 1894, Johanna ter Meulen

On November 22, 1893, Octavia Hill wrote to a friend: 'I have with me (…) a charming young lady, Miss Ter Meulen from Amsterdam, who is spending a few months in England, to prepare for taking up houses in her own country. She is full of power, brightness and sweet human sympathy.'[76]

Image 5.5 Johanna ter Meulen, around 1915

From September till December 1893, Johanna ter Meulen (1867-1937) worked in London under Octavia Hill's supervision.[77] In those years, an economic depression was causing massive unemployment. The emerging socialist movement and radical journalists, lawyers and businessmen, attacked the regent class in Amsterdam with reform proposals. Johanna's social interest was awakened. She hoped for reforms which could bridge the gap between rich and poor, in order for a society to arise that matched her ideals of friendship, love and fidelity. Arnold Kerdijk, member of the House of Representatives, front man of the Social Liberals, and since 1887 chief editor of *Sociaal Weekblad* (Social Weekly), asked her to translate articles from foreign journals.[78] In house Kerdijk she met Emilie

---

[76] Quote from Whelan 2005, p. 340
[77] Van der Linde, 2009b.
[78] Because of the friendship with her cousins Agneta and Elisabeth Matthes, Johanna ter Meulen got right in the middle of a group of inspired social liberal

Knappert, who was doing club work with factory girls in Leiden. Johanna was friends with the daughters of Willem Spakler, director of a major sugar refinery. He was also a social liberal. With him Johanna spoke about improving the housing in the *Jordaan*-area, Amsterdam's own 'East End'.

In 'Our Home' (*Ons Huis*) on the Rozenstraat – based on the example of London's Toynbee Hall – which opened in 1892, Johanna met Hélène Mercier. Her articles in *Sociaal Weekblad* on workers housing, were very close to Johanna's heart.[79] Reading Mercier led Johanna to the work of Octavia Hill. That was the kind of work Johanna was looking for: no charity, but working towards better housing in combination with social support to families. She told Spakler she would love to do that kind of work. In 1892, he entrusted her the management of his houses on the Laurierstraat. She took the weekly rent, oversaw compliance with the rent regulations, and allowed repairs. She also mediated in disputes between neighbours. It turned out to be a failure due to her lack of experience, which tenants found out soon enough. Johanna was very disappointed (in herself), but learned from it that it is a profession which requires knowledge, practical experience and good people skills. And what was a better place to learn this profession than with Octavia Hill in London?

Back in Amsterdam, Spakler provided the capital to purchase a number of houses on the Tuinstraat in the Jordaan neighbourhood. The houses were renovated, slums were demolished and new houses were built. Ter Meulen made these houses part of Housing Society Old-Amsterdam

---

reformers of the eighties and nineties of the nineteenth century. Agneta Mattes (1847-1909) was, together with her husband Jacques van Marken (1845-1906), the driving force behind the groundbreaking social policy of the Dutch Yeast- and Alcoholfactory in Delft. She herself was also a businesswoman. Together with her husband she wrote history with the first representative body (De Kern, 1878), the first company newsletter (*De Fabrieksbode,* 1882), the first head of personnel (1808), various savings and insurance schemes, such as the voluntary occupational health scheme (1880), the first company social worker (Maria Kruseman, 1883-1889) and housing for staff in the garden village Agnetapark (1883), laid behind the factory.

Elisabeth Matthes (1849-1902) was married to Arnold Kerdijk (1846-1905), who, as social liberal director and politician, was incredibly active, i.e. editor of the Social Weekly (*Sociaal Weekblad*), as a member of the House of Representatives, and in 1899 as the first chairman of the Training institution for Social Work, which was renamed 'School for Social Work' (*School voor Maatschappelijk Werk*) in 1903.

[79] Mercier, 1887.

(*Woonmaatschappij Oud-Amsterdam*), of which she herself became director and home supervisor. She did not extend the amount of houses to more than 94, since she thought 100 houses to be the maximum number for a responsible house management, ensuring personal contact with the families.[80]

From 1894 till her death 43 years later, Johanna ter Meulen remained home supervisor. From her small office on 149 Anjelierstraat, she reached out. When 'her' families asked for help, she was unstoppable. There are plenty of examples in her handwritten *Dagboek mijner woningbemoeiing* ('Diary of my home supervision'), which she kept from 1894 to 1896.[81] From later years as well, stories of her activities have survived. She was looking for work for a man who got fired. She asked for advice when a family had to pay too high a premium for an insurance policy. For the eldest daughter of a family where the mother had died, she asked for a placement in the Amsterdam home science school. She advised on choice of school and further education. She applied for scholarships for the study costs of her tenants' children. If tenants would keep creating nuisance, even after repetitive complaints, she would stop the contract.

Johanna ter Meulen thought the privacy of her tenants had to be respected. That meant no unsolicited interference in their private affairs, and certainly no entering their homes uninvitedly. In 1918, she wrote in the newsletter of the National Housing Council: 'Those who believe do not haste. That is the proverb the home supervisor has honoured. She has to wait till one trusts her, never does she force herself onto someone. Reverent and humble be her actions in all personal affairs. (…) That is how, over the years, the home supervisor can become the trusted counsel of many of her families. Thus a great influence can emanate from her.'[82] In her office she founded a library for the children of her tenants. Once a week they could borrow new books; a service that was used extensively. Mothers had questions regarding infant nutrition, diseases and physical complaints of the children. To gain knowledge on these topics, and in order to be able to refer her clients, in 1897 Johanna did an internship with an outpatient clinic for child diseases. She collected her notes into a little book called: 'Some Hints for Young Mothers' (*Eenige Wenken aan Jonge Moeders*).

---

[80] Ottens, 1981.
[81] Ter Meulen, 1896.
[82] Ter Meulen, 1918, 1921 [transl. eds.]

At the symposium 'Vocational training' during the National Exhibition of Women's Labour in The Hague (1898), Johanna explained her view on her new profession. 'Housing work' was eminently a task for the civilized woman. The salary could be raised from the rental income. Women were expected to be better able to maintain personal contact then male supervisors. They would also be better suited to detect negligence, and find ways to deal with that.[83]

In 1903, together with seventeen other home supervisors, she founded the national Society for Female Home Supervisors (*Landelijke Vereniging van Woningopzichteressen*). It was the first professional representative body in the field of social work. Together with the School for Social Work – which was founded in 1899 – a training program was designed for the home supervisors. The Society took care of the practical component of the training. Johanna was chairwoman till 1915. In 1928 she forfeited her membership, because she thought the society insufficiently defended the importance of social housing management towards the municipal Amsterdam Housing Service. As a member of the Amsterdam Housing Council, she was on top of the implementation of the Housing Act of 1901. She wrote the book 'Housing of the poor in Amsterdam' *(Huisvesting van Armen te Amsterdam)*, a thorough report of in 1903 still existing abuses, supported with statistical material.[84] From this book comes the poignant quote: 'I must look for a smaller property, because my family becomes too large.'[85] Her study must have been inspired by Octavia Hills *Home of the London Poor* from 1875. Besides her work in the Jordaan neighbourhood, she was appointed director of the 'Society of Housing Contruction North of the IJ' (*NV Maatschappij van Huizenbouw benoorden het IJ*). She was also active in other areas, such as in the child protection sector, as a member of the Guardianship Council.

There are still Amsterdam residents who have known Johanna ter Meulen personally. Wim Bongers, born in 1920 on 170 Tuinstraat, and later moved to number 99, remembers her vividly: 'Every Thursday I borrowed books from her library at the Anjelierstraat. She advised my brother to keep studying, and brokered for a scholarship for the train operator school. When he passed his exams, she gifted him a nice pair of compasses.' How she dealt with her tenants? 'She was the boss. But very likable. She was very empathic and has done much good. Everyone who

---

[83]   Ter Meulen, 1898; Grever & Waaldijk, 1998, p. 129, 255.
[84]   Ter Meulen, 1903.
[85]   Ter Meulen, 1903, p. 38 [transl. eds.].

has known her, will remember her as a distinguished lady who wanted the best for the working population.'[86]

Johanna ter Meulen's enduring values:
- Social entrenpreneurship.
- Critical of traditional charity, which does not try to take away the causes of poverty.
- Small-scale organizing of her housing corporation.
- Integrated services.
- Personal contacts, respecting the privacy of its tenants.
- Municipal governance of the housing of the population is needed.
- National social legislation: the Housing Act.
- Work in social housing management as suitable work for women.
- Paid work also for women from the upper middle class.
- Professional training in a work environment that becomes more complex.

5.7 Conclusion

Let me round up with five observations about what struck me in the study of these pioneers.

Outreaching

Firstly, I am struck by the personal and social commitment and involvement of the five pioneers. They match with many of the statements on the ten point program of the *Eropaf!*-manifest.[87] They worked outreaching and context oriented. They drew people back into society, but treated them with respect. They pointed out the responsibilities of citizens and authorities. Their actions were aimed at 'self-help' and restoration of autonomy, but they were not afraid to act when necessary. They were honest. Their activities are known till today.

The problems they dealt with have not been solved, for they are inherent to every society and they are still here today. This makes these five almost our contemporaries. Even today, the prison regime and an effective, human way of working in rehabilitation are issues on the

---

[86] Interview with the author.Amsterdam, January 10, 2009; Fentener van Vlissingen, 1937; Pijnappel, 1937.
[87] Räkers & Huber, 2010, p. 19-48

agenda. Neighbourhood-oriented work has been at the centre of discussions for years. Person-centred care continues to be subject of method development. Reading about the hundreds of 'visitors of the poor' – in Glasgow, London, Elberfeld, Amsterdam – who were trying to establish a relationship of trust with families in trouble, who advised on debt relief, mediated with work, showed the way to health care and education, etc., makes me think of today's social workers who also carry out similar inspirational, 'strength oriented' activities.[88]

Values

Secondly, I am struck by the large role that general Christian and Humanist values have played in the thoughts and actions of the pioneers and their supporters. Of course, financial motives and motives of public order and employment have been motives for governments, managers and entrepreneurs. How could it be otherwise? But values such as compassion, mercy, humanity and justice have played a vital role in the work of the pioneers. They combined a practical approach, a great sense of compassion and a liberal view on (people's own) responsibility, and were inspired by religious values from the Christian tradition. This is most clear with Fry and Chalmers, but it also counts for others. Fry was part of the Quaker tradition, and Chalmers of the evangelical revival movement. The combination of support and evangelizing is obvious to them, as it was obvious later to William Booth, founder of the Salvation Army.

By 1850 there was a turning point, a separation between support and conversion. Missionary work was not a theme for Octavia Hill and Johanna ter Meulen. They devoted themselves to improving their own personal possibilities (and of others). Light, air and space. Hill and Ter Meulen were inspired by their Christian faith, but against 'conditional support' in the sense of 'you only get help if you accept that Christ has also died for you', for according to them this was incompatible with the Gospel's spirit of inclusivity. For Octavia Hill, her faith was an ethical and moral foundation from which she acted, but she did not impose it onto others. Meanwhile, she was not to be trifled with; she was unyielding, soldierly, and tenacious in her quest for a better life for the bottom layer of the population. We can say the same about the other pioneers of the modern care for the poor: Hélène Mercier, Marie Muller-

---

[88]   Penninx & Sprinkhuizen, 2011.

Lulofs, Louis Blankenberg, Johanna ter Meulen. No carrousel of projects, but durable and reliable presence, sometimes for decades.

Early women

Thirdly, for us (Dutch), who always start the story of public and militant action of women with Aletta Jacobs in the seventies and eighties of the nineteenth century, it is breathtaking to read about the women that practised their belief in human values already fifty years (!) earlier: at the beginning of the nineteenth century. Their activity and commitment were unheard of before that time. They were vigorous, effective, checked if promises were kept, and knew how to gain influence at the highest levels and with the parliament. For the generations before us, this was no secret. Mrs. W.H. Posthumus-van der Goot, dedicated a chapter of her standard 'From mother to daughter' (*Van moeder op dochter*), to Elizabeth Fry, Barbara van Meerten-Schilperoort and other women of the forefront.[89] How is it possible that we so easily forget about the vital contributions of our pioneers?

Generalists: touched and militant

Fourthly, for decades now, regularly the discussion arises within the social work education and profession, whether the social worker needs to be a generalist, a specialist or both.

For the nineteenth century voluntary visitor of the poor, this was not an issue. He or she dealt equally naturally with housing problems and advise on education of the children, as with debts or finding work. For many it was equally natural that their social work was a part of a larger social movement aimed at elevating and developing the people. They acted because they were touched; touched by the distress of others. Touched by the fact that so many did not receive what they were humanly entitled to. They wanted to help, but also listen; they wanted to look for solutions, together with their clients. They were militant and helpful. But let's not be mistaken. The pioneers were also great organizers, with a businesslike attitude, and, already by the end of the nineteenth century, in favour of training and professionalization.

Practice researchers of the knowledge centres of social faculties in higher education advocate for the broad social (neighbourhood)professional. See for example the plea of Haarlem social work professor Margot

---

[89]   Posthumus-van der Goot & De Waal, 1977, p. 28-31

Scholte: the social worker as generalist-specialist and mediator.[90] The Utrecht professor Hans van Ewijk, since 2009 holding the Marie Kamphuis Chair 'Foundations of Social Work', argues for 'less segregation and more connection', for a social worker who works integrated and is a well-known person in the neighbourhood, next to the local policeman, neighbourhood care, and General Practitioner: 'a basic professional who knows the neighbourhood and its people, and in return is known by them'.[91] In recent practical experiences and studies we have beautiful material to once again study this question of a generalist approach versus specialism. The historical perspective will offer help and inspiration here.

On the shoulders of nineteenth century giants

Fifthly, when speaking about these recognizable problems of hundred fifty to two hundred years ago, one has to point out how society was different at that time. Everything was organized more small-scale, not yet modernized by means of technology, education, infrastructure and public transport, and by modern means of communication.[92] The pioneers were active in the heyday of laissez-faire capitalism, at least in Britain, while in Holland and Germany the industrial revolution still had to start. The interdependence of state and society was not there yet. There was no talk of social legislation, the welfare state was still beyond the horizon.

To me, it's fascinating to look at these pioneers again, in a time where that same old capitalism has led, in new shapes, to a worldwide economic crisis, with all its consequences. The welfare state has been under attack since Thatcher and Reagan. A renowned journalist writes about London: "Dickens' gap between rich and poor has returned".[93] London cuts the budgets of youth work, education, rental subsidies and public facilities and also has 73 billionaires. The gap between the rich and poor is back at the level of the early nineteenth century. The August 2011 riots in London also hit the neighbourhoods where Octavia Hill worked. She could get back to work. Toynbee Hall, founded by her friends in 1884, works overtime anno 2012. People are queuing up for consultations for debt settlement.

---

90 Scholte, 2010, p. 92-93
91 Van Ewijk, 2010b, p. 21-25. Van Ewijk, 2010c. [transl. eds.]
92 Van der Woud, 2010a.
93 Ketelaar, 2011. [transl. eds.]

In the Netherlands, far-reaching budget cuts and pleas for a 'caring society' led to the Social Support Act (*Wet Maatschappelijke Ondersteuning*, 2007), in which principles can be recognized that were taken for granted in the nineteenth century. This also applies to the Social Assistance Act (*Wet Werk en Bijstand*, 2004), which will be reformed into a new Act 'work according to ability'. Are we going back to the nineteenth century? What opportunities does the 21st century offer for a 'Welfare New Style'? Study of history shows that most problems and dilemma's aren't new.[94] The exciting thing about this history is that we can investigate how the pioneers have solved these dilemmas. Or at least have tried to solve them. Their solutions have lost nothing of their relevance for today. Together with their sympathizers they have laid the foundation for modern social work in Europe, or rather: the Western world. They did so in their time: before social legislation, before social sciences and before the rise of the welfare state. In this article, I have listed some enduring values of every pioneer. If I try to mention the most essential values out of those, I would come to the following list:

Elizabeth Fry:
>   Compassion, the rights of depreciated people, Go for it! (*Eropaf!*)

Thomas Chalmers:
>   Solidarity in the neighbourhood, guidance towards self-help.

Daniel von der Heydt:
>   Local government in cooperation with volunteers.

Octavia Hill:
Social entrepreneurship, the right to quality of life, culture and education.

Johanna ter Meulen:
>   The value of small scale, legislation and professionalism.

---

[94]   See the essays at www.canonsociaalwerk.nl

Bibliography

Adriani, J.H. (1940). *Voorlezingen over Armenzorg en Maatschappelijk Werk.* (3de druk). Zutphen.

Agnew, E.N. (2004). *From Charity tot Social Work. Mary E. Richmond and the Creation of an American Profession.* Chicago.

Bervoets, L. (1999). Een voorbeeldig pionier. Marie Muller-Lulofs 1854-1954. In B. Waaldijk, J. van der Stel & G. van der Laan (red.), *Honderd jaar sociale arbeid. Portretten en praktijken uit de geschiedenis van het maatschappelijk werk* (pp. 21-36). Assen.

Beutel, H. (2007). *Die Sozialtheologie Thomas Chalmers und ihre Bedeutung für die Freikirchen.* Göttingen.

Bijbel (1975). Willibrordvertaling. Boxtel.

Bijlsma, J. & Janssen, H. (2008). *Sociaal werk in Nederland. Vijfhonderd jaar verheffen en verbinden.* Bussum.

Blomberg, W.C. (1985). *Aan de bakermat van de Amsterdamse volkshuisvesting. Louise Went (1865-1951).* Amsterdam.

Blond, Ph. (2010). *Red Tory. How left and right have broken Britain and how we can fix it.* Londen.

Bogaers, L. (1997). 'Geleund over de onderdeur. Doorkijkjes in het Utrechtse buurtleven van de vroege Middeleeuwen tot in de zeventiende eeuw. *Bijdragen en Mededelingen betreffende de Geschiedenis der Nederlanden, 112,* 336-363.

Bogaers, L. (2008). *Aards, betrokken en zelfbewust. De verwevenheid van cultuur en religie in katholiek Utrecht, 1300-1600.* Utrecht.

Bogaers, L. (2010). Gericht op saamhorigheid. Utrechts buurtleven door de eeuwen heen. *Maatwerk, vakblad voor maatschappelijk werk,* juni, 9-12.

Bok, P. de (1997). Interview met Geertien Pols, divisiemanager Opvang en Wonen van het Rotterdams Centrum voor Dienstverlening: De voorwaarden van derden zijn hefboom voor hulpverlening. *Tijdschrift voor de Sociale Sector, 6,* 20-24.

Bruijn, J. de (1954). *Thomas Chalmers en zijn kerkelijk streven.* Nijkerk.

Calisch, N.S. (1851). *Liefdadigheid te Amsterdam. Overzigt van al hetgeen er in Amsterdam wordt verrigt, ter bevordering van de stoffelijke, zedelijke en godsdienstige belangen, voornamelijk der minvermogenden en behoeftigen.* Uit echte bronnen bijeengebracht. Amsterdam.

Costa, I. da (1974). *Bezwaren tegen de geest der eeuw.* Uitgave Bleiswijk, in hedendaags Nederlands overgezet door K. Exalto.

Darley, G. (2010). *Octavia Hill. A Life* (nieuwe uitgave). Londen.

Deben, L. (1988). *Van onderkomen tot woning: een studie over woonbeschaving in Nederland, 1850-1969.* Amsterdam.

Dercksen, A. & Verplanke, L. (1987). *Geschiedenis van de onmaatschappelijkheidsbestrijding in Nederland, 1914-1970*. Meppel.

Doorn, L. van (2002). *Een tijd op straat. Een volgstudie naar (ex-)daklozen in Utrecht, 1993-2000*. Utrecht.

Doorn, L. van (2004). *Outreachende hulpverlening. Praktijkervaringen van 10 experimentele projecten*. Arnhem.

Doorn, L. van, Etten, Y. van & Gademan, M. (2008). *Outreachend werken. Handboek voor werkers in de eerste lijn*. Bussum.

Drenth, A. van (1995). De groote verantwoordelijkheid van haar vrouw zijn. Woningopzichteressen en de professionalisering van sociale zorg in Nederland (1880-1940). In A. van Drenth, M. van Essen & M. Lunenburg (red.), *Sekse als pedagogisch motief* (pp. 171-185). Baarn.

Drenth, A. van & Haan, F. de (1999). *The rise of caring power. Elisabeth Fry and Josephine Butler in Britain and the Netherlands*. Amsterdam.

Duyvendak, J.W. (2005). Hans Achterhuis na dertig jaar herlezen. Ongekend radicale kritiek op het welzijnswerk. *Tijdschrift voor Sociale Vraagstukken, 9*, 12-16.

Eerenbeemt, H.F.J.M. van den (1977). *Armoede en arbeidsdwang. Werkinrichtingen voor 'onnutte' Nederlanders in de Republiek 1760-1795*. Den Haag.

Egging, J. (2005). Willem Hendrik Suringar als propagandist en intermediair van praktische filantropie. *Documentatieblad voor de Nederlandse kerkgeschiedenis na 1800, 28*(53), 63-64.

Engbersen, G. (2006, 11 februari). Emancipeer de onderklasse: bied honderdduizend stages. De Sociale Agenda 3. *De Volkskrant*.

Ewijk, H. van (2010a). *European Social Policy and Social Work. Citizenship based Social Work*. Abingdon.

Ewijk, H. van (2010b). *Maatschappelijk werk in een sociaal gevoelige tijd*. Utrecht.

Ewijk, H. van (2010c). Met de basiswerker terug naar meer eenvoud. Interview *MO/Samenlevingsopbouw, 29*, 4-8.

Fentener van Vlissingen, J.S. (1937). In memoriam Johanna ter Meulen. *Tijdschrift voor Armwezen, Maatschappelijke Hulp en Kinderbescherming*, maart, 8.

Fentener van Vlissingen, J.S. (1953). Het pionierswerk van onze eerste woningopzichteressen. *Tijdschrift voor Volkshuisvesting en Stedebouw*, maart, 70-72.

Franke, H. (1990). *Twee eeuwen gevangen. Misdaad en straf in Nederland*. Utrecht.

Fuchs, J.M. (1971). *Ik zal doen wat in mijn vermogen is. Honderd jaar Amsterdamse liefdadigheid*. Amsterdam.

Geertsema, H. (2004). *Identiteit in meervoud. Een identiteitsbeschrijving van het maatschappelijk werk*. Dissertatie. Groningen.

Gewin, E. (1917). De bakermat van het Elberfelder stelsel. *Tijdschrift voor Armenzorg en Kinderbescherming, 18,* 151-153.

Grever, M. & Waaldijk, B. (1998). *Feministische openbaarheid. De Nationale Tentoonstelling van Vrouwenarbeid in 1898.* Amsterdam.

Haan, F. de (1995). Niet langer cellulair, nog steeds Elisabeth Fry. *Nemesis,* 59-76.

Henselmans, H. (1993). *Bemoeizorg, ongevraagde hulp voor psychotische patiënten.* Delft.

Hes, J. (m.m.v. J. Veldhuis) (2000). *Recht doen aan de buurt.* Dordrecht.

Hill, O. (1970). *Homes of the London Poor* (heruitgave). London.

Hilton, B. (1988). *The Age of Atonement. The Influence of Evangelicalism on Social and Economic Thought, 1795-1865.* Oxford.

Hubregtse, P.H. (1930). De sociale taak der woningopzichteressen. In *Maatschappelijk Werk. Opstellen aangeboden aan Emilie C. Knappert op haar zeventigsten verjaardag 15 juni 1930* (pp. 205-213). Amsterdam.

Hubregtse, P.H. (1949). Sociaal woningbeheer. Geschiedenis, ontwikkeling en perspectieven. In M.J. de Haas et al. (red.), *Problemen van het Maatschappelijk Werk. Gedenkboek ter gelegenheid van het 50-jarig bestaan (1899-1949) van de school voor maatschappelijk werk* (pp. 302-312). Amsterdam/Purmerend.

Jagt, L.J. (2008). *Van Richmond naar Reid. Bronnen en ontwikkeling van taakgerichte hulpverlening in het maatschappelijk werk.* Houten.

Janse, M. (2007). *De afschaffers. Publieke opinie, organisatie en politiek in Nederland 1840-1880.* Amsterdam.

Ketelaar, T. (2011, 30 augustus). Dickens' kloof tussen rijk en arm is terug. *NRC Handelsblad.*

Kok, P.Th. (2000). *Burgers in de bijstand. Werklozen en de ontwikkeling van de sociale zekerheid in Leeuwarden van 1880 tot 1930 .* Groningen.

Koning, P. de (2003, 30-31 augustus). Bemoeizucht. Steeds meer mensen uit huis gezet vanwege overlast of huurschuld. *NRC Handelsblad.*

Krutzen, M. (2007). *Elisabeth Fry.* Uitgeverij Boekenbent.

Krutzen, M. (2009). 'Mensch! Help u zelf en God zal u helpen!' Anna Barbara van Meerten-Schilperoort (1778-1853), reclasseringsmedewerkster van het eerste uur. *Tidinge, Tijdschrift van historische vereniging Die Goude,* juli.

Kuypers, P. & Lans, J. van der (1994). *Naar een modern paternalisme. Over de noodzaak van sociaal beleid.* Pamflet. Amsterdam.

Lange, C.C. de (1965). Johanna Elisabeth ter Meulen. *Jaarboek van het genootschap Amstelodamum, 57,* 145-166.

Lans, J. van der (1994, 10 augustus). Het vuile werk van de verzorgingsstaat. *De Groene Amsterdammer.*

Lans, J. van der (2003). De ontdekking van de leefwereld. Nogmaals modern paternalisme. *Tijdschrift voor de Sociale Sector,* november, 4-11.

Lans, J. van der (2011a). *Ontregelen. De herovering van de werkvloer* (9de druk). Amsterdam.

Lans, J. van der (2011b) *Eropaf! De nieuwe start van het sociaal werk* (4de druk). Amsterdam.

Lans, J. van der, Medema, N. & Rekers, M. (2003). *Bemoeien werkt.* Amsterdam.

Leeuwen, M.H.D. van (1992). *Bijstand in Amsterdam, ca. 1800-1850. Armenzorg als beheersings- en overlevingsstrategie.* Zwolle.

Linde, M. van der (2009a). Octavia Hill. Het recht op schoonheid, licht en ruimte. *SoziO,* 88, juni, 18-21.

Linde, M. van der (2009b). Johanna ter Meulen. Voorvechter van volkshuisvesting en pionier van outreachend sociaal werk. *SoziO,* 87, april, 40-43.

Linde, M. van der (2010). *Basisboek Geschiedenis sociaal werk in Nederland* (4de druk). Amsterdam.

Linde, M. van der (m.m.v. T. Limperg) (2011a). 'Onweerstaanbare drang naar menschenliefde door daden'. Louis Blankenberg (1852-1925), promotor van de individuele hulpverlening. *SoziO-SPH, 101,* augustus , 26-29.

Linde, M. van der (2011b). *Doe wel, maar... zie om. Een pleidooi voor historisch besef in het sociaal werk.* Openbare les. Utrecht.

Loch, C.S. (1910). *Charity and Social Life. A short study of religious and social thought in relation to charitable methods and institutions.* Londen.

Mak, G. (1991, 4 september). Een volkomen afgeschreven uithoek van de stad. *NRC Handelsblad.*

Mak, G. (1992, 28 maart). 'Ruik eens even door de brievenbus.' Drie middagen op stap met Henk Plenter. *NRC Handelsblad.*

Mak, G. (1995, 14 maart). De ontbinding van het huisbezoek. *NRC Handelsblad.*

Maurice, C.E. (Ed.).(1913). *Hill, Life of Octavia Hill as told in her letters.* Londen.

Melief, P.B.A. (1955). *De strijd om de armenzorg in Nederland 1795-1854.* Groningen.

Menger, A. (1997). Voorwaardelijk, gedwongen, outreachend, bemoeizorg of gewoon AMW? *Tijdschrift voor de Sociale Sector,* 6, 10-13.

Menger, A. (2009). Wie werkt? Over het vakmanschap van de reclasseringswerker. In J. Hermanns & A. Menger, *Walk the line. Over continuïteit en professionaliteit in het reclasseringswerk* (pp. 69-110). Openbare les maart. Hogeschool Utrecht.

Menger, A. & Bouwes, J. (1995). *Activerende hulpverlening. Rapport methodiekontwikkeling.* Hogeschool Rotterdam & Omstreken.

Menger, A. & Roskam, H. (1997). Hoe het mis had kunnen gaan... Voorwaardelijke hulpverlening aan langdurig werkzoekenden in Den Haag. *Tijdschrift voor de Sociale Sector, 6*, 14-15.

Mercier, H. (1887). *Over Arbeiderswoningen.* Amsterdam.

Mercier, H. (1895). Octavia Hill. *Mannen en vrouwen van beteekenis in onzer dagen, 26*, 273-320.

Meulen, J. ter (1896). *Dagboek mijner woningbemoeiing, 9 juli 1894 – 12 oktober 1896.* Manuscript in Archief van de Woningmaatschappij Oud-Amsterdam, Stadsarchief Amsterdam.

Meulen, J. ter (1895, 23 november). Over de werkwijze van Octavia Hill. *De Amsterdammer. Weekblad voor Nederland*, nr. 962.

Meulen, J. ter (1898). *De beschaafde vrouw als opzichteres van arbeiderswoningen.* Amsterdam.

Meulen, J. ter (1903). *Huisvesting van armen te Amsterdam.* Haarlem.

Meulen, J. ter (1918). De woningopzichteres. *Woningbouw, mededelingen van de Nationale Woningraad*, 1 april.

Meulen, J. ter (1921). *De woningopzichteres.* Dordrecht.

Muller-Lulofs, M.G. (1906). Het werk van den vrijwilligen armbezoeker. In *Wat een armbezoeker weten moet* (pp. 27-64). Amsterdam.

Muller-Lulofs, M.G. (1916). *Van mens tot mensch.* Utrecht.

Münsterberg, E. (1903). Het Elberfelder stelsel. *Tijdschrift voor Armenzorg en Kinderbescherming, 4*(115), 236-252.

Nijenhuis, H. (red.) (1997). *De lerende professie. Hoofdlijnen van het maatschappelijk werk.* Utrecht.

Ottens, E.S. (1981). 'Oud-Amsterdam' in de Jordaan, of: de volkshuisvestings-praktijk van Johanna ter Meulen. *Ons Amsterdam*, 75-78.

Ottens, E.S. et al. (2000). *Wonen – Woning – Wet. 100 jaar woningwet.* Amsterdam.

Pama, G. (2003, 18-19 oktober). Werken aan woonbeschaving. Woningcorporatie de Nieuwe Unie wil bewoners opvoeden en binden aan hun wijk. *De Volkskrant.*

Penninx, K. & Sprinkhuizen, A. (2011). *Krachtgerichte Sociale Zorg.* Utrecht.

Pierson, A. (1889). *Een schrede voorwaarts.* Rede, uitgesproken in de Unie op 7 december 1888. Haarlem.

Pierson, A. (1982) *Oudere tijdgenooten* (4de druk). Amsterdam.

Pierson, N.G. (1872). Armverzorging. *De Gids, 36*, 45-70.

Pijnappel, E.A. (1937). In Memoriam Johanna ter Meulen. *Tijdschrift voor Volkshuisvesting en Stedebouw, 18*(3), 29-30.

Posthumus-van der Goot, W.H. & Waal, A. de (red.) (1977). *Van moeder op dochter. De maatschappelijke positie van de vrouw in Nederland vanaf de Franse tijd* (herdruk). Nijmegen.

Räkers, M. (2008). De ontruiming van meneer De Haan. In S. Spinder et al., *Krachten en kansen. Initiatieven voor vernieuwing in zorg en welzijn* (pp. 63-74). Houten.

Räkers, M. & Huber, M.A. (2010). *Eropaf! 2.0. Manifest. Tien kernwaarden.* Amsterdam.

Räkers, Marc & Jong, Carolien de (2006). *Eropaf! Outreachend samenwerken in welzijn en wonen.* Amsterdam

Regt, A. de (1986). *Arbeidersgezinnen en beschavingsarbeid. Ontwikkelingen in Nederland 1870-1940* (3de druk). Meppel.

Sachße, C. & Tennstedt, F. (1998). *Geschichte der Armenfürsorge in Deutschland. Vom Spätmittelalter bis zum i. Weltkrieg.* Stuttgart.

Savornin Lohman, J. de & Raaf, H. (2008). *In de frontlinie tussen hulp en recht* (3de, herziene druk). Bussum.

Scholte, M. (2010). *Oude waarden in nieuwe tijden. Over de kracht van maatschappelijk werk in de 21^e eeuw* (2de, herziene druk). Haarlem.

Simpelaar, L. (2011). *Mijn grootste fout is dat ik voor de fouten van de rijken niet hetzelfde geduld opbreng als voor die van de armen. Marie Muller-Lulofs (1854-1954).* Utrecht. Beschikbaar via venster 1870 H. Mercier van Canon Sociaal Werk.

Soetenhorst-de Savornin Lohman, J. (1990). *Doe wel en zie om. Maatschappelijke hulpverlening in relatie tot het recht.* Amsterdam/Lisse.

Spinder, S. et al. (2008). *Krachten en kansen. Initiatieven voor vernieuwing in zorg en welzijn.* Houten

Swaan, A. de (2004). *Zorg en de staat. Welzijn, onderwijs en gezondheidszorg in Europa en de Verenigde Staten in de nieuwe tijd* (6de druk). Amsterdam.

Thompson, E.P. (1980). *The Making of the English Working Class.* Pelican Books.

Tjeenk Willink, M. & Treurniet, A (1958). Voortgang en Samenhang 1908-1958. In *Motief en functie. Bewogenheid en beweging in het maatschappelijk werk 1908-1958* (pp. 281-373). Haarlem.

Tonkens, E. (2008). *Mondige burgers, getemde professionals. Marktwerking en professionaliteit in de publieke sector* (volledig herziene en uitgebreide 4de druk). Amsterdam.

Tonkens, E. & Duyvendak, J.W. (2001). Paternalisme tussen verguizing en omarming. Bemoeizorg en bemoeizucht van sociale professies na 1950. *Justitiële Verkenningen, 6,* 8-18.

Traas, M. (1996). *Waarom zou ik? Waarden en motieven in de maatschappelijke hulpverlening.* Baarn.

Trattner, W.I. (1999). *From Poor Law to Welfare State. A History of Social Welfare in America* (6th ed.). New York.

Verzelen, W. (2005). *Sociaal werk. In- en uitzichten.* Antwerpen/Apeldoorn.

Vries, C.W. de (1916). *Handboek voor Armbezoekers*. Haarlem.

Waaldijk, B. (1996). *Het Amerika der Vrouw. Sekse en geschiedenis van het maatschappelijk werk in Nederland en de Verenigde Staten*. Groningen.

Waaldijk, B., Stel, J. van der & Laan, G. van der (red.) (1999). *Honderd jaar sociale arbeid. Portretten en praktijken uit de geschiedenis van het maatschappelijk werk*. Assen.

Webb, B. (1950). *My Apprenticeship (nieuwe uitgave)*. Londen.

Whelan, R. (1998). *Hill, Octavia Hill and the Social Housing Debate. Essays and letters by Octavia Hill*. Londen: IEA Health and Welfare Unit.

Whelan, R. (2005). *Hill, Octavia Hill's Letters to Fellow-Workers 1871-1911*. Londen.

Woud, A. van der (2010a). *Een nieuwe wereld. Het ontstaan van het moderne Nederland* (8ste druk). Amsterdam.

Woud, A. van der (2010b). *Koninkrijk vol sloppen. Achterbuurten en vuil in de negentiende eeuw* (3de druk). Amsterdam.

6. New avenues for reducing recidivism?

Jo Hermanns and Anneke Menger

6.1 Introduction

Reducing the high to very high rates of recidivism among offenders in the Netherlands (average rate of 70%) has proved to be a difficult task. In the year 2009 over 35,000 adults left prison. Over 80% of them already had a criminal record. Over the next two years roughly half of them were expected to be convicted again of what is generally a serious crime, and end up back in prison. Continuity in criminal behaviour seems to be an essential part of the lifestyle of the majority of offenders. A diligent worldwide search is therefore underway, for effective programmes that can help to turn around the criminal way of life in which a large proportion of offenders have become caught up. This contribution briefly describes the two main strategies: behavioural interventions and socio-ecological approaches. A third strategy (the wraparound model) described here is an attempt to combine the strengths of the first two strategies and add an extra element, namely a management component to translate all the different activities that have to be undertaken into a single integrated and managed process. Finally, some thoughts are offered on a new approach of the organization and the professional content of rehabilitation, departing from the wraparound care model as a service delivery model.

6.2 The 'What Works' approach as the dominant strategy

This article focuses on offenders who have been sentenced to a term of imprisonment. The offenders in question sometimes undergo structured interventions lasting anything from a few weeks to a few months either during or after their stay in prison based on the 'what works approach'. The core of the theory developed by Andrews & Bonta about the psychology of criminal behaviour, on which the 'What Works' approach is based, is that the attitudes, interpretations, and decisions of individuals in the context of risks and criminogenic needs determine whether or not they commit an offence (Andrews & Bonta, 1998). Andrews and Bonta assume that cognitive behavioural interventions are the best basis for action.

Cognitive behavioural interventions (training or treatment) are based on the notion that offenders lack the cognitive skills they need if they are to fulfil their personal wishes in a manner acceptable to others. This means that they continuously get into difficulties. Interventions are designed to rectify this cognitive deficit by getting them to realize that their present perception of social reality is based on wrong thinking and fallacious ideas. They are then taught new ways of perceiving social situations, for example, by interpreting other people's behaviour more realistically and putting themselves in other people's shoes, and more effective ways of resolving problems. These cognitive skills are practised on the assumption that this will prevent undesirable behaviour such as criminality.

The Washington State Institute for Public Policy recently published a survey of 'What Works and what does not' (Aos, Miller, & Drake, 2006). It found 291 evaluations of individual adult corrections based on rigorous research. Interventions in the category of the cognitive-behavioural approach were indeed often found to be effective. Examples of well-known forms of socio-cognitive interventions in the Netherlands are social skills training, aggression regulation training, and lifestyle training for drug-involved offenders.

The survey by Aos et al. showed that effective cognitive behavioural interventions could achieve a reduction in recidivism averaging 8.2% among the general offender population. In the Netherlands this would mean that the current 2-year rate of recidivism among the general offender population could be cut from 54% to 45.8%, if all prisoners were to be offered cognitive-behavioural interventions that are in keeping with their recidivism risk, criminogenic needs, and personal circumstances. The systematic application of effective interventions would in that case produce a great social gain, both in terms of the quality of life of victims and offenders, and in terms of the material social costs.

Interesting in this context are the findings, summarized by Aos et al. (2006) and Cullen & Gendreau (2000) that behavioural interventions that are community-based, i.e. take place in the actual life and social context of the offender, are for more effective than the same interventions in penitentiary institutions. This already points to the importance of a broader, contextual perspective.

6.3 The socio-ecological approach

This approach, which is sometimes referred to by researchers as the classical social casework approach, lays the emphasis on solving

114

practical problems and working on social relationships, which are necessary after imprisonment in order to be able to integrate into society. It is evident from a series of studies that the problems which prisoners and ex-prisoners experience cannot be attributed solely to 'cognitive defects'. The results of risk assessments of over 11,000 offenders by the Dutch probation service to measure criminogenic needs produced the following Top 5 list (Knaap, Leenarts, & Nijssen, 2007):

1. training, work, and learning

2. ways of thinking, behaviour, and skills

3. attitudes

4. relationships with friends and acquaintances

5. drug-taking

A Dutch study of the needs of prisoners after release showed that 22% of them encounter ID-related problems (no ID document or the inability to retrieve it), 40% have income-related problems, 30% have accommodation problems, and 8% have health care problems (Kuppens & Ferwerda, 2008). According to the researchers themselves, the last of these figures is an underestimate owing to the research methods used. In view of the high percentages in the different categories it may be assumed that many former prisoners encounter a combination of these problems simultaneously. In addition, a relatively large proportion of ex-prisoners have mental health problems or addictions or both. A problem that is also often overlooked is that an unknown but probably substantial proportion of the prison population are functionally illiterate and/or dyslexic (Hudson, 2003). Solutions will have to be found to all these obstacles to the participation of former prisoners in society.

Despite the long tradition of the classic social work approach, there has been a failure to adopt an evidence-based policy. In line with the social casework and inspired by 'positive psychology' are the *Desistance approach* (McNeill, 2006) and the *Good Lives Model* (Ward & Brown, 2004). In both these, the approach of working on criminogenic risks is expanded to working towards goals that are positively valued by the client. Supporting the development of positive values such as intimate relationships (romantic partnership, or parenthood), education, work, and personal achievements is seen as important. In a longitudinal study on the life course of more than 4500 imprisoned offenders, Blokland, Nagin,

& Nieuwbeerta (2005) showed that a marriage was related to a reduction in recidivism of 27%. Few behavioural interventions have an effect of that size. The assumption is that recidivism can only partially be achieved by means of psychological intervention, but a criminal life course can be changed only by making an alternative life more realisticly possible. In this approach, it is not just the offender, but also his or her social environment that has to be involved in the programme. Delinquents must not just be 'pushed' into another live through the judicial and care systems, they must also be 'pulled' into the society through its prevalent social systems.

6.4 Wraparound care

An intervention model that has become known by the name 'wraparound' – sometimes referred to as the *wraparound care model* – seems able to combine the strengths of effective behavioural interventions and the contribution of the socio-ecological approach, and adds an important extra element: namely the planning and coordination of all activities. Wraparound was originally designed as a case management process for the better organization of help provided to client systems with complex needs. After all, providing care to multi-problem families and their children involved dealing with the same problems as occur in supervising and counselling persistent re-offenders.

The first aim of wraparound was to develop a strong case management system which could bring all the necessary activities under unified control (Brown & Hill, 1996). The help, care, and support was organized and directed by the case manager using a specific plan of action. The loose elements were, as it were, wrapped around the client system. Wraparound has now become more than a form of case management. In practice, a substantive vision evolved of how to bring about changes in the lives of people who display serious and chronic problematic behaviour. The National Wraparound Initiative Group, under the direction of Bruns (Bruns et al., 2004), formulated a number of principles that now belong to the quality or integrity criteria that can be assessed by reference to standardized observation scales (Bruns, Suter, & Leverentz-Brady, 2006).

Unfortunately, there is only limited empirical evidence about the efficacy of this approach in reducing recidivism, and even this relates only to young offenders. The only randomized controlled trial that can be found in the literature shows that during and immediately after the programme, a group of young offenders who received wraparound services did not play truant, get expelled or suspended from school, run away from home, or get picked up by the police as frequently as those members of a control group who received the juvenile court conventional services (i.e. referral by a case manager to a number of separate services) (Carney & Buttell, 2003). During a short measuring period of a few months after the programme, there was no difference between the very low rates of recidivism between the two groups. Unfortunately, no data were collected on recidivism in the longer term. The wraparound approach can therefore not yet be called evidence-based. However, practice-based would be a fair description.

The key elements of the substantive thinking behind wraparound are that lasting changes in client systems can take place only if:

a) the interventions are in keeping with a plan designed by a team of professionals and persons from the client's own network and the client system;

b) the plan sets out definite objectives to be achieved in the circumstances of the client's life;

c) the necessary activities are jointly controlled by a case manager and the client;

d) where necessary, interventions by both the client's own social networks and by professional organizations from a variety of sectors such as social work, health care, and general support can be arranged;

e) the plan is implemented in the surroundings which are least restrictive in the given circumstances, preferably in the client's own home and community.

The wraparound model is protocol-based.[95] Besides the case manager there is an assistant with a very low case load who provides day-to-day support for the client system in implementing the plan, preparing team meetings, and monitoring progress. In principle, a wraparound programme involves support in all relevant fields of life such as housing,

---

[95] In the USA millions of families receive services under hundreds of different programmes described as 'wraparound', all of which, by no means, fulfil the minimum quality requirements. This chapter refers only to protocol led and structured programmes as described and studied in the literature referred to here.

family, cognitions, behaviour and emotions, occupational qualifications and training, legality, relationships and social networks, safety and medical care.

The wraparound process consists of 13 steps. In the case of the services provided to former prisoners to prevent recidivism, these steps are as follows:

1. identify the key persons in the client's life;

2. explain to those concerned how wraparound works;

3. form a wraparound team;

4. decide which professional services should be provided to the client and select which services are necessary (or still necessary);

5. draw up a plan with measurable objectives;

6. decide what training or counselling the key figures need;

7. draft a plan for crisis situations and decide the conditions for implementation of the plan;

8. search for assistance, treatment, and support which is necessary but not yet available;

9. arrange for the funding of the plan;

10. implement the plan;

11. evaluate progress and adjust the plan as necessary;

12. determine the rounding up of the process and devise a long-term plan; and

13. determine the extent to which the objectives have been achieved, as input for the further development of the programme.

The team meets only a few times (usually once every three months). The responsibility for implementation lies mainly with the client, the case manager, and the assistant. The programme is implemented under the direction of a single case manager who is active throughout the entire process. In the case of programmes for combating recidivism, the process must start during the imprisonment stage and continue thereafter until the defined objectives have been achieved. On the basis of the experience with the reintegration projects for prisoners, Taxman (2004) estimated that the post-imprisonment wraparound stage can take anything between one month to two years.

Finally, an important element of the wraparound model is the conviction that the client system is a part 'owner' of the problem, and that changes are not possible without the intrinsic motivation of the client. This is why the client, or the clients in the case of a family, is/are always members of the wraparound team. This may appear at first sight to be at odds with the fact that the wraparound model is often applied in situations where there is a mandatory framework, such as juvenile criminal law and child protection, but is not (Trotter, 1999; Menger & Krechtig, 2010).

6.5   New avenues for the probation service?

What we have described above is an ideal desistance process. The logic of combating recidivism is in this way juxtaposed with the logic of the criminal justice chain. Reasoning backward from important life goals of and for offenders, the probation service can devise a plan involving a combination of activities that must be undertaken by the offender himself, by his (future) social network, and by professional care workers and support staff (sometimes from multiple agencies). Evidence-based behavioural training will generally be part of the plan that is drawn up. But social networks and social institutions also play an essential role in this respect. This involves a unique project for each prisoner individually, which can be carried out only with strong 'project management' and a 'support base' among all concerned. Such projects must not be seen as a form of aftercare (i.e. after the sentence has been served), but as a coordinated range of activities which are implemented during and after the imprisonment, as part of a single continuous process. The intensity and duration of the programme is geared to the seriousness of the recidivism risk, and the programme is based on the concrete needs of the offenders in various aspects of their life. Each 'project' is therefore unique and takes account of the individual characteristics of the offender.

Since 2006 the reintegration process for prisoners in the Netherlands has, broadly speaking, taken the following form:

1. During imprisonment, behavioural interventions are possible, under the responsibility of the penal institution concerned.

2. During imprisonment, offenders receive advise from the social services staff of the prisons, who provide help with problems in

four areas (identity papers, income, accommodation, and health care) and collaborate with the municipal authorities.

3. After release, prisoners with a moderate or high risk of recidivism are offered supervision and counselling by one of the three probation organizations. Here too, use is made of behavioural interventions. The probation service remains active as long as the sentence still exists. This is the case, for example, where a prisoner is released on licence.

4. Once a sentence has formally ended, the responsibility passes on to the municipal authorities under the Social Support Act. Each municipality should therefore have a liaison officer for cooperation with the social services staff, and for the provision of care in the municipality.

Once again, each of these four links in the reintegration chain involves a variety of organizations, each with its own responsibilities: the Public Prosecution Service, the courts, the (mental) healthcare institutions, social services, municipal and regional institutions, educational establishments, and so forth. The number of case managers and professionals with whom a former prisoner comes into contact within a period of say six months can vary, but in most cases the number could not be counted on the fingers of two hands. Often, it is found that essential activities in the chain are not carried out (Kuppens & Ferwerda, 2008). For example, when this survey was carried out 83 municipalities had still not appointed a liaison officer for former prisoners. The quality of the information transferred between the social services and the municipalities also often left something to be desired.[96]

But even if the chain were to function as intended, this complex process involving countless risks of failure in relation to transfers and forms of bilateral collaboration would be a very ambitious, even utopian undertaking. What plays a role in this connection is that each link in the chain often has its own management, funding, regulation, and production targets. Other factors include differences in organizational culture, professional autonomy, privacy protection, and institutional interests. An essential difference between the sequential organizational structure of the reintegration process and the wraparound model described above is that

---

[96] The social services staff themselves can hardly be blamed for this, as there are only just under 200 of them available to deal with the 35,000 people who leave prison.

the latter is based not on a diagnosis or problem analysis, but on analysis of what objectives should be achieved. Any obstacles that are anticipated or occur in achieving these objectives require attention, but only in the context of achieving the final objectives. As noted, this model does not create sequential actions that can be placed in a timeline, but a chain that can be forged around the prisoner/former prisoner in such a way as to create a circle rather than a classical line. Naturally, a time schedule forms part of the wraparound plan, but this can be visualized as a circle which moves over time. Part of the circle adjusts to the stage in which the prisoner or former prisoner is at the moment in question. Strong case management with continuity over time is a precondition. Coherence and collaboration are not sufficient. A form of overall control is necessary.

6.6   What next?

Based on the comparison between the present procedure for reintegrating former prisoners on the one side, and the proposed 'ideal type wraparound model' on the other, the first conclusion of this chapter is that it is unlikely to achieve a substantial reduction in the recidivism of Dutch prisoners with the current way of working. If the wraparound model is used, pragmatic solutions for the current prisoners must be sought through the collaboration that exists in the present system. This chapter is not the place to resolve such a complicated issue from behind the keyboard or *ex cathedra*. Nonetheless, a number of conceptual exercises could perhaps be informative.

The main obstacle to introducing the wraparound process in the present structure (besides a number of substantive professional difficulties which are beyond the scope of this article) is the lack of continuity in the approach to and management of the overall process. If we are to fantasize about specific solutions, the following probation model would not seem such a bad idea. On the premise that it is necessary in the case of the wraparound model to reason backwards from final objectives, the obvious course of action would seem to be the grafting of the management of the process on to these final objectives, and to appoint a professional (facilitator) who has the ultimate responsibility for achieving these final objectives as far as possible. The facilitator should form a wraparound team from the start of the prison sentence, and manage the team, both during the imprisonment and after release, until social participation takes place smoothly and the client poses no security risk to society. The contribution to be made by the other institutions and staff involved should form part of the plan managed by the facilitator and the client. The objectives of the wraparound plan could be determined, in principle, by using the instruments currently available to the probation service, such as offender assessments. Arrangements could be made, for example, for a professional researcher to join the team temporarily. Effective behavioural interventions can be used to achieve definite objectives relating to cognitions, emotions, and behaviour. The various effective behavioural interventions available to the team can be regarded as the 'toolkit' of those who facilitate the wraparound plan for prisoners and former prisoners. An important part of the plan will be objectives that can be achieved in or by organizations that form part of ordinary society, such as schools, social services, debt management services,[97] businesses, social networks, and so forth. In this approach it is therefore necessary for representatives of these institutions to be members of the wraparound team.

The question then is who could act as a professional facilitator. Since reintegration revolves largely around the system of local facilities but the probation service is best equipped professionally, the obvious course of action would be for the municipalities to use ('hire') the probation service to manage the overall reintegration process. Probation officers are the ideal wraparound workers. After all, changing a criminal lifestyle into something more socially acceptable is their profession. They are experienced in working within a correctional setting, in other words the context created by the criminal law for part of the change process.

Experiments with the wraparound care model to reduce recidivism are currently being carried out in the Netherlands. Evaluation studies are part of these experiments. There is however, no doubt that increasing continuity throughout the judicial chain in the rehabilitation process of offenders will contribute to its effectiveness.

---

[97] In the Netherlands, two-thirds of all prisoners have debts (Kuppens & Ferwerda 2008).

Bibliography

Andrews, D., & Bonta, J. (1998). *The psychology of criminal conduct*. Cincinnati: Anderson Publishirg Co. .

Aos, S., Miller, M., & Drake, E. (2006). *Evidence based adult corrections programs: what works and what does not*. Olympia: Washington State Institute for Public Policy.

Blokland, A., Nagin, D., & Nieuwbeerta, P. (2005). Life span offending trajectories of a Dutch conviction report. *Criminology, 43*(4), 919-954.

Brown, R., & Hill, B. (1996). Opportunity for change: Exploring an alternative to residential treatment. *Child Welfare League of America, 725*, 35-57.

Bruns, E., Suter, J., & Leverentz-Brady, K. (2006). Relations between program and system variables and fidelity to the wraparound process for children and families. *Psychiatric Services 57*(11), 1586-1593.

Bruns, E., Walker, J., Adams, J., Miles, P., Osher, T., Rast, J., et al. (2004). *Ten principles of the wraparound process*. Portland: Portland State University.

Carney, M., & Buttell, F. (2003). Reducing juvenile recidivism: evaluating the Wraparound Servics Model. *Research on Social Work Practice, 13*(5), 551-568.

Cullen, F., & Gendreau, P. (2000). Assessing correctional rehabilitation: policy, practice, and prospects. *Criminal Justice 3*(109-175).

Hudson, C. (2003). Basic skills provision for offenders on probation supervision: beyond a rethoric of evidence-based policy? *British Journal of Educational Studies, 51*(1), 64-81.

Knaap, L. v. d., Leenarts, L., & Nijssen, L. (2007). *Psychometrische kwaliteiten van de Recidiev Inschattingsschalen (RISc). Interbeoordelaarsbetrouwbaarheid, interne consistentie en congruente validiteit (*Psychometric qualities of the Recidivism Estimation Scales (RISc). Inter-assessor reliability, internal consistency and congruence validity). Den Haag: WODC.

Kuppens, J., & Ferwerda. H. (2008). *Van binnen naar buiten. een behoefteonderzoek naar de aard en omvang van nazorg voor gedetineerden* (From inside to outside. A needs survey by reference to the nature and scope of the aftercare for prisoners) . Arnhem: Advies- en Onderzoeksgroep Beke.

McNeill, F. (2006). A desistance paradigm for offender management *Criminology and Criminal Justice, 6*(39-62).

Menger, A & Krechtig. L(2010: Het Delict als Maatstaf, Basismethodiek voor werken in gedwongen kader, *Amsterdam: SWP* (Dutch general professional method for working with mandated clients).

Taxman, F. (2004). The offender and reentry. *Federal Probation, 68*(2), 31-35.

Trotter, Ch. (1999): Working with involuntary clients. A guide to practice. *St. Leonards NSW Australia*.

Ward, T., & Brown, M. (2004). The good lives model and conceptual issues in offender rehabilitation. *Psychology, Crime & Law, 10*(3), 243-257.

7. *Kwartiermaken*, creating space for otherness[98]

Doortje Kal

7.1 *Kwartiermaken*: Introduction and Background

Background

In their book *Arbeidsrehabilitatie in een vernieuwde geestelijke gezondheidszorg*[99], Jaap van Weeghel and Jacques Zeelen (1990) introduce the concept of *kwartiermaken*. They define this concept as the efforts aimed at visualizing, making accessible and, if needed, adapting social *work* situations. In my opinion this concept also applies to other situations. It is about making (work- or other) places suitable not just for the individual client, but likewise setting out a collective environment strategy for the humanization of work or of society as a whole.

When I started working in 1990 at a well-functioning day activity centre (*DAC*), I could immediately step into this conceptual framework: *kwartiermaken* as a collective environment strategy, for the humanization of society. After all, the many visitors at the *DAC* underlined with their arrival the inhospitality of society. Together with the prevention worker at the time, Kees Onderwater of *Riagg*[100], we visited the boards of city districts to lobby (both financially and politically) for what we called 'categorical community work', community work for people with psychiatric disabilities. In short, the aim of this project was (in the terminology of that time):

'promoting an infrastructure that enables participation in living, working, knowing, and well-being of people with a psychiatric disability. The project is aimed at the social integration of people who all too often lead a marginalized existence. It targets precisely that area where the influence of organized mental health care fails, and where community involvement is required. (...) It is not a normalization process in which

---

[98] *Kwartiermaken* is originally a Dutch term meaning the preparation of a camp (or 'quarters') for troops; the word **kwartiermaken** is used metaphorically here to refer to a process of preparation of institutions and individuals for the integration of former psychiatric patients into the community. **Kwartiermaken** is also the name of a project in Zoetermeer, the Netherlands, which aims to prepare institutions and individuals for the integration of former psychiatric patients into their midst.

[99] *Occupational rehabilitation in a renewed mental healthcare.* [transl. eds.]

[100] Riagg is an outpatient mental health care organization.

patients are adjusted to society. But it is a matter of accepting and revaluing the 'being different', of creating inclusive space in society, of a focus on survival of vulnerable people.' (Brochure *Psychiatrie Opbouwwerk Samenleving*, 1991)

Sisyphus' view

In psychiatry, social contexts are becoming less of an issue. With the somewhat oppositional compendium *Sisyphus' view* (*Het uitzicht van Sisyphus*, Baars & Kal, 1995), I tried, as a prevention worker, to give an impetus to a discussion on the importance of social contexts, and to bring a more contextual approach into the agenda again. In this compendium we showed how psychological problems *also*, at the least, link to the structure of our society. In this way the book was a prelude to the new *Kwartiermaken* project, which I started in 2007 in Zoetermeer,[101] together with Gerda Scholtens and Geesje Tomassen. In 2001, I did my PhD on a description of and reflection on this project, at the University of Humanistic Studies in Utrecht. In this chapter, I shall mainly present my philosophical reflection on the project.

7.2 *Kwartiermaken*: On strangeness, hospitality, and suspension

Introduction

At the base of my *kwartier* activities there is the request of clients to, as one of them once formulated, 'become a member of the world' (Scholtens & Kalo, 1999, transl. eds.). This is not a natural process for people with a psychiatric background. I cite Keefman, alias Jan Arends (1972): 'Things happen in the world by appointment or by intercession. And since psychiatrically impaired people are often not understood, there is a problem.' For a long time psychiatry has not only imprisoned its patients in (total) institutions, but also still, and in a certain sense more and more, imprisons itself as a discipline.

Initiated in the eighties, the policy of *socialization* attempts to reintegrate or retain people with psychiatric problems in society. Care closer to home and social support have to better enable the process of 'becoming a member of the world'. The paradoxical situation however, is that simultaneously the orientation of the psychiatric discipline increasingly narrows itself down to the medical-biological discourse. The process of

---

[101] A city close to The Hague.

de-institutionalization seems to bypass psychiatry as a discipline. This is a serious situation. The dominant biomedical discourse in psychiatry, makes it difficult for both clients as well as other citizens to think in terms other than (the dichotomous) 'mentally ill' and 'healthy'; it makes it hard to think differently about being different.

And it is precisely this that is important to achieve social integration. The increase in biomedical knowledge has not increased the potential for integration. More biomedical knowledge has indeed led to better identification of psychiatric problems, but not to more understanding of and tolerance towards people 'with a psychiatric background'. In the following sections I will introduce a philosophical reflection on the notion of 'making space for the strange other' and how to realize this space in practice. But first I will focus on the categorization that I employ.

Categorization – a paradoxical strategy

Making space for people who are different? Doesn't that encourage stigmatization just as much, and doesn't that prevent the restoration of reciprocity? I chose for the categorization for the following reasons:

1. Not naming 'the otherness', not talking about it, will not bring the group out of the margin.

2. In order for people to integrate, 'the other' (however relative) needs to get a chance to appear 'in its otherness'. This is necessary to be able to develop a counter position. Identifying the group as a category is necessary for detecting and addressing the excluding effect of normality. *The categorization functions as an intermediate step.* This step is made, precisely in order to offer the possibility of integration (in other words: connection with others), and at the same time prevents an equalizing assimilation in which there is no recognition of otherness or difference.

I have found support for this line of thinking in, among others, Luce Irigaray's theory of difference.[102] The theory of difference motivates the cultivation of values that encourage the respect of and engagement with the otherness of others. The theory of difference makes the categorization, that is in itself perilous, a productive undertaking. It

---

[102] As discussed in Irigaray (1992), as well as in the theses of Halsema (1998) and Van den Ende (1999).

offers a 'vocabulary of difference', where the otherness of the other appears in its relation to the conventional. By noting the otherness as a relative problem, the other side, normality, is also called into question. The normal world and reality are thus put to question in order to make space for 'the strange other'.

a. Strangeness and conflict

In relation to the acceptance of the one who might be experienced as strange, I use terms such as 'the other' or 'the strange' or 'the unmentionable'; I write about 'non-presentable suffering' and 'unmentionable conflict'. For the French thinker Lyotard who theorized on difference, *conflict* has the special meaning of a dispute over a dispute, which he calls *differend*. This arises when the other does not acknowledge the dispute as such. Hence, the experience becomes non-presentable. This is a crucial notion for *kwartiermaken*. It involves an experience that cannot be discussed by the person in general intelligible or recognized terms. This puts the person in a position of speechlessness and thus of isolation. The core of the differend is the suffering from the injustice that one's own position (experience, perception, condition, memory) cannot be expressed in a situation in which precisely this position is at issue. That brings us to the question of how to work on optimizing the conditions for making the speechless heard.

'I would like to call a differend the case where the plaintiff is divested of the means to argue and becomes for that reason a victim. (...) A case of differend between two parties takes place when the regulation of the conflict that opposes them is done in the idiom of one of the parties while the wrong suffered by the other is not signified in that idiom.' (Lyotard, 1988, p. 9)

With the identification of these kinds of non-expressible injustices, Lyotard appeals to giving a voice to the injustice that cannot be articulated within a certain discourse, within a certain language game. This requires new idioms, or when it concerns, for example, people with a serious mental handicap, also non-language related hermeneutic competences (Meininger, 1997, 2007). Lyotard points out that the satisfaction that can come from this, will always remain partial. The new idioms run the risk of becoming contested themselves, since they are deployed in the conversation in an already mapped out way and have an excluding effect on other speakers and 'actors'.

b. Hospitality

With this experienced strangeness and conflict in mind, *kwartiermaken* aims at making society hospitable.

In his essay *Of hospitality,* French philosopher Jacques Derrida (1998) asks himself if we can expect from the stranger to act like the others and speak the language of the others *before* he is welcomed. Is it then possible to still speak of providing hospitality? Is the stranger then still a stranger? Hospitality only arises, says Derrida, when there is a person one does not know yet, who might also not let himself be known easily. It is important to realize that 'the stranger' (the 'strange guest') depends on hospitality. And secondly, that the act of providing hospitality also makes the host a bit of a stranger, in the sense that he or she enters into unknown territory with the provision of hospitality. He says: 'A hospitable attitude towards the other presumes that something else than I can have priority.'

For Derrida, hospitality; giving access to the stranger or to otherness, is linked to a symbolic space – call it the 'space between' or a free zone – where mediation and border crossings can happen between oneself and the other, *without one having to lose oneself in the other and the other having to assimilate to the one's identity.* What consequences does this have for the normal course of affairs? In other words: which (intermediate) steps needs to be taken to achieve true hospitality?

c. An intermediate step towards creating niches of hospitality

In order to provide hospitality, a suspension of the norm that defines normality is required. *If the house is not maintained, the meeting cannot take place.* The 'house' must be made suitable for reception, the thresholds need to be removed. Not once, but over and over, since strangeness can arise yet again, threatening at exclusion. Furthermore, offering a place to 'someone one cannot place' is a matter of trying, a matter of trial and error. Offering hospitality provides a tension that one cannot shy away from. We have looked for things that could help us handle that tension. The idea of an *intermediate step* or *suspension* seems useful. The host or hostess should not have to surrender to the other. In holding hostage there is no meeting. The intermediate step is needed to find out how normality, and the host(ess) as a part of that normality, are preventing a true encounter. The maintenance of the house therefore, primarily involves a critical examination of one's own identity. The quality of the accessibility for 'strange others' depends on the willingness and the ability of society (institutions, professionals, and citizens) to make this intermediate step and the suspension of the conventional a reality.

The term 'niche' is a concretization of hospitality. *Kwartiermakers* create niches in social and volunteer work, and at all the places where people want to participate in society. In niches, vulnerable people find others who are emotionally supportive and have time; there are activities which are experienced as meaningful by them. Niches are environments in which self-esteem is fed. The quality of these niches is based on buddies, people who assert themselves as allies and, if necessary, as mediators. Buddies can be organized by, for example, a 'hospitality officer' or 'case manager', but when the awareness of the importance of these niches has grown, it could be that buddies step forward of their own account. This is important, because not everyone with a psychiatric or other problem will report themselves as such.

Intermezzo 1: The portrait of Karen Soeterik – An anthropologist as a *kwartier*-maker

"In part, I experience my work as *kwartiermaker* with *Stichting Prisma*[1] as the work of an anthropologist in the field: I must empathize with people who are strange to me, I investigate where people experience obstacles in participation, I build networks and talk with key figures. Lastly, I 'translate' the social environments and experiences of 'the strange others' into the language of policymakers and professionals. (...)

Besides the people with an intellectual disability themselves, *kwartiermaken* is also aimed at the care institutions, the welfare and other social organizations which are active in the neighbourhood, and at the management of the particular city district. Over the past two years we worked in Amsterdam East/Watergraafsmeer. The aim was to promote a welcoming and safe environment for people with intellectual disabilities in regular leisure centres. You could call it working with niches. If people from the neighbourhood can make use of these facilities, they will often expand their social network and feel less lonely. It also creates more awareness of this special group among professionals and the other users of these facilities, which reduces their getting cold feet.

I worked for the first time in this district with two extra staff members (from the field of social integration and participation) from *Cordaan* (merged partner of *Prisma*), and that has paid off. They had time to calmly get to know people, to see what they wanted, and to make people talk about the possibilities in the neighbourhood themselves. They could bind people to themselves and literally pull them along, since they were trusted."

(Also see: www.kwartiermaken.nl/publicaties; *Dat het gewoon is dat we er zijn* (That it is simply that we are there, transl. ed.) and *Kwartiermaken in sociaal-cultureel werk in Amsterdam Oud-West* (*Kwartiermaken* in social-cultural work in the Amsterdam Old-West district, transl. eds.)).

Intermezzo 2: The portrait of Gerda Baerveldt – *Vriendendienst* brings people together[103]

Gerda Baerveldt is *kwartiermaker* at *Amsterdamse Vriendendiensten,* and participated in the training *kwartiermaken* for experienced experts. *Vriendendienst* to her has everything to do with *kwartiermaken*. The spearhead of this 'friendship service' is the one-on-one buddy contact. People from society are brought into contact with people with psychiatric backgrounds to help them enter into that society. This kills two birds with one stone: you bring people into contact with each other, which expands both their lifeworlds, and you bring people into society; 'bring people among the people', as the motto of Vriendendienst reads.

'What inspires me are the stories of people. Volunteers tell me that they would have otherwise never met someone with a psychiatric background, they would have never discovered how to really be there for another; they make clear that it really affects them.

And sometimes the buddies are actually friends. (…)

I think our *Open Houses* are a real *kwartiermaken* activity. We do this now in 5 or 6 neighbourhood centres. We organize a lunch with an activity afterwards, and try to motivate other people from the neighbourhood to come as well, which is quite successful!'

7.3   Research – Organizing 'critical dialogues'

Over the next two years I want to tackle five themes head-on within the research programmes of the Knowledge Centre for Social Innovation. I want to introduce all these themes by organizing - in the words of Adri Smaling (2008) - a *critical dialogue,* in order to arrive, from this dialogue with divergent stakeholders of a shared problem, at more

---

[103]   The Dutch name *Vriendendienst* is chosen since it has two meanings. Literally, it means 'friendship service', figuratively a 'kind turn'.

precise research questions. I believe that Smaling's concept of critical dialogue makes way for strangeness, contributes to hospitality, and calls for suspension. I will try to show this in the coming part of this chapter.

The critical dialogue as a qualitative research method

In his farewell speech, Smaling (2008) argues for organizing critical dialogues as a method of research. These dialogues are about understanding, assessing, and possibly correcting or improving an argument, a reasoning. Smaling states that this critical dialogue is not limited to a cognitive rational discussion aimed at consensus. Participants are not stripped of their polyphony and multiple diversity; unanimity is no longer the highest goal. The critical dialogue is however aimed at making clear, understanding, respecting, and communicating similarity and difference of opinion.

The critical dialogue is of vital importance in participatory research methods. Especially so, since stakeholders are also seen as competent co-researchers in participatory research. In addition we will also bet on action research, whereby researchers are also social change agents.

Empathic understanding

Empathy is a prerequisite for being able to carry out a dialogue. It helps to do more justice to others, morally and ethically, but also with regard to the knowledge that one wants to acquire. Empathic understanding improves the dialogue and vice versa. The knowledge gained from experience with the research subject is an advantage. This provides one with an, as it were, (empathic) antenna.

Smaling (2008) claims that perhaps much too little is done to further develop our capacity in society for dialogue and empathy. This capacity would be good for both human society as well as for social scientific research.

7.4 Research Themes

A. Critical dialogue on the value of a kwartiermaker in a district team

> 'When writing the text for this folder, I mainly went back to my memory of the time when I was in a deep crisis myself and felt completely isolated. In that memory I looked for words that would have been able to arouse my interest in *kwartiermaken*. I found out that this was not at all easy. When I was suffering from depression I found society nothing but terribly scary, and I only looked for places where I could hide from that 'society'.

> But who knows, at the moments I felt pushed into action (for example by the Public Employment Service) and realized I had to at least do something, I would have liked to been given a folder on *kwartiermaken*. I hope we have succeeded with this folder to attract your attention, and that it will invite you to meet us.'

> (An experienced *kwartiermaker* in the folder *Ik mag er zijn, jij mag er zijn* (I'm ok, you're ok), Van Bergen & Sok, 2008, transl. eds.)

In a district, too many organizations and professionals work at cross purposes. The Knowledge Centre for Social Innovation is developing district teams, which ensure that citizens who need it get the right support in the field of housing, care, and participation; teams with present and widely approachable new social professionals.

The question is: How can these social district teams be organized and arranged in such a way that they offer effective support to people in the district and contribute to participation and social cohesion?[104] I want to explore the added value of *kwartiermaken* and the use of experiential expertise. Furthermore, it is important to research and develop further the competencies and methods that make up the work of *kwartiermaken*. I will hereby build on previous research that was carried out by the research group on *participation, care and support* (Scholtens, 2007).

---

[104] Also see Van Ewijk (2010), who described the Netherlands as a country of institutions par excellence: the top in terms of beds in mental health care, care for people with an intellectual disability, and children in special education. Even in times of the 'socialization of care' and the *Wmo* (Social Support Act), the budgets for specialized care have doubled in the past decade, but the number of social workers remained stable or have decreased, depending on the sector.

B. Critical dialogue on civic friendship

> 'Since one year I have a buddy who also had the same training as I did. (…) Now I think that it would have been better if projects such as these would have been there in the past, when I was younger. If I would have had a friend of my own age, I would not have felt so lonely.' (Başar, 2010)

Citizenship is a central concept in the *Wmo* (Social Support Act). To improve social participation (and hence citizenship) of vulnerable groups, the Wmo depends on the participation of, in my words, more resilient citizens. The motto here is: from welfare state to participation society.

Friend services and buddy projects seem to be an excellent opportunity to live up to this double participation claim. What started as a volunteer project for people who had become isolated because of their psychiatric background or otherwise needed a buddy to overcome societal obstacles, has grown into a movement with diverse projects such as the food bank buddies, sports buddies, walking buddies, phone and e-mail buddies, study buddies, buddies for youth, homeless, people with mental disabilities, and people with a migrant background, buddies for refugees and former prisoners. And last but not least the 'buddy at the location' where someone wants to participate in an activity which is not right away experienced as safe, inviting, or welcoming.

We could entitle this form of citizenship, according to the ethicist Hans Reinders (1999), as *civic friendship*. It does not straightaway mean a relation in the private sphere; the friendship denotes a public virtue which makes an actual society possible. Civic friendship exists where citizens are each other's fellow citizens; one participates in another's life, so that everyone can thrive.

But what about the municipal support for such projects, now that the mental health care has to withdraw as a financier? Under what conditions do citizens become 'concerned citizens' or civic friends? What social infrastructure is needed to make civic friendships succeed, and how do we train social professionals for this?

C. Critical dialogue on an economy of inclusion – working on niche diversity

Kwartiermaken supports an inclusive society where even people with small and big handicaps get the chance to socially participate according to their own desire and ability, at an income that improves their situation rather then condemning them to eternal poverty.

Both a sustainable and steady economy as well as an inclusive economy seem to benefit from a higher niche diversity in society. The concept of niche diversity comes from biology/ecology; a niche refers to a specific place of significance to the preservation of a certain (vulnerable) population. Niches in their turn are beneficial to the ecological system as a whole. Niche diversity must offer the possibility for people with diverse handicaps to participate in society in a humane, sustainable, and inclusive way, making this society a different one.

Through the special research group on *Kwartiermaken* I want to organize a critical dialogue with, among others, the *Platform Duurzame en Solidaire Economie* (Platform Sustainable and Inclusive Economy, transl. eds.) to make clear what the overlap is between a sustainable economy and an inclusive economy, and to research how these two can strengthen each other – both in theory as well as in practice.

Can we, together with students, professors, and other stakeholders, amongst whom there are definitely people from the assumed target groups, perform an explanatory study from a common vision in order to support concrete initiatives and existing practices?

D.   Critical dialogue on 'exclusion makes ill'

A violated group identity

We all know it: one's self-understanding is not created in isolation. Identity formation is a dialogical process. People are dependent on the recognition of others for their own sense of self, which makes us all vulnerable. Denial can deeply affect a person's identity. Since we can only develop an attitude towards ourselves from the standpoint of others and the social world around us, we cannot remain unaffected by the contempt and humiliation of others. Moreover, denial does not only cause pain and sadness, it may also hinder the individual in the development of his capabilities and talents. Latent capacities can be blocked by a fundamental lack of confidence, an inability to see yourself as a person who is able to bring a specific task to a successful conclusion. Contempt and negative stereotyping have self-repressive effects. To understand this, we must pay attention to both the *internal self-doubt* that can arise in the longer term when someone takes over a negative image, as well as to the *external threat* that can come from personal encounters with negative stereotypes about one's group.

In other words, it is important to realize that prejudices produce their own reality. Dominant groups can lead minorities to see themselves as inferior. A violated group identity is born, since the particular group begins to believe in its own unworthiness. The limited appreciation starts getting in the way of self-esteem. Based on this violated image, people start looking at each other with mixed feelings. Again, the human dependency on recognition for one's interpretation of self makes minority groups and marginalized groups very vulnerable. We almost always fail to do justice to their pain and internal struggles (Van Leeuwen, 2003).

I believe this text underlines the similarity between people with a psychiatric background and the Muslims who are being disregarded by the Dutch politician Geert Wilders' party PVV. I will use this similarity as a prelude to a critical dialogue on how exclusion can itself be a cause of mental illness, and on stigma and discrimination of others. Then we will examine how society and its institutions and citizens can be a place where more people feel at home, and how *kwartiermaker*s can be of importance in this process.

A further question is: how can the *kwartiermaken* movement mean more to people with a migrant background, in order for them to also feel more welcome in society and reduce their chances of becoming psychiatric patients?

There is a mutual intention to work together on this theme between our research group and Ihsan, *Islamic institute for social activation work*. Ihsan wants to improve the involvement of Muslim communities in the Netherlands with social issues, and hence improve their commitment. One of the pillars of the programme is participation in the public debates on social issues such as multiculturalism, responsible citizenship, and combating impoverishment and exclusion.

E.   *Organization of a kwartiermaker festival at the university under the motto: In praise of visibility*

Over the past decade around 25 *kwartiermaker* festivals (often lasting several days) have taken place all over the Netherlands. By organizing cultural events, a *kwartiermaker* festival aims to bring about meetings between people with and people without a psychiatric background. People with a psychiatric background in general, and at the Arnhem festival people with a mental disability as well, present themselves in artistic productions (theatre, music, poetry, exhibitions) and in doing so, try to bring about a shift in the public imagination and representation with regard to themselves.

Kwartiermaker festivals help people from vulnerable groups to come out in the open. They make themselves known in an artistic way. The participants 'as others' long for being recognized for what is important to them, their artistic qualities, but also, in the words of Ellie van Steensel (2008), bringing to attention their 'slightly less obvious being in the world'. Thus the festival is also an agenda; through the arts and other activities it involves our attention on the importance of this double recognition.

The Flemish philosopher Rudi Visker (2007) points at the importance of this 'coming out in the open' with his book *Lof der Zichtbaarheid* (In Praise of Visibility, transl. eds.). He claims that showing oneself in word and deed to others, brings about a change in people. In that sense, the public space is a productive space. For example, the public space enables the amateur or professional artist to not be alone in his otherness; an otherness that makes him a minority and possibly oppresses him. Most people – not everyone – attach importance to participating in a public space that is wider than that of just the like-minded. This has to do with a form of respect, with the experience that one also matters in the 'normal world' – without having to give up one's otherness. It is most certainly not my purpose to absolutize otherness as an all-determining category, or to degrade 'being together with peers' as something of less quality. But with this festival we want to show that the public space does not only belong to 'standard people', to a small majority of 'big me's' (*dikke-ikken*, Kunneman, 2006). The public space is a space that allows for liberation. It is as if the person says: 'My otherness need not continuously be on the foreground of my concern, but can find a home in the public space offered by means of this festival.' The importance of entering the public space is powerfully articulated by Barbara Douwes, participant of the Amsterdam *kwartiermaker* festival in 2008:

> "I think my participation is wonderful; I finally get the space to show
> my world. It's important to have an opening to the world. Someone
> with a psychiatric background is often cut off from the world, not
> easily allowed into it." (In: Zandinga, Koelmans & Swart, 2009, transl.
> eds.)

In her inaugural speech as professor in the field of active citizenship in early 2009, Sandra Trienekens placed art at the heart of society. Trienekens suspects that (community) art can help to generate the 'soft civic competencies' of citizens and organizations. With these competencies she means, among others, the ability to live with, sometimes insoluble, differences, and the ability to give diversity a positive position in the public domain; in other words to not push everything that is different to the private domain. Soft civic competencies involve the ability to accept imperfection and deal with difference.

The *kwartiermaker* festival at the university will be organized in cooperation with the university departments of Creative Therapy, Cultural Social Development, and Social Pedagogic Care, precisely in order to also stress the community building aspects of artistic activities, next to the therapeutic aspects.

Bibliography

Arends, J. (1972). *Keefman*. Amsterdam: De Bezige Bij.

Baars, J. & Kal, D. (red.) (1995). *Het uitzicht van Sisyphus. Maatschappelijke contexten van geestelijke (on)gezondheid.* Groningen: Wolters Noordhoff.

Başar, B. (2010). *Ik wil niet meer onzichtbaar zijn. Autisme in de allochtone cultuur in Nederland.* Pica.

Bergen, A.-M. van & Sok, K., met bijdragen van Hanneke Henkens (2008). *Buitengewoon: kwartiermaker en ervaringsdeskundigheid in maatschappelijke steunsystemen. Beschrijving zorgvernieuwingsprojecten in Eindhoven en randgemeenten.* Utrecht: Movisie.

Brons, R. (1997). *Lyotard: tussen openbaarheid en sprakeloosheid.* Amsterdam: uitgave in eigen beheer.

Derrida, J. (1998). *Over gastvrijheid.* Essay. Amsterdam: Boom.

Ende, T. van den (1999). *In levende lijven. Identiteit, lichamelijkheid en verschil in het werk van Luce Irigaray.* Leende: Damon.

Ewijk, H. van (2010). *Maatschappelijk werk in een sociaal gevoelige tijd.* Inaugurele rede Grondslagen van het maatschappelijk werk, Universiteit voor Humanistiek. Amsterdam: SWP Humanistic University Press.

Irigaray, L. (1992). *Ik, jij, wij. Voor een cultuur van het onderscheid.* Kampen: Kok Agora.

Halsema, A (1998) Dialectiek van de seksuele differentie. De filosofie van Luce Irigaray, Amsterdam: Boom

Kal, D. (2001). *Kwartiermaken. Werken aan ruimte voor mensen met een psychiatrische achtergrond.* Amsterdam: Boom.

Kunneman, H. (1996). *Van theemutscultuur naar walkman-ego. Contouren van postmoderne individualiteit.* Amsterdam/Meppel: Boom.

Kunneman, H. (2006). *Voorbij het dikke-ik. Bouwstenen voor een kritisch humanisme.* Amsterdam: SWP.

Leeuwen, B. van (2003). *Erkenning, identiteit en verschil. Multiculturaliteit en leven met culturele diversiteit.* Leuven: Acco.

Meininger, H. (1997). *'... Als u zelf'. Een theologisch-ethische studie van zorg voor verstandelijk gehandicapten.* Amersfoort: Vereniging 's Heeren Loo.

Meininger, H.P. (2007). *Verbindende verhalen en de ruimte van de ontmoeting.* In

H.P. Meininger (red.), *Plaatsen waar plek is. Perspectieven op onderzoek naar sociale integratie van mensen met een verstandelijke handicap.* 's Heerenloo.

Reinders, H. (1999). *De toekomst van de Nederlandse gehandicaptenzorg. Bespiegelingen over zorg, burger- en vriendschap.* In *Handboek Mogelijkheden, vraaggerichte zorg voor mensen met een verstandelijke handicap.* Maarssen: Elsevier Gezondheidszorg.

Scholtens, G. (2007). *Acht keer kwartiermaken. Een verkennend onderzoek naar de methodische aspecten van kwartiermaken*. Amsterdam: SWP.

Scholtens, G. & Kal, D. (1999). *'Ik verlang ernaar lid van de wereld te worden'. Kwartiermaken in buurt- en sportverenigingen en vrijwilligersorganisaties.* Zoetermeer: Reakt.

Smaling, A. (2008). *Dialoog en empathie in de methodologie.* Amsterdam: SWP, Humanistics University Press.

Steensel, H.F. van (2008). Na de Beeldend Gesproken Kunstprijs.

Trienekens, S. (2009). *Kunst in het hart van de samenleving: over burgerschap en culturele dynamiek.* Public class. Amsterdam: Hogeschool van Amsterdam.

Visker, R. (2007). *Lof der zichtbaarheid. Een uitleiding in de hedendaagse wijsbegeerte.* Amsterdam: SUN.

Weeghel, J. van & Zeelen, J. (1990). *Arbeidsrehabilitatie in een vernieuwde geestelijke gezondheidszorg.* Utrecht: Lemma.

Zandinga, H., Koelmans, H. & Swart, A. (2009). *Kwartiermaken doe je samen! Landelijk onderzoek naar de werkzaamheid van kwartiermakersfestivals.* Graduation thesis for the Master Programme Social Pedagogic Care. Utrecht: Hogeschool, Utrecht.

8. Promoting interethnic relations by strengthening social networks: 'Connecting through football'

Stijn Verhagen

8.1 Introduction

In the previous chapters we have already mentioned how, in the field of care and social work, The Netherlands is a 'country of institutions' par excellence. Few other countries in the world refer people with problems so quickly to specialist support agencies such as child welfare, mental health or special education (Eurydice, 2005; Van Ewijk, 2010). So far, this observation has led to two conclusions. Firstly, in the provision of care there is often an underestimation of the strength of people's social networks (cf. Mirsky, 2003). Secondly, social professionals can be useful in mobilizing this strength, although this requires a different type of social professional. The aim of these *new* social professionals, as opposed to their predecessors, must be to lessen their own role in providing care. It is often better to enable the social network of the person involved to offer the necessary support (Verhagen, 2009; Hilhorst, 2011).

This chapter builds on the idea of the new social professional. I would like to add here however, that the role of the new social professional extends beyond just strengthening the network of those who need *support*. Even people without this need will benefit from vital social environments. Equally important is the fact that by creating strong social environments, people can be *prevented* from becoming vulnerable and relying on specialist care. Research shows, for example, how strengthening of associations, schools and neighbourhoods is a crucial factor in the prevention of addictions (Benson, Roehlkepartain & Sesma, 2004), aggression (Junger, 2006), nuisance (Garbarino et.al, 1997) and interethnic tensions and polarization (Snel & Boonstra, 2005).

The case considered in this chapter is the project 'Connecting through Football' (*Verbinden door Voetbal*), which started three years ago at football club Zwaluwen Utrecht 1911, situated on the edge of the Utrecht districts Kanaleneiland and Rivierenwijk. Rivierenwijk is a district where the majority of residents are native Dutch whereas the residents of Kanaleneiland are mainly of Turkish or Moroccan descent. Out of these two districts, Kanaleneiland is mainly the one with problems. These problems – deprivation, lack of safety and little mutual trust between residents – are so large that they cannot be solved by the district alone (see also City of Utrecht, 2008). In this setting, football club Zwaluwen Utrecht 1911 wants to be a relaxed, problem-free place for residents in this part of town to come to, not just for the club itself, but also to create a positive impression on the other districts around. More precisely, Zwaluwen wants to stimulate relaxed interethnic relations in this strongly segregated environment. With this aim, three years ago, the club got in touch with the department of participation and social development (Dutch: Participatie en maatschappelijke ontwikkeling) of the Hogeschool Utrecht.

In the following sections I will describe respectively, the conceptual vision, and the practical design of 'Connecting through football'. Then I will address the results of this project: In which way is 'Connecting through football' successful? What can be improved? In conclusion, I will discuss the significance of this project for social work.

8.2   Conceptual vision

In recent years, the Netherlands has seen a large number of initiatives to promote contact between citizens and improve behaviour in the public sphere. Many of these initiatives are aimed at reducing the distance between the 'natives' and 'foreigners'. Such initiatives include multicultural street festivals, debates on Islam and world music festivals. Studies by Fast en Boonstra (2005) and the *Sociaal en Cultureel Planbureau* (2007) show however, that these initiatives generally do not lead to lasting interethnic contact. The main reason is that these initiatives are generally organized too haphazardly with way too much stress on the theme of 'ethnicity' (Raad voor Maatschappelijke Ontwikkeling (RMO), 2005). In order to achieve positive group contact, we need more than just bringing people together.

Socio-psychological insights

According to Allports sociopsychological contact hypothesis, four conditions must be met to avoid negative perceptions between groups (Allport, 1954) The first is that, with contact between people, there needs to be *sufficient opportunity* to get to know each other. This condition is consistent with the concerns that RMO (2005) has about one-time contact moments. These moments are too incidental and too forced to really get to know each other and to renounce any possible prejudices. 'The story is told of a lady of goodwill who planned an interracial tea', in the words of Allport. 'When the guests came she insisted that they sit in alternate chairs – first a white lady then a coloured lady. The tea was a failure.'(Allport, 1954: 279)

The second condition is the importance of shared goals and common interests, *irrespective of* ethnic background. This condition implies that in order to promote interethnic contact, one should focus on ethnicity *transcending* activities, such as sporting together (Chu & Griffey, 1985; RMO, 2005). Through the shared will to win, or the shared need for fun, cooperation can arise, rendering ethnicity inconsequential.

These two conditions, structural contact and ethnicity transcending contact, are however, not sufficient to combat prejudice or tensions between groups. Allport's third condition is that the power status of those in contact should in principle be the same. In spite of social or socio-economic differences, people need to experience the same power status *within the sub-domains in which they function* (eg. sports clubs, classroom, company). How annoying it can be to experience status differences within a sub-domain, is illustrated by the Dutch Creole jazz singer Giovanca, who, reflecting on her youth, said she had felt herself to be just a citizen of Amstelveen. "I was not aware of differences in colour and class, until I was 15 years old. Then one of the mothers told me it was so admirable for me to be in pre-university school, since it was harder for our kind. I really freaked out for a moment. Who are you then? Don't I belong to you? And why is it harder for us? I had a period after that where I thought: well, if it is 'you', then 'you' is what you'll get." (Volkskrant magazine, 24th December 2010: 83) [transl. eds.]

The fourth condition for countering interethnic tensions concerns the management of the (ethnically mixed) organizations. They have to support and endorse the importance of positive interethnic contacts. The directors, trainers and coaches of football clubs need to unequivocally convey the importance of good and respectful contact.

Allport's contact hypothesis has been widely researched. The research indicates that the more these conditions are satisfied, the better the group relations in that particular situation will be. The effects, although not large, are significant, both for children as well as for youth and adults (Pettigrew & Tropp, 2006).

Pedagogical insights

For those wanting to understand and improve group relations, pedagogical insights are also important. Allport's conditions for example, can hardly be realized without pedagogical sensitivity on the part of those involved. Soccer trainers will have to give their pupils self-confidence and make them feel at home in order to be able to bring/hold them in equal status positions. More generally, they will have to create surroundings where children (and others) feel safe, and are offered skills to, for example, resolve quarrels and prevent conflicts.

For a healthy educational climate in the association/organization, it is also required to apply the principle of participation, not only as an educational principle, but also as a way of increasing the opportunities for interethnic contacts (De Winter, Horjus & Van Dijken, 2009). Having youngsters *actively* participate in activities, and letting them make decisions about the state of affairs, helps them learn what it means to co-exist. They also learn to deal with possible differences of opinion and interests. Such participation gives the youth a voice and responsibilities, and consequently teaches them to deal with these, in effect paving the way for positive *interethnic* group relationships. 'In factories, neighbourhoods, housing units, schools,' says Allport (1954), 'common *participation* [emphasis added; SV] and common interests are more effective than the bare fact of equal-status contact.' (p. 276)

8.3 Practical design 'Connecting through football'

Three years ago, the department of Participation and Social Development[105], part of Hogeschool Utrecht (Utrecht University for Applied Sciences), started the project 'Connecting through football'. This project has multiple goals: stimulating respectful behaviour, increasing volunteerism, and promoting interethnic contacts. This chapter focuses on the latter.

The department started this project at the request of the ethnically mixed amateur football club Zwaluwen Utrecht 1911, situated on the edge of the disadvantaged district Kanaleneiland in Utrecht. Firstly, the project induces the involvement of board members and volunteers, which include trainers and coaches. Secondly, the association manager of the club plays an important role. The association manager is a social worker and plays a central role in the web of activities set up by the 'Connecting through football' project. Not only does he try to provide space for volunteers' initiatives, he also looks for support within the club for plans taken up by the board, or the ideas proposed by the university or other external parties.

---

[105] Dutch: *lectoraat Participatie en maatschappelijke ontwikkeling*. The corresponding Dutch project title is *'Verbinden door Voetbal'*.

144

Thirdly, around five social work students every year from the Hogeschool Utrecht also play an important role in supporting and, to some extent, establishing and developing the activities at the club. These students also play an important role *in researching* the results of 'Connecting through football'. The independent Dutch social scientific research institute Verwey-Jonker Instituut, has also been involved, mainly in order to prevent the people who have been responsible in realizing this project from working too much from their their own perspectives. Fourthly, the city of Utrecht, FC Utrecht, the KNVB (the Royal Dutch Football Association) and a number of other parties too are involved. They facilitate the project to a certain extent by providing manpower and resources, and play a role in spreading awareness about the project in the region.

The activities that have been set up by 'Connecting through football' (see intermezzo), are consistent with the previously mentioned socio-psychological and pedagogical insights. First and most notable is that the activities set up by this project are *not* focused on people's ethnicities, but on ethnicity transcending themes that can connect the target groups, especially the shared wish to behave respectfully and according to the rules of *fair play*. Secondly, the activities are not organized just once, but are carried out on a regular basis. They happen more or less throughout the whole season. Thirdly, the board of the club supports the activities, and endorses the importance of positive (interethnic) behaviour at the club. Fourthly, the status positions of the people involved in the activities are the same: in principle, anyone can participate. And lastly, the people involved do not just participate in the activities, but also have a voice and are partially responsible for carrying them out(participation principle).

Intermezzo: three examples of 'Connecting through football' activities

A number of activities are organized under the project 'Connecting through football'. Out of these the three most important ones are: the social internships, the Fair Play Cup and the 'positive coaching' track. Considered alone, these activities can not be expected to produce significant changes at the club level. However, when considered together and in combination with the other activities undertaken through this project, we can aim at making a difference.

1. Social internships

Zwaluwen offers youth the opportunity to develop themselves as game leaders/trainers through the medium of internships. In this way, the youth develop an understanding for the opportunities of children, learn to deal with them in a respectful manner, and mediate disagreements. In these participatory roles, they learn the importance of setting a good example, and can experience the value of positive contacts.

2. Fair Play Cup

For the E and D pupils (footballers aged between 9 and 12 years old), a Fair Play Cup is organized. Earlier, youth teams were rewarded for displaying sportsmanship, but in a rather ad hoc manner. With the introduction of the Fair Play Cup, this practice has attained a structural character. The Fair Play Cup starts at the beginning of the season with a football clinic organized by FC Utrecht, giving great attention to the theme of respect. Then the players, trainers/leaders and parents of the respective participants are monitored for their display of sportsmanship. The developments occurring in this sportsmanship competition are available and can be followed on the club's website. At the end of the season, the winning team is rewarded the Fair Play Cup and receives medals from an FC Utrecht player, and are given the chance to play a match at the FC Utrecht stadium.

3. Positive coaching

Under the 'positive coaching' track, leaders/trainers/parents are taught the skills of coaching in a positive manner, and how in doing so, a positive club culture can be created.

8.4   Better behaviour?

To gain insight into the development of the atmosphere and prevalent (interethnic) behaviour, a 'before and after' study was carried out at Zwaluwen between 2008 and 2010, which included a limited number of interviews. The estimated response rate for these two measurements (before and after) was 35% and 65% respectively. However, as it was exactly during this period that the 'Connecting through football' activities were introduced and implemented, we cannot make indisputable *causal* statements about whether any improved behaviour can be attributed to these activities. However, we can suggest the extent to which the theoretical assumptions of the project can explain the found results.

What are the most important outcomes of the 'before and after' study? The first outcome is that the atmosphere at Zwaluwen has improved (see Table 7.1). The score that members give to the atmosphere at the club has risen from 6.5 (on a 10-point scale) in 2008, to 7.6 in 2010. One interviewed volunteer also indicated that the atmosphere has changed positively. 'I see a positive trend, and of course there are quarrels, hassles or disagreements every now and then, but that is to be expected in any place where many people come together.' In line with this positive development, the score for sportsmanship has also increased. In 2008, the members gave the prevalence of this quality a rating of 6.1, and two years later a 6.9.

Table 7.1 Scores given to atmosphere and sportsmanship at the club

	2008 (N=69)	2010 (N=136)
Atmosphere	6.5	7.6
Sportsmanship	6.1	6.9

A second result is that not only the *general* behaviour (atmosphere, sportsmanship), but also the *interethnic* behaviour has improved. Respondents gave the relationship between immigrant and native members of Zwaluwen a higher score in 2010 than in 2008 (see Table 7.2). Whereas interethnic behaviour was rated as moderate or even insufficient in 2008, in 2010 it is seen as being rather good. Though the score that the parents of the athletes give to cross-cultural relationships within the club is indeed one tenth of a point lower in 2010 than at the start of the project, the evaluations of the athletes and volunteers have risen.

Table 7.2 Scores given to interaction between immigrant and native members of Zwaluwen

Athletes		Parents		Volunteers	
2008(N=34)	2010 (N=112)	2008 (N=26)	2010 (N=15)	2008 (N=9)	2010 (N=9)
5.7	7.5	6.9	6.8	5	7.2

Two important side remarks have to be mentioned at this stage. Firstly, despite improved interethnic relations at the club, there appear to be certain *in-group preferences*. The analysis indicates that the group of indigenous respondents clearly fosters more negative feelings against the ethnic immigrant Dutch than these immigrant respondents themselves (65° as opposed to 76°). Conversely, the immigrant respondents clearly think more negatively about the indigenous Dutch than the indigenous respondents themselves (66° as opposed to 74°). Secondly, there is the methodological issue relating to respondent groups. Although the surveyed athletes, parents and volunteers at both measuring moments had roughly the same profile in terms of age, gender and ethnicity, the size of these groups is statistically limited. Besides, the percentage of *athletes* (as a percentage of the total respondent group) is relatively higher in the 'after' study. These differences in respondent groups between the 'before' and 'after' studies may bear influences on the outcomes.

8.5   Better behaviour on account of 'Connecting through football'?

Are the mentioned improvements in the atmosphere, sportsmanship and interethnic contact at the club to be attributed to the activities introduced by 'Connecting through football'? The answer to this question seems to be affirmative, though there are no *causal* evidences.[106]

However, the question of causality can be addressed based on the available theoretical insights. In line with these insights we could indeed conclude that the 'Connecting through football' activities have made more favourable (interethnic) group relations possible. These activities largely fulfill Allport's four – previously (empirically) proven – conditions for positive group relations. So why should these activities have *no* effect in the case of Zwaluwen? Furthermore, qualitative research can provide additional insights. As an addition to the 'before

---

[106] This is only possible if we set up a randomized control trial (RCT) with an experimental group and a control group. For practical reasons, however, this is not possible.

and after' study, students of the Hogeschool observe the participants of the Fair Play Cup on a weekly basis, and athletes, parents, volunteers and board members are interviewed about their experiences with the different 'Connecting through football' activities. Do they think the improved atmosphere and interethnic manners are to be attributed to 'Connecting through football', or do other developments in the club play a role as well? We can not derive a definite answer to the question of causality. However, if the qualitative data correspond with the quantitative results, the *plausibility* of our statements can be enhanced.

The fact that the 'Connecting through football' activities, the development of which was based on theoretical insights, have benefited football club Zwaluwen, does not mean that no further improvements can be made. Firstly, the *interpretation* of the four conditions can be improved in many ways. The structural nature of the activities for example (condition 1), could be enhanced by developing initiatives for a wider group of members; most of the current activities focus on youth alone. Moreover, the shared experience of the activities could improve further (condition 2); the Fair Play Cup competition has still not gained popularity among all the teams. In other words, the more the 'Connecting through football' activities are organized in line with Allport's findings, the greater the chance that interethnic contacts at Zwaluwen will improve.

Secondly, Allport's hypothesis also has its limits. This is evident from the fact that, for example, in spite of the observed positive developments at Zwaluwen, there is a certain 'like knows like' atmosphere. Football does not just connect people, it also reflects differences (Atyeo, 1979; Verweel & Wolterbeek, 2011). Clubs are not only meeting places for people who are different, but also places where the 'like-minded' meet and, knowingly or unknowingly, exclude 'others' or make it difficult for them to gain access to the group (cf. Bourdieu, 1984, 1991). People have a certain sociopsychological need for (ethnic) group formation and security (Verkuyten, 2005). And it matters to them if their background is 'Dutch', 'Moroccan' or 'Turkish', even though it may only be because 'others' often tend to confirm this identity.

Ramsahai (2008) shows, for example, how migrants playing football in their own circle feel more secure and at home at their club than migrants playing in mixed clubs. They also tend to spend more time at their own clubs than footballers who sport in mixed clubs, and more often consider the club to be like a second home. Ramsahai claims to have found no convincing evidence indicating that migrants playing in their own circles are less integrated into society, although his analysis does show that migrants sporting in their own circles are less emotionally affectionate towards natives than migrants who sport in mixed clubs. Moreover, migrants sporting in mixed clubs have far more native friends than migrants sporting in their own circles.

The above things considered, it seems that activities that on the one hand transcend ethnicity, such as the 'Connecting through football' activities, and on the other hand clearly give space for (experiencing) one's own identity, are most likely to provide positive group relations (cf. Wetenschappelijke Raad voor het Regeringsbeleid [transl. The Scientific Council for Government Policy], 2007). For example, research by Verkuyten (2010) shows that Turkish-Dutch Muslims are most positive about other groups if they have both, a strong Muslim as well as a Dutch identification. Gaertner and Dovidio (2000) found the same for American youth; those who see themselves as members of their ethnic minority and also as Americans have the most positive perception of others.

Putnam (2000) talks about people's desire for bonding and bridging in this context, and states that *both* aspects are crucial for the development of strong communities. Finding the right balance between these two concepts is however, easier said then done. An illustrative case in point is the (failed) attempt by the Utrecht people's club *Rivierenwijkers,* which also wanted to make things attractive for its Turkish players (see for a detailed account Verweel & Vermeulen, 2011). They started playing Turkish music alongside the songs of Dutch folk singer André Hazes at the club parties. For the (young) Turkish players this music was too old-fashioned and alienating, and thus worked counterproductive. It did *not* establish the bond with the Turkish players that the club had sought to achieve. Though the players did appreciate the club's gesture, nevertheless, all of them left the club within the next few years. This example reminds us of the 'lady of goodwill who planned an interracial tea', in paragraph 7.3. Or of Giovanca's feeling when she succinctly pointed out: 'If it is 'you', then 'you' is what you'll get.'

8.6 The value of 'Connecting through football' for social work

The project 'Connecting through football' is only partially conducted by social workers. These comprise mainly just the club manager who has a social work background, and the social work students. Still the project offers some valuable lessons for social work, even if they suggest that it is maybe not a good idea to have many social workers being present at clubs such as Zwaluwen after all.

To begin with, it is important that social workers operate as much as possible from substantive and preferably scientific knowledge of – in this case – interventions to promote interethnic contacts. This may seem obvious, but it is not. For years, social workers have been disqualified as being semi-, quasi-, pseudo-, or sub-professionals (Macdonald, 1995). These are professionals who hardly have more relevant knowledge than laymen. The fact that citizens/clients often have a rich expertise based on experience, and are often more scientifically well informed, does not however mean that they do not deserve 'real' professionals. These 'real' professionals should be social workers who understand the (latest) scientific developments in their field, and use these to support initiatives of citizens/clients or give proposals for improvements themselves. Furthermore, they should be able to point out the *limits* to possibilities.

Although social workers (should) have substantial expertise, their position is not superordinate to citizens/clients. On the contrary, their role is subservient. Their task is mainly to (further) enhance the strength and social networks of people. If this strength would completely be taken over by professionals or the government, we would be stuck in an inefficient, unpopular and bureaucratic process. But, as Hilhorst (2011) also suggests, the logic in this case should also not be that everything the government can no longer realize, must be resolved by the people themselves.

What this signifies is that we need a *new* interpretation of solidarity, where citizens take the lead and social professionals provide support. Sometimes subtly and relatively invisible, sometimes directly and more in the foreground. In the short term, it takes extra time for professionals to mobilize people's social networks, and to provide people with facilities that enable them to participate and take control of their own lives. In the long term however, this investment will fetch returns. After the first intensive phase of introducing and implementing the 'Connecting through football' activities, we are now already witnessing an improvement in the atmosphere and social behaviour at the club. The interethnic contacts have improved, and with time, the willingness to engage in voluntary work has also increased. Athletes give this willingness in volunteering a score of 7 in the 2010 survey whereas in 2008, this score was a mere 5.5.

That 'Connecting through football' *encourages* the mutual solidarity within the club (instead of taking over that solidarity), can in my view, not be separated from the specific relationship of cooperation between researchers, professionals and volunteers within 'Connecting through football'. This cooperation is characterized by the fact that the actors involved work *together* to improve the club environment, not by carrying out textbook interventions, but by developing and implementing a customised mix of interventions that suit the club. Hilhorst (2011) also states that many (welfare) organizations are not judged by the proceeds of their interventions, but by the interventions themselves. 'This is easy when delineated products are delivered: these many home visits, these many clients put in a project, these many checks carried out' (p. 154) [transl. ed.]. But in the complex field of preventive social intervention, such as in the case of 'Connecting through football', where multiple and confounding (side) effects play a role, this is a route leading to a dead end (cf. Banks, 2011; Rouw en Verhagen, 2009).

Therefore, 'Connecting through football' chose for a process of joint research and learning, in order to realize improvements in practice. Since the work of Argyris and Schön (1978) and Schön (1983), the importance of learning civil organizations and reflective practitioners in the prevention and solution of problems, has been pointed out. Nevertheless, contemporary scholars indicate that many organizations still find it difficult to flesh out this commitment (Schouw, 2009; Walraven en Pen, 2011; WRR, 2006). Therefore, in many organizations a cultural change must occur. Whereas organizations currently mostly see researchers as the ones bringing knowledge to the institution, with the professionals and volunteers being the ones implementing this knowledge, *modern* organizations will have to set up more durable, internal processes of learning. This means that there will be much more scope for knowledge sharing between colleagues, and that there will be more structural cooperation with parties that can contribute to the learning of professionals.

In the case of 'Connecting through football', the university researchers, and the professionals and volunteers of the club worked together from the outset. They had (and have) a lot of contact and are relatively flexible and communicative about both their research as well as their development activities. Working this way creates a circle in which the researchers tailor their research to practical real life questions, but in which these real life questions also partially arise from the insights based on the research. Zwaluwen thus operates as a *learning organization*, which not only benefits the (interethnic) contacts at the club, but can possibly also serve as a source of inspiration to schools, music clubs, shopping malls, discos, leisure facilities and other urban organizations in The Netherlands and abroad, in order to achieve what they want to achieve.

Bibliography

Allport, G. (1954). *The Nature of Prejudice*. New York: Basic Books.

Argyris, C. en Schön, D. (1978), *Organizational Learning: A Theory of Action Perspective*. Reading: Addison-Wesley.

Atyeo, D. (1979). *Blood & Guts: Violence in Sports*. Londen: Paddington Press.

Banks, S. (2011). Ethics in an Age of Austerity: Social Work and the Evolving New Public Management. *Journal of Social Intervention*, vol. 20, issue 2, 5-23.

Benson, P., Roehlkepartain, E. & Sesma, A. (2004). *Tapping the Power of Community. Building Assets to Strengthen Substance Abuse Prevention*. Search Institute Insights & Evidence, 2(1), 1-14.

Bourdieu, P. (1984). *Distinction. A social critique of the judgement of taste*. Cambridge: Harvard University Press.

Bourdieu, P. (1991). Sport and Social Class. In C. Mukerji & M. Schudson (red.), *Rethinking popular culture. Contemporary perspectives in cultural studies*. Berkely: University of California Press.

Chu, D. & Griffey, D. (1985). The contact theory of racial integration: The case of sport. *Sociology of Sport Journal*, 2(4), 323-333.

Eurydice (2005). *Key Data in Europe on Education 2005*. Luxembourg: Office for Official Publications for the European Communities.

Ewijk, H. van (2010). *Maatschappelijk werk in een sociaal gevoelige tijd*. Amsterdam: Uitgeverij SWP.

Gaertner, S. L. en Dovidio, J. F. (2000). *Reducing Intergroup Bias: The Common Ingroup Identity Model*. Philadelphia, PA: Psychology Press.

Garbarino, J., Kostely, K. en Barry, F. (1997). Value Transmission in an Ecological Context. The High-Risk Neighborhood. In: J. Grusec en L. Kuczynski (red.) (1997). *Parenting and Children's Internalization of Values. A Handbook of Contemporary Theory*. New York: John Wiley.

Gemeente Utrecht (2008). *Monitor Diversiteit en Integratie. Diversiteit en integratie in Utrecht 2008*. Utrecht: Gemeente Utrecht.

Hilhorst, P. (2011). Sociale veerkracht als vangnet. *Socialisme en Democratie*, 5/6, 149-158.

Junger, M. (2006). Naar een kosteneffectief beleid ter voorkoming van antisociaal gedrag. In: I. Doorten & R. Rouw (red.) (2006), *Opbrengsten van sociale investeringen*. Amsterdam: SWP.

Mirsky, L. (2003). *Family Group Conferencing World Wide. Restorative Practices eForum* (www.restorativepractices.org). Bethlehem, Pennsylvania. International Institute for Restorative Practices.

Macdonald, K. (1995). *The Sociology of the Professions*. Londen: Sage Publications.

Pettigrew, T. & Tropp, L. (2006). A Meta-analytic test of intergroup contact theory. In *Journal of Personality and Social Psychology*, 90(5), 751-783.

Putnam, R. (2000). *Bowling Alone. The Collapse en Revival of American Community.* New York: Simon en Schuster.

Raad voor Maatschappelijke Ontwikkeling (2005). *Niet langer met de ruggen naar elkaar. Een advies over verbinden.* Den Haag: Raad voor Maatschappelijke Ontwikkeling.

Ramsahai, S. (2008). *Thuiswedstrijd in een vreemd land. Een sociaal wetenschappelijke analyse van voetbal in eigen kring.* Zeist: Uitgeverij BOX Press.

Rouw, R. en Verhagen, S. (2009) Insights into Proceeds from Social Investments: Beyond Numbers Fetishism and Relativism. *European Journal of Social Work, vol. 12, no. 4, December 2009:* 435-446.

Schouw, G. (2009). *Een slimme stad is een lerende stad.* Den Haag: Nicis/ Uitgeverij Jan van Arkel.

Schön, D. (1983). *The Reflective Practitioner: How Professionals Think in Action.* New York: Basic Books.

Snel, E. & Boontstra, N. (2005). De waarde van interetnisch contact. Een onderzoek over initiatieven en beleidsprojecten om interetnisch contact te bevorderen. In RMO, *Niet langer met de ruggen naar elkaar. Een advies over verbinden.* Den Haag: Sdu.

Sociaal en Cultureel Planbureau (2007). *Jaarrapport Integratie 2007.* Den Haag: SCP.

Verhagen, S. (2009). *The Participative Society. Why Social Work Professionals should focus on environment rather than behaviour.* Inaugural lecture Utrecht University of Applied Sciences. Utrecht: HU.

Verkuyten, M. (2005). *The social psychology of ethnic identity.* Hove: Psychology Press.

Verkuyten, M. (2010). *Identiteit en diversiteit. De tegenstellingen voorbij.* Amsterdam: Amsterdam University Press.

Verweel, P. & Vermeulen, J. (2011). De kracht van het alledaagse sporten. In P. Verweel & M. Wolterbeek (red.), *De alledaagse kracht van de sport.* Amsterdam: SWP.

Verweel, P. & Wolterbeek, M. (red.) (2011). *De alledaagse kracht van de sport.* Amsterdam: SWP.

Walraven, G. & Pen, C.J. (2011). *Van de maakbare stad naar de lerende stad: de praktijkgerichte bijdrage van lectoraten.* Leuven/Apeldoorn: Garant.

Wetenschappelijke Raad voor het Regeringsbeleid (2006). *Lerende overheid. Een pleidooi voor probleemgerichte politiek.* Amsterdam: Amsterdam University Press.

Wetenschappelijke Raad voor het Regeringsbeleid (2007). *Identificatie met Nederland.* Amsterdam: Amsterdam University Press.

Winter, M. de, Horjus, B. & Dijken, M. van (2009). *Vreedzaam komt van school. Onderzoek naar de vreedzame wijk.* Utrecht: Universiteit Utrecht.

9. Participation of the lower-educated in The Netherlands

Rob Gründemann and Ben Fruytier

9.1 Introduction

In the spring of 2008, *Statistics Netherlands* announced that the proportion of lower- and higher-educated people in the age group of 15-64 was roughly equal in 2007 (Centraal Bureau voor de Statistiek (CBS), 2008a). At that time there were 2.5 million lower-educated, 3.7 million medium-educated, and 2.4 million higher-educated people (amongst the people between 15-65 years of age who were not following education) in the Netherlands. The lower- and higher-educated thus make up almost 30% of the population. The medium-educated are, at 40%, still the largest group. This development is due to a growth in the number of higher-educated and a shrinkage in the number of lower-educated people in the Netherlands. This process has been occuring for a much longer period of time. It is a positive development, since for decades the demand for high-skilled work has been growing steadily in the labour organizations of our western economies. A decline in the number of lower-skilled workers, however, does not mean that they need no more attention; rather the contrary. Firstly, it is questionable if the demand for lower-educated professionals in the market will fall (Josten, 2010). And even if that should be the case, then the development of the economy and the demand for labour by companies and institutions would only constitute one of the reasons for deciding whether or not lower-skilled workers deserve extra attention. Besides labour participation, participation in society is an equally important, if not more important, reason.

Many different surveys and statistics indicate that the socio-economic status of the lower-educated in the Netherlands structurally lags behind that of the medium- or higher-educated, both within organizations as well as in society as a whole. In this chapter we will further address the situation of the lower-educated. To that end, we will first give a brief explanation of the terms 'workforce participation' and 'social participation' and their interrelated nature. Next we will give a description of the situation of the lower-educated. We will look at their chances in the labour market, their position in labour organizations, and their health and living situation. We will conclude with a brief summary.

9.2 Workforce participation and social participation

Participation means being part of something. Perhaps 'being part' is too passive an expression; it is more about actively taking part in, or even stronger, being involved with something. Involvement not only expresses the activity, but also the intention. There is commitment, a connection to something. That something can be a company or organization one works for, but also the house one lives in with another, or the street, the neighbourhood, the city, or more generally the society one lives in. This, in other words, is social participation. Verhagen (2008, p. 18) observes, rightly, in his inaugural speech as Reader at the Hogeschool Utrecht, that till the late 1990s participation was mostly seen as *workforce* participation. The purpose of this was to avoid poverty, unemployment and welfare dependency. It would indirectly be a contribution to the welfare of society. For various reasons - which we shall refrain from elaborating here - the focus in this century has shifted to participation as a social issue. Social cohesion and safety have been the central issues of the first decennium of the 2st century. When it comes to workforce participation, growth has remained an important factor, no longer just for economic reasons, but also for social reasons. Figure 9.1 visualizes this shift in focus. Most of the attention now goes to growth of workforce participation as a solution for social issues on the societal level.

Figure 9.1. Changes in the focus on growth in workforce participation: from economic issue at the level of organization and society, to social issue (source: Fruytier, 2008, p.24)

Growth in workforce participation	Economic issue	Social issue
Societal level	Increase of prosperity in the society 1	Contribution to social integration, safety and emancipation 2
Organizational level	3 Enough and well-qualified employees	4 Good workplace Corporate social responsibility

The fact that the focus on workforce participation has grown to include more social reasons than in the last century, does not imply that the effects of a growing workforce participation have changed. The economic and social effects on organization and societal level are far too interconnected for this: the fact that the growing workforce participation brings about jobs and welfare for more people, has a positive impact on the social effects, and vice versa. It is more, and especially, a guaranteed income that makes an important contribution to social integration, safety in society, and empowerment of vulnerable groups in the labour market. And in a safe environment with involved citizens, economic activities have better chances for success. Every entrepreneur of small- and medium-sized enterprises (SMEs) settles preferably in a business park within or near an area with a well-educated and, especially, well-motivated (potential) labour force living in good houses. But such a positive relation between labour demand and labour supply does not apply to every form of work. It applies to labour under reasonable terms and conditions, which appeals to the talents of workers. However, unhealthy, badly paid routine work, executed by workers being hired and fired whenever needed, without any security about the extent of the contract, does not fall in this category. 'Good workplaces' and 'corporate social responsibility' are about mitigating the risks borne by employees, about measures that establish the rights of workers to healthy and challenging work, about good working relations and participation in work meetings. In that way, 'corporate social responsibility contributes to a solution for widely acknowledged social issues in education, vocational training, participation, safety and quality of life' (Kok, 2001 [transl. ed.]). It is exactly these characteristics of labour that are insufficiently developed among the lower-educated, as compared to the medium- and higher-educated. In the remainder of this chapter, we will deal with this in more detail.

9.3 Characteristics of the lower-educated

There are approximately 2.5 million people in the Netherlands that fall under the category of the lower-educated, i.e. without basic qualifications.[107] These are more often men than women: around two out

---

[107] A basic qualification is, according to the Dutch government, the minimal level of education that is needed to have a serious opportunity for durable skilled work in the Netherlands. A HAVO (higher vocational education) or VWO (pre-university) diploma counts as basic qualification. A VMBO (pre-vocational) diploma gives access to the next level of vocational education, but is *not* seen as basic qualification by the government. A basic qualification here is a vocational diploma, with the exception of v:level1 (assistant practitioner). For more information on the Dutch education system, refer to
http://en.wikipedia.org/wiki/Education_in_the_Netherlands

of three lower-educated workers is a man. This has both to do with the fact that women are generally higher-educated than men, as well as that women participate less often in the labour market than men, especially so for lower-educated women. Also, the proportion of immigrants is relatively large amongst the lower-educated workers. 7% of the total working population in the Netherlands is of foreign origin. Amongst lower-educated workers the share of immigrants is 12.5%, and amongst those with just primary education even 20%. Finally, the working lower-educated have a relatively high average age (39 years). This is due to the increase of the educational level amongst the younger population.

The lower-educated work relatively often in temporary jobs and are concentrated in cyclically sensitive sectors (De Vries, Wolbers & Van der Velden, 2004). An overview of the professions and sectors is given as table 9.1.

Table 9.1. Professions and sectors with the highest percentage of lower-educated workers (De Vries et al., 2004)

Professions	Sectors
— office helpers	— meat and fish
— metal workers	— wood and building materials
— interior carers and cleaners	— horticulture
— civil engineering labourers	— road and rail
— construction workers	— plastics
— mechanical operators	— metal products
— catering and care assistants	— construction
— drivers, loaders and unloaders;	— catering
— department store assistants	— paper

Of the professions mentioned in this table, 65%-80% is constituted by the lower-educated. Within these listed sectors, the amount of workers without a basic qualification lies between 44% to almost 60%.

9.4   The labour market situation of the lower-educated

The lower-educated often have a relatively low job security. People with a vocational training diploma are, on an average, more often working, and more often they have a permanent contract than people with only primary education or upper secondary school (*MAVO*) or preparatory vocational education (*VMBO*) (De Vries et al., 2004). Also, the future employment perspectives are more favourable for people with a basic qualification. According to the Ministry of Education and Culture, youth with a vocational training diploma are twice as likely to have a job as youth without such a diploma.[108] The non-working lower-educated are less likely to find a regular job and more likely to end up on welfare than the non-working with higher education. Two out of three claimants of welfare are lower-educated (CBS, 2007). Moreover, the lower-educated are usually on welfare for a longer time. Of the welfare claimants who have at the maximum a primary education, almost 50% are on welfare for five years or more, whereas this number is substantially lower, at 35% amidst the higher educated.

The lower-educated are also more often unemployed (De Graaf-Zijl, Groot & Hop, 2006). Perhaps partly as a consequence, they are less voluntarily mobile/flexible than the medium- and higher-educated (Gesthuizen & Dagevos, 2005; Zwinkels, Ooms & Sanders, 2009). This is in line with Beckers (1964) and Polachek & Siebert's (1993) *human capital theory*. According to this theory, higher-educated people are more attractive to employers, not only because their education has given them more knowledge and skills, but also because they are expected to have a higher work motivation because of their education. Their options for employment are extra wide, because they can also accept jobs below their level. In this way, the lower-educated run the risk of being displaced by higher-skilled workers (Wolbers, 2009). This displacement happens both with the transition from work to unemployment or inactivity as well as vice versa (Gesthuizen & Wolbers, 2010). The occupation by higher-skilled workers of jobs previously done by lower-skilled people even seems to be a structural phenomenon. Seen in this light, the investigation by the Netherlands Bureau for Economic Policy Analysis (CPB) which revealed that the amount of lower-educated jobs has remained practically the same since the 1980s (Josten, 2010), doesn't necessarily imply an improvement of the situation of the lower-educated. Moreover, the employment prospects of lower-skilled workers will be further pressurized if labour migration from Eastern Europe grows stronger.

The lower-educated also appear to show greater reluctance in changing jobs, even when they notice that their characteristics and qualities do not meet the desired job characteristics and qualities (Gesthuizen & Dagevos, 2005). However, even with an active attitude, the career opportunities of lower-educated workers are limited on the external

---

[108] See: www.rijksoverheid.nl/onderwerpen/aanval-op-schooluitval/startkwalificatie

labour market (Raemdonck, De Grip, Thijssen & Valcke, 2008). In the long run, voluntary mobility on the part of the lower-educated appears to have a positive effect on finding another job. It also contributes to faster reintegration after a possible loss of work (Heyma, Van der Werff & Prins, 2009).

9.5 The work situation of the lower-educated

The lower-educated are more often in physically demanding and stressful occupations, and consequently run greater risks of physical deterioration (Allen & De Grip, 2007; Jettinghof & Smulders, 2008). Data from the National Survey of Working Conditions (NEA), held yearly since 2005, shows that the lower-educated have a higher physical work pressure than the medium- or higher-educated (De Vries, 2010). Higher physical work pressure refers to working conditions requiring greater force and involving repetitive movements. This difference can partially be explained by the fact that the lower-educated are working in professions that involve a high degree of physical exertion, such as industrial and agricultural occupations. In these occupations, 40% of the labour employed, for example, is engaged in tasks requiring regular physical exertion, whereas when considering the overall average including all workers, this number amounts to only 20%.

To add to this, the lower-educated also run a higher risk that their available knowledge and experience declines in value due to obsolescence of qualification (Allen & De Grip, 2007; Steemers, 2010). This can happen, for example, because of technological and organizational innovations in the work process, such as automation and task enrichment (De Beer, 2006), but also because both the employers of the lower-educated as well as the lower-educated themselves invest less in training than the higher-educated (Fouarge, De Grip & Nelen, 2009). Participation in trainings and courses remains consistent amongst the lower-educated, but rises among the medium- and higher-educated.

9.6 Health situation of the lower-educated

The lower-educated in the Netherlands generally have poorer health than people with medium- or higher-education. At least one in five lower-educated people, experiences one's own health as less than good. For the higher-educated this statistic is only one in ten (CBS, 2010). This has to do with less favourable material conditions, less favourable socio-psychological factors, and more unhealthy (lifestyle)behaviour (National

Institute for Public Health and the Environment (RIVM), 2011). Research shows, for example, that the lower-educated eat less healthy (Meeusen, Vanm Wijk, Hoogendam, Ronteltap & Van 't Riet, 2010), and are more (severely) overweight (RIVM, 2011). There are more people overweight (body mass index (BMI)) ≥ 25 kg/m^2) among the lower-educated (52%) than among the medium- (44%) and higher-educated (33%). A similar situation applies to being seriously overweight, or obesity (BMI ≥ 30 kg/m^2). The percentages among lower-, medium- and higher-educated are 17%, 11% and 7% respectively (RIVM, 2011). There are also more smokers among the lower-educated (33%) than among medium- (29%) and higher-educated (20%). Another important factor is that a sizeable part of the lower-educated group deals with problems on multiple fronts, such as housing, relationships and finances (RIVM, 2011).

Besides these physical differences, there are also differences in mental health. The higher-educated have less psychological problems the lower-educated (Driessen, 2011). Amongst the group of people with a college or university education, around 9.7% suffer from mental problems, in contrast to 23.8% amidst people who have only finished primary education. This relationship between lack of mental health and educational level persists when corrected for differences in age and sex between the different social groups.

Lastly, the (healthy) life expectancy of the lower-educated is lower than that of the medium- and higher-educated (see Table 9.2).

Table 9.2 Life expectancy in years (at birth) against level of education (CBS, 2008b)

	Life expectancy		Healthy life expectancy		Life expectancy without physical limitations	
	Men	Women	Men	Women	Men	Women
Higher education	79.1	83.8	69.0	69.2	74.6	74.3
Higher secondary education	77.1	83.7	63.7	65.6	70.9	71.8
Lower secondary education	74.6	81.1	59.6	61.3	67.4	68.5
Primary education	72.2	78.1	50.2	52.8	61.9	60.5
Difference high – low	*(6.9)*	*(5.7)*	*(18.8)*	*(16.4)*	*(12.7)*	*(13.8)*

The differences in life expectancy (at birth) between the levels of education are not trivial. They concern a substantial number of years. The lower-educated not only live shorter, but also spend fewer years of their lives in good health. The difference there is even the largest; more than 15 years (!). The differences are generally larger between men than between women. Only in the case of life expectancy without physical limitations, the difference between the higher- and lower-educated is (slightly) larger for women.

Moreover, persons who work, generally have a better health than the non-working (CBS, 2010). The proportion that feels unhealthy among the unemployed (26.5%) is twice as high than among the working population (13.3%). In 77% of the cases, disability comes together with health that is experienced as less good, but this (high percentage) is obviously not surprising.

These figures show how important it is for people to participate actively in the work process. Unfortunately, this participation is much lower for the lower-educated than for the medium- and higher-educated (CBS, 2006). For the higher-educated the gross labour participation (including people seeking work) is between 80% and 90%, for the medium-educated between 75% and 80%, and for the lower-educated between 50% and 60%.

9.7 Housing situation of the lower-educated

A recently published report by the Council for Social Development (RMO) states that the Netherlands is increasingly becoming a country where the lower- and higher-educated are living in separate worlds; where it is no longer descent, but education that is key for the social world one lives in (RMO, 2011). This is also reflected in the housing situation. The lower-educated live relatively often in poor neighbourhoods in big cities. Measures to improve the situation in these areas have on the one hand aimed at reducing the physical and social problems of the area, and on the other hand at improving the (socio-economic) position of individual residents. In 2011 the Netherlands Institute for Social Research (SCP) published the results of its study on the effectiveness of this policy (Wittebrood & Permentier, 2011).

They concluded that the government's specific policy for these areas had little effect. The situation in the poor neighbourhoods has hardly changed between 1999 and 2008. Creating more green spaces, and sports and play facilities had little demonstrable impact on the liveability and safety in these neighbourhoods. Replacing social housing by private property however, appeared to have a positive effect on the experience of safety and residents' satisfaction with the housing and living environment. The deterioration of the area and the crime rate concurrently decreased. The researchers hypothesize that in this different ownership relation, residents invest more in their house and feel more connected to their house and living environment. In addition, more and more non-Western Dutch middle class residents move into these studied neighbourhoods. On the other hand, it appears that middle and upper class native Dutch more often leave these areas, for lower income groups to return. Thus, the segregation of lower- and higher-educated native Dutch only seems to increase.

9.8 Summary

In this chapter the situation of the lower-educated in the Netherlands has been described. We started with a brief explanation of the concepts of work participation and social participation. Participation means being actively involved with something. Until the 1990s, participation was seen mostly as economic participation or work participation in the Netherlands. Recently the focus has shifted to participation as a social issue; actively participating in society.

At this moment, there are as many lower- as higher-educated people in the Netherlands. Both groups form about 30% of the population. The lower-educated are more often male than female, and more often immigrant than native. They work relatively more often in temporary jobs and cyclically sensitive sectors. Partially due to this fact, they have a relatively low job security and are also more often unemployed.

The lower-educated in the Netherlands generally have poorer health than the medium- and higher-educated and often have an unhealthy lifestyle. Even the (healthy) life expectancy (at birth) is considerably lower for the lower-educated than for people with higher levels of education. This situation is mainly caused by poor living and working conditions and a reduced access to care of the lower educated.

Lastly, we looked at the housing situation of the lower-educated in the Netherlands. It was observed that higher- and lower-educated people in the Netherlands increasingly live in their own worlds and meet each other lesser and lesser. This also counts for the housing situation. We find the lower-educated more often in poor neighbourhoods. It is mostly the medium- and higher-educated native Dutch that move into better neighbourhoods.

Bibliography

Allen, J. & Grip, A. de (2007). *Skill Obsolescence, Lifelong Learning and Labor Market Participation*. Maastricht: Researchcentrum voor Onderwijs en Arbeidsmarkt.

Becker, G. (1964). *Human Capital: A Theoretical and Empirical Analysis, with Special Reference to Education*. New York: National Bureau of Economic Research.

Beer, P. de (2006). Perspectieven voor laagopgeleiden. *Tijdschrift voor Arbeidsvraagstukken, 22(3)*, 218-233.

Centraal Bureau voor de Statistiek (CBS) (2006). *Hogere opleiding, hogere arbeidsparticipatie*. Webmagazine, 18 april.

Centraal Bureau voor de Statistiek (CBS) (2007). *Tweederde bijstandsontvangers laagopgeleid*. Webmagazine, 14 november.

Centraal Bureau voor de Statistiek (CBS) (2008a). *Bijna evenveel hoog opgeleide als laag opgeleide Nederlanders*. Webmagazine, 14 april.

Centraal Bureau voor de Statistiek (CBS) (2008b). *Gezondheid en zorg in cijfers 2008*. Den Haag.

Centraal Bureau voor de Statistiek (CBS) (2010). *Mensen met beroepen van lager niveau voelen zich minder gezond*. Webmagazine, 25 augustus.

Driessen, M. (2011). *Geestelijke ongezondheid in Nederland in kaart gebracht. Een beschrijving van de MHI-5 in de gezondheidsmodule van het Permanent Onderzoek Leefsituatie*. Den Haag: CBS.

Fouarge, D., Grip, A. de & Nelen, A. (2009). *Leren en Werken*. Maastricht: ROA.

Fruytier, B. (2008). *Productiviteit en participatie. Samenspraak of tegenspraak?* Oratie. Utrecht: Hogeschool Utrecht.

Gesthuizen, M. & Dagevos, J. (2005). *Arbeidsmobiliteit in goede banen: Oorzaken van baan-en functiewisselingen en gevolgen voor de kenmerken van het werk*. Den Haag: Sociaal en Cultureel Planbureau (SCP).

Gesthuizen, M. & Wolbers, M.H.J. (2010). Kansen van laag opgeleide mannen: structurele en cyclische verdringing in Nederland. In R. van Galen, J. Sanders, W. Smits & J.F. Ybema (red.), *Dynamiek op de Nederlandse arbeidsmarkt; de focus op kwetsbare groepen*. Den Haag: CBS.

Graaf-Zijl, M. de, Hop, J.P. & Groot, I. (2006). *De weg naar werk - Onderzoek naar de doorstroom tussen WW, bijstand en werk voor en na de SUWI-operatie*. SEO rapport 887. Den Haag: Raad voor Werk en Inkomen (RWI).

Heyma, A. Werff S. van der, & Prins J. (2009). *Baten van baan-baanmobiliteit: eindrapportage*. Amsterdam, SEO

Jettinghoff, K. & Smulders, P.G.W. (2008). Wie kan en wil er doorwerken tot 65-jarige leeftijd? *Tijdschrift voor Arbeidsvraagstukken, 24(1)*, 88-100.

Josten, E. (2010). *Minder werk voor laagopgeleiden? Ontwikkelingen in baanbezit en baankwaliteit 1992-2008*. Den Haag: CPB.

Kok, W. (2001). *Toespraak Minister President tijdens bijeenkomst Voorzittersoverleg MKB Nederland 6 maart.* http://www.minaz.nl/Actueel/Toespraken/2001/03/

Meeusen. M.J.G., Wijk, E.E.C. van, Hoogendam, K., Ronteltap, A. & 't Riet, J. van (2010). *Eetgewoonten van laagopgeleiden*. Wageningen: LEI.

Ministerie van Economische Zaken (2010). *Handboek wijkeconomie*. Den Haag.

Polachek, S.W. & Siebert, W.S. (1993). *The economics of earnings*. Cambridge/New York: Cambridge University Press.

Raad voor Maatschappelijke Ontwikkeling (RMO) (2011). *Advies: nieuwe ronde, nieuwe kansen. Sociale stijging en daling in perspectief*. Den Haag.

Raemdonck, I., Grip, A. de, Segers, M., Thijssen, J. & Valcke, M. (2008). Zelfsturing in leren en loopbaan als predictoren van employability bij laaggeschoolde werknemers. *Gedrag & Organisatie, 21*, 386-405.

Rijksinstituut voor Volksgezondheid en Milieu (RiVM) (2011). *Nationaal Kompas Volksgezondheid (versie 4.4, 15 juli 2011)*, Bilthoven.

Steemers, F. (2010). *Blijvende inzetbaarheid in langere loopbanen*. Leiden: Sidestone Press.

Verhagen, S. (2008). *Participatie en maatschappelijke ontwikkeling*. Oratie. Utrecht: Hogeschool Utrecht.

Vries, J. de (2010). Lichamelijke belasting op het werk en ziekteverzuim. *Sociaaleconomische trends, 2de kwartaal*, 55-60.

Vries, M.R. de, Wolbers, M.H.J. & Velden, R.K.W. van der (2004). *De arbeidsmarktpositie van schoolverlaters en werkenden zonder startkwalificatie*. Den Haag: RWI.

Wittebrood, K. & Permentier, M. (2011). *Wonen, wijken & interventies. Krachtwijkenbeleid in perspectief*. Den Haag: SCP.

Wolbers, M.H.J. (2009). Gedwongen baan werklozen leidt tot verdringing. In *Tijdschrift voor Arbeidsvraagstukken, 25(2)*, 226-227.

Zwinkels, W., Ooms, D. & Sanders, J. (2009). *Omvang, aard en achtergronden van baan-baan-mobiliteit*. Den Haag: RWI.

10. The new social professional

Being in-between

Jean Pierre Wilken

10.1 Introduction

New times require new professionals. The field of social work is diligently searching for a new identity. To a large extent, this is a reaction to budget cuts by governments due to the economic recession. Against this backdrop of reduced public money, professional care becomes scarcer. Procedures for the allocation of resources and accountability become more and more important. Professional care is only resorted to if no other solutions are possible.

A second trend is the transformation of the welfare state into a participation state, represented by the ideas of *civil society*. Professional help is no longer a matter of course. Citizens are expected, and also demand to care for themselves and to help others. Only if self-care and mutual care turn out to be insufficient, does professional care come into the picture.

This second trend corresponds to the first one. Governments may use this transformation to a civil society as the basis for legitimizing budget cuts, as is the case in the Netherlands under the current right-wing cabinet.

The domain of professional social work has to deal with these developments, which can be seen both as a threat, and as a challenge. It is no doubt true that extensive expenditure cuts are threatening the quality of social work. On the other hand, social work is offered the opportunity of repositioning itself in a way which can lead to a new and stronger identity. It is an opportunity to get rid of old practices, for example of practices which are based on a 'care for' instead of a 'care with' vision.

In this article I will explore the identity of a 'new social work', of a 'new social professional'. I would like to state at the outset that 'new' is a relative word. There will always be new social professionals, simply because an old generation will continuously be replaced by a new young generation. But some basic aspects of social work will always remain the same, like the contribution it wants to make to the improvement in the quality of life of individuals and communities, and the use of basic professional competences like social and communication skills, assessment skills and problem-solving skills. New visions and methods are often based on already existing knowledge.

I use the term 'new' to refer to letting go of old visions and paradigms and replacing them with new ones, and making way for the acceptance of professional methods that these new visions bring along with them. We have reached a point in time, where social work seems ready for a major innovation. Although this innovation can also be regarded from an organizational point of view, I shall limit myself here to the innovation of social professionalism. I will also limit myself to a number of fundamental principles, which in my view can be broadly applied by all social professionals, regardless of their discipline and function. I will not elaborate on issues belonging to specific domains within social work and how they relate to the basic principles that I shall discuss in this chapter, since this is a discussion that extends beyond the space available here.

10.2 Social work and the civil society

'Civil society' is broadly defined as the space in society where citizen action takes place (Knight, Chigudu and Tandon 2002). It is the space where individual members of society voluntarily come together, in formal or informal gatherings, groups, associations, or organizations, to participate in public life. Civicus, the World Alliance for Citizen Participation, speaks about "the arena, outside of the family, the state, and the market where people associate to advance common interests." (Civicus, 2005). In theory, the institutional forms of civil society are distinct from those of the state and market; though in practice, the boundaries between state, civil society, and market are often unclear. Civil society commonly embraces a diversity of forms, varying in their degree of formality, autonomy, and power. Civil society often consists of organizations such as registered charities, development non-governmental organizations, community groups, women's organizations, faith-based organizations, professional associations, trade unions, self-help groups, social movements, advocacy groups, and coalitions. In the policy belonging to the ideas of New Public Management, which since the eighties is aiming at efficiency in the social sector, the care sector, and the educational sector, the notion of civil society is nowadays often used to cut down expenses.

I consider the idea of civil society as an endeavour to revitalize community life, encouraging social networks where people can work and support each other together. This is in line with ideas of empowerment and community development. Civicus considers itself a social movement, promoting communities of "informed, inspired, committed citizens who are actively engaged in confronting the challenges facing humanity". Civil society is also understood as an arena where individual citizens are empowered and where crucial skills related to democratic power sharing, negotiation, and collective action are developed (Diamond, 1994).

Social work can be situated in the centre of this arena, though at the same time it also has to relate to the state and the market. It can choose to place itself at the mercy of the waves, or to take a clear stand.

In my view, professional social work is an indispensable pillar for the quality of our society. I state this not only because I am a social professional myself, but also because research shows that postmodern communities are generally not able to generate sufficient 'community care', and of the quality desired to cover the needs of all members of the community.

A number of developments seem to act against a more caring community: ageing populations, more chronically ill people, greater distances between relatives because of increased mobility, and the pressure on people to work more and longer leaving less time for voluntary activities (Cameron and Moss 2007).

A completely autonomous caring community is a utopian ideal. But a more 'caring community', the way back from an individualistic society to a community in the original sense of the word - living together, sharing common interests, providing support to each other- is certainly realizable, as is shown by numerous local initiatives in many neighbourhoods, and cultural and religious communities.

10.3 Active citizenship

Modern civil society is making an appeal to people to be active citizens. Van Ewijk (2010) mentions three principles for active citizenship (p. 27-28):

1. *The principle of self-responsibility or self-reliance.* This principle refers to the idea that people should take care of their own life and should be held fully responsible for their own behaviour.

2. *The principle of human and social rights.* This is endorsed in numerous declarations and conventions. Social rights refer mainly

170

to the right of access to education, labour, housing, health, healthy environment, and safety. Resources to assure these rights are not only to be provided by the state, people have to make contributions themselves as well.

3. *The principle of social responsibility.* This refers to responsibility for people around you, for your neighbourhood, for caring for and supporting fellow citizens.

Van Ewijk argues that this last principle has been given the least attention in western societies. There was a strong emphasis on liberty and equality, but 'fraternity': the commitment to the community, was rather forgotten. It is now however, back on the agenda through the aim of promoting social cohesion.

In the new Social Support Act in the Netherlands, introduced in 2007, active citizenship is a key notion. It regards social cohesion as the product of participation. An important condition for participation is self-reliance. The paradox in this line of thinking is that the act also presupposes that social cohesion is already present, because people are supposed to be supporting each other. In reality, social cohesion is not obvious. It often takes a lot of effort to create the 'bonding' needed for social cohesion, and social professionals are often playing an important 'bridging' role here.

Active social professionals

Social professionals can intervene at the level of self-reliance, participation, and social cohesion. The level at which the interventions take place, will depend on the specific function and role of social professionals. In my point of view, however, social professionals should always work in a contextual way, connecting the three levels to each other.

Van Ewijk (2010, p. 71-72) mentions a number of core tasks for the social professions. I will categorize these tasks, and some additional ones, according to the three levels of intervention.

Table 10.1 Objectives and tasks of social professionals

Core objectives:	*Enhancing self-reliance*	*Enhancing social participation*	*Enhancing social cohesion*
Core Tasks:	To help solve individual problems	To help solve group problems	To help solve community problems
	To activate people to take care of their own living and working conditions	To implement social rights and duties	To endorse and promote social responsibility
	To support the development of social competences	To support persons with reintegration; create 'facilitating environments' which enable participation	To act as an 'intermediary' in order to improve social cohesion (bridging and bonding)
	To manage care around an individual or a group of individuals	To manage and coordinate social services and social interventions	

An additional task is to supervise and control, and to intervene in case of serious problems of criminality, compulsory care, etc.

Body of knowledge

The body of knowledge needed by social professionals is related to the objectives and tasks mentioned above. I will not go into details about the competences specifically needed for each task, but restrict myself to the sources of knowledge which can be used. Traditionally, there are two sources: (1) the knowledge from scientific research and theories on social work and health care (2) and the knowledge gained from professional practice and experience. Over the last decade a new source of knowledge has come into the picture: the experiential knowledge of service users. In my opinion this is a very valuable source, a source which is indispensable for offering good services (Wilken, Ravelli & Van Doorn, 2009). First of all, the experiences of the service user help us to get to know the person and to understand his needs better. Second, we need the experiences with regard to the support we are providing as professionals, as feedback to know if the person is satisfied with our services or not. A constant dialogue is essential to connect need and intervention, and to assess the quality of our work. Although we have our professional standards, only our clients can decide whether or not we are delivering service of good quality.

10.4   Research on the experiences of service users

I will now report on the outcomes of a study investigating the ideas of service users about 'good care'. Good care is defined in the study as care (or services) perceived by a receiver of care as beneficial and helpful. The study was conducted amongst long-term users of mental health care services, and consisted of two parts: a systematic review of international literature, and a narrative case study in the Netherlands including thirteen individuals (Wilken, 2010). Two types of analysis were applied. The first one was a qualitative analysis including all the different aspects people mentioned with regard to their experiences with professionals and professional institutions. A second analysis researched the underlying notions. Although this study is situated in one particular domain of professional intervention: mental health care, I think the results of the second analysis of underlying notions can be generalized to apply to the broader professional field.

Categories of professional acts

The themes coming to the fore in the analysis can be clustered into five categories: connecting, understanding, affirming, securing, and strengthening. The categories are characterized in terms of active verbs, to indicate that they relate to an active and dynamic process.

The first category entails the establishment of a *personal connection*. Although it is a separate category, consisting of a number of elements, personal connection can only develop and obtain meaning through the acts within the other categories. Connecting can be regarded as a process that may start with a glimpse of sympathy from the professional that deepens over the course of time. Sympathy can be evoked by the empathic attention the professional gives, by the respect he or she shows, or by the humour he or she uses. The connection can deepen through reciprocity in the relationship, through dialogical conversation and a continuing presence, and through acts of commitment and dedication. The connecting process may result in a feeling of togetherness or companionship. The relational and communicational notions identified above create a so-called *interpersonal space*. This is a psychological and metaphorical notion that expresses a number of qualities that are needed for constructive collaboration, and as an embedment for professional interventions. In this safe space there is room for being, room for expression and dialogue, and room for development. It seems that a connection and collaboration between the professional and client are only established if there is a kind of reciprocity or responsiveness from both sides.

The second category refers to the person feeling *understood*. This can be an understanding of the situation or of him- or herself as a person. Feeling understood strengthens the personal connection with the professional. The notion of understanding is connected to the sensitivity of the professional for the personhood of the other and his or her situation and experiences. The person feels understood on the basis of the presence and expressions of the professional. The professional can also contribute to a better understanding by the person him- or herself; by letting the person tell his or her story, by asking clarifying questions, and by helping to put experiences in a larger perspective.

Another important act is that the person has the experience of being *acknowledged*. This constitutes the third category. Again, this may be an acknowledgement of the personal situation, but also of vulnerability and strengths. By this recognition the person feels seen and respected. I have chosen the term 'affirming' to express that by being recognized and acknowledged (especially), people in vulnerable dispositions experience something to hold on to. Being recognized as a unique human being means that one's personal identity is revealed and affirmed. At the same time, it is an expression of value and an important element to increase self-confidence. The notion of affirming has a threefold meaning. The first is that the professional answers to the need of the person to be recognized as a worthwhile human being, with a personal autonomy and a unique identity. The second is that the person's personal experiences and knowledge are acknowledged (as being valid and valuable). The third is that the professional expresses that he or she attaches him- or herself to the other and expresses engagement and support. The personal–professional connection is affirmed, also from the side of the client.

The fourth category is *securing*. Although affirming is also a form of securing, securing encompasses all elements that help the person to feel safe (or safer). From the analysis it became clear that the mere presence of a professional who is trusted by the person and who offers companionship provides the needed safety. Different active forms of securing came to the fore in the study; varying from a quick response, to a desperate phone call, to arranging a network of friends who can be reached in case of need. The attachment between professional and client provides a form of security, which answers to the need of feeling safe and of having someone to hold on to. Within the act of securing, other, more specific elements are also visible, such as assistance to take care of the personal niche and the offering of reassurance. The professional may also serve as a form of 'social insurance' by offering companionship.

The fifth category is called *strengthening*. The study showed overwhelming evidence that good care is aimed at making people stronger and helping them in their coping or development process. Strengthening starts with recognizing the strong (healthy) side of the person and focusing on possibilities. Clients value professionals who have an optimistic point of view, who provide encouragement and inspiration. An important form of strengthening is by supporting people to learn from past and present experiences. One might say that securing, understanding, and affirming are the basis of a supportive relationship. Although this helps the person to feel connected, to feel recognized, and to feel safe, which in themselves are basic human needs, this may not be enough for the person to become more independent. From the perspective of the participants in the narratives, acts of strengthening should also be added to the care. This may include acts aimed at increasing self-confidence, developing skills, and social participation. Important empowering acts involve helping the other to 'learn by experience', emphasizing talents and achievements, offering inspiration and encouragement, working on a future perspective, and connecting people to environments that offer space for growth.

10.5 Realizing a good practice

The five categories described above can be considered as interrelated dimensions of the work of social professionals. What happens within these dimensions will be different for every client. It is the task of the professional to connect to persons in a way that leads to desired outcomes. In every situation a 'good practice' should be established. I follow here the notion of MacIntyre who states that the professional responsibility is "to achieve those standards of excellence which are appropriate to, and partially definitive of, that form of activity, with the result that human powers to achieve excellence, and human conceptions of the ends and goods involved, are systematically extended" (MacIntyre, 1985, p. 187). A practice is realized by and within the relationship between the professional and the client.

The logic of good care is embedded in a theory of *ethics of care*. Building on the work of Tronto (1993) and other scholars such as Baart (2001) and Van Heijst (2005), I shall assert that a practice of good care is embedded in a dialectical, reciprocal relationship that is based on human dignity and the well-being of people in a vulnerable position. In this relationship, recognition is essential (Honneth, 1995). The relationship is based on presence and the recognition of the other as a fellow human being (equality) *and* as a unique, special individual (inequality). In this ethical frame, frailty is acknowledged and conserved. The practice revolves around the recognition and restoration of human integrity and human dignity. Good care is both, aimed at the preservation of vulnerable people as well as on inclusion and empowerment. The caring relationship revolves around the discovery of what is considered 'good'. In the conception of the good, it also becomes apparent what value should be strengthened, supported, and obtained.

10.6 Tenets for a good practice

On the basis of the ethics of care, six fundamental tenets of good care can be distinguished, namely presence, shared perspective, diversity, recognition, autonomy and vulnerability, and empowerment. Each of these areas can be considered separate theoretical frameworks, although they are interrelated. My assumption is that they are all of equal importance. Ignoring any one of them will weaken the foundation of good care. I approach these areas as *tenets*, indicating that in each practice (as defined by MacIntyre, see above) the challenge is to use these frames and to discover how they can be applied.

The core of the tenet of *presence* is to become and to be present in such a way that this beneficiality is experienced. The tenet of presence is to become, to be, and to remain present in a way that provides a dedicated connection with a person. The tenet requires that ways are found to come close, to be attentive in an open but intense mode, and to relate to the social environment of the person (Baart, 2001). This requires calmness, sensitivity, and loyalty. It requires the professional to be open to the experiences and emotions of the other, and not to avoid them or push them away. It requires an effort to connect to the person on multiple levels, to be compassionate, to recognize what is at stake, and to do what should be done. The mere presence of the professional, as typified by the mentioned characteristics, already contributes to affirmation, safety, and strengthening.

The tenet of creating a *shared perspective* is related to the categories of connecting and understanding. This notion is meant to provide a way of thinking and working, which enables the connection of the two perspectives of the professional and the client. Good care can only be conceived through dialogue between the perspective of the person and the perspective of the professional. The tenet of shared perspective seeks to create the interrelational space of a common understanding. The core idea of a shared perspective is that the professional is able to change (in) his or her position to (understand) the perspective of the other. This serves three goals. One goal is to really understand the client and his or her needs. The second is to be able to create a relationship in which good care is possible. The third goal is to see oneself, as a professional, from the position of the other. This enables one to monitor one's own behaviour through its effects on the other. Achieving a shared perspective can be realized through a process of discovery and learning. From this study it is apparent that this process by itself, is already an important part of good care. Thus, working on the creation of a shared perspective is both *part of* and a *condition for* good care.

The exposure to the perspective of the other and the attempt to understand, entail being confronted with a world that is often quite different from the personal world of the professional. This brings into play the tenet of *diversity*. The core task here is that the client *is* and *can be allowed* to be different, and that this difference is *kept intact*. The role and position of a care recipient are different from those of a professional. There may be differences in gender, age, cultural background, religion, skin colour, and so on. I also consider a different biography, coloured by experiences with a serious disease, disabilities, and the care system, as an important aspect of diversity (see Kal, 2001; Van Heijst, 2005; Ghorashi, 2006; and Meininger, 2007 about issues related to the recognition of alterity).

The tenet of *recognition* means seeing and affirming the other as a worthwhile fellow human being, and acknowledging his or her experiences, needs, and desires. To be able to offer recognition, a professional has to understand the person and his or her situation, and be sensitive to the needs connected to recognition. The work of Honneth (1995) can be used to differentiate between different elements of recognition. Honneth distinguishes three forms of recognition, namely *love*, *respect*, and *solidarity*. Honneth offers an excellent framework by relating the notions of identity, vulnerability, and autonomy to each other, and makes a connection with social exclusion and inclusion. In love, we recognize the acts of attachment and the provision of basic trust and security as a means to contribute to a unique identity. Good care is based on the sympathy for another human being and compassion for the tragedies he or she experienced. Respect for the other, in all of its aspects, contributes to the restoration of autonomy, which is connected to self-determination and awareness of rights. Solidarity can be connected to valuation and the promotion of self-esteem. It is also connected to the notions of dedication and commitment, of staying present and offering sustainable support. Finally, recognition can be connected to empowerment, since it offers the foundation for recovery, personal development, and increased well-being.

The tenet of *autonomy and vulnerability* builds on the tenet of recognition. Good care contributes to the preservation and restoration of autonomy. Autonomy can be conceived as (re)attaining self-direction. It is related to the notions of control, agency, and responsibility, according to which human beings are conceived as the agents of their own life and as responsible actors in the human community. The main feature attributed to autonomy seems to be that (finally) people themselves are the ones in control of decisions. Good care leaves people in control and restores the ability to exercise control as much as possible. This conception of autonomy is based on respect for human dignity and freedom of self-determination, *and* on the notion of interdependence. Autonomy is also related to social inclusion. It can only be realized if people allow each other to participate as valued, respected, and contributing members of society. Social inclusion calls for the validation and recognition of diversity as well as recognition of the commonality of lived experiences and the shared aspirations among people.

Increasing capacity to take care of the vulnerability, the development of an autonomous identity, and increasing social participation as forms of increasing autonomy, can also be regarded from the perspective of the tenet of *empowerment*. For the professional, this tenet refers to helping the person to become stronger, both individually and in collaboration with others. The tenet requires a good understanding of concepts and mechanisms of power and powerlessness within the caring relationship, in the social environment of the person, in the health system, and in society. The ideas of Jacobs (2001), Van Regenmortel (2002), and others can be used to clarify this tenet further. Within the relationship between the professional and client, good care is aimed at equalizing the power balance. The relationship that develops in this interpersonal space should provide the client with opportunities to become stronger and more powerful. Powers should be recognized and made visible, correctable, and developable. Here I use the notion of *mutual power*, which is aimed at the development of empowering relationships (Freedberg, 2009). Power is not something that is a given fact, but an *expanding commodity*, something that is developed in the collaboration between different parties (Israel *et al.*, 1994).

The role and contribution of professional care may differ, but a common orientation can be characterized by certain aspects. The first is that the professional not only considers deficits and problems, but also positive aspects, such as the person's abilities and lessons learned from experiences (good and bad). The professional's role in making the person stronger may refer to the person gaining health, coping better with problems, or having increased self-confidence and social skills. The second is that the professional uses encouraging communication. He or she articulates the values that he or she observes, and encourages the use of personal strengths. The third aspect is that in the actions of the professional, there are always strengthening elements. The professional's actions are aimed at reinforcing the client, either directly or indirectly, by creating facilitating resources. An aspect of an empowering approach is to help the person to connect to 'empowering environments' in the community. The tenet of empowerment requires that good care is not only aimed at an individual level, but also at an organizational and a community level. Empowering care also includes the creation of safe environments and gaining better access to and control over resources. In this regard, professionals can function as intermediaries or bridges.

10.7 Objectives

The *ultimate aims* of good care are physical, psychological, social, and existential by nature. Physical and psychological aims concern offering security, encouragement, and hope, and increasing strengths and possibilities. The professional offers this (already) in the relationship itself, and uses the relationship and the actions that are a response to needs and aspirations, as a means or bridge to connect the person with his- or herself and the world (extending social participation). In the relationship, this is done by offering companionship and attachment. Good care offers a bridge between the person and the world, either in a narrow sense, such as the connection with family, neighbours or a workplace, or in a broad sense, such as the connection with society or being acknowledged as a full citizen. In this respect, the professional not only acts as a fellow human being, but also as a fellow citizen. He or she symbolically represents the world, and can act as a bridge between the world of the person and the world at large.

The ultimate aim of good care, seen from the perspective of the community and the society, is social inclusion. I have argued that social inclusion requires a culture in which the elements of good care are reflected. Social inclusion requires respect for differences and the willingness of every citizen to remove barriers and to create room for each other's vulnerability, to value strengths and to value contributions to social capital.

10.8 Qualities of the professional

In the practice of good care, basic qualities can be narrowed down to a sound ethical basis that provides the integrity to be there for the other (with preservation of one's own position), to respect diversity (to see the other as being different but not crazy, acknowledge suffering and vulnerability, recognize knowledge and competences), and to support the other in improving his or her quality of life (expressed in terms of the restoration or fortification of identity, overcoming of vulnerability and increased autonomy). A thorough awareness of all these elements is necessary for good care. It requires a professional attitude of wanting to establish a personal–professional connection, and of dedicating oneself and one's knowledge and access to resources to the benefit of the person. The professional should also have the communicational and relational competences to establish a relationship. In this process, understanding and recognition are key notions. Through understanding and recognition, the other can be consolidated on the levels of identity, needs, and desires. The two main practical acts of the practice of good care are thus, securing and strengthening.

The basic relational configuration for good care can be characterised as *partnership*. Care recipients conceive good professionals as people with whom they can form an alliance. The notions of symmetry, reciprocity, and interdependence play an important role here. Professionals can take different positions. A valued position is that of companionship or friendship. This position expresses the value clients attribute to a professional who is near to them, who is personally engaged and is willing to engage in a reciprocal relationship. The position expresses the intention of wishing a good life for the other. Another aspect of the social professional's identity is the professional as a citizen. This position can be a foundation for friendship, and it enables the promotion of equality and connects the person to the community.

Since good care has a normative foundation, it is important that a professional is able to reflect on what is experienced in practice. Here I use the concept of the normative–reflective professional as developed by Kunneman (1996) and others. A central question in the discourse on good care is: Is what I am doing as a person and a professional, beneficial to the person I am serving? In order to answer this question, conceptions of beneficiality and quality of life should be reflected upon. These conceptions are formed by norms and values not just of the professional and the client, but also of the community and the society.

We can distinguish between three types of qualities in this profession. The first are *virtues*, composed of commitment and dedication, benevolence and attentiveness. The second are *dispositions*, such as open-mindedness and open-heartedness, authenticity and positivity. Or, being disturbable, interruptible and approachable; this means that a professional is open and available, and is not hidden in an office, or behind procedures and agendas. The third are *abilities*. Besides the specific competences belonging to the profession, these abilities include empathic sensitivity and responsiveness.

10.9 Care responsiveness

Under the notion of 'care responsiveness', I place the service user in the position of *actor*. From the point of view of the service user, care responsiveness concerns the response to the susceptibility of the professional with regard to the needs of the person (often experienced as or expressed in an empathic and understanding way), and to the actions the caregiver undertakes with regard to meeting the needs of the service user. What is essential in this process from the part of the professional is that he or she should constantly monitor how the service user reacts to his or her acts of expression. The crux of a productive collaboration is that the other perceives the presence of the professional as being supportive and (potentially) beneficial. The concept of care responsiveness requires a great deal of perceptiveness and sensitivity. Responsiveness is not only expressed in verbal communication but also in non-verbal communication. The professional constantly attunes him- or herself to the other and his or her environment. In order to be(come) a responsive professional, the working principles of the theory of presence are valuable. These principles are letting oneself become free, become open, become involved, become inserted, become moved, become lent and become controlled (Baart, 2001).

10.10 The professional as a citizen

Besides fulfilling a 'personal-professional' role in the contact with clients, the professional role can also be regarded from the perspective of *citizenship*. I will now briefly discuss five aspects of this role.

(1) Citizenship is a foundation for collaboration

A professional is not 'just' a professional, but also a (fellow) citizen. Professional service provision is sketched in a domain that lies across the spheres of the personal and the public. For the professional, the interpersonal space that is created in concurrence with the client crosses both his or her own personal space and the public space in which he or she is employed. Within this limited intersection, he or she searches for and establishes collaboration and a working alliance. This alliance is always embedded in the conception of citizenship.

(2) Citizenship promotes equality

There are other reasons for using citizenship as a framework for regarding the professional role. One is that by doing so, at the level of citizenship, both actors are equal. On a human level, they share the same basic vulnerability and dependency. On a political level, they share the same rights and duties as other citizens within a given society. This does not mean that there is no inequality in the way citizenship is or can be 'practised'; on the contrary, these differences may be quite large. By articulating these differences, the professional may, given his or her available resources, help the person to achieve 'full' citizenship.

(3) Citizenship enlarges the professional domain

The notion of the professional as a citizen enlarges the scope of the professional. When working with an individual, the social context of the person is always taken into account. The professional does not operate outside a social system or in a separate social system, but is part of the 'larger world' and also represents this world for the care receiver. This includes a representation of the reality that counts for every person in a given society.

(4) Citizenship brings matters of injustice into sight

A fourth aspect, a political one, is that citizenship brings matters of injustice into sight. It may place the professional in the position of an advocate. Where (citizen's) rights are at stake, the professional could play a role to help solve such problems.

(5) Citizenship involves bridge building

A fifth aspect is that citizenship places the professional in the position of a 'bridge' or 'bridge builder' between the client and the community. The scope of the professional extends beyond the individual client to his or her position in the community. This community might be his or her personal social network, but also the neighbourhood in which he or she lives, and his or her position in the labour community and the social welfare system. If what is valuable to a person is related to, or can be found in, the community, good care (also) has to involve actions towards the community. I connect here the role of the professional as a citizen to the objective of *social inclusion*. Professionals and the agencies they are working for should incorporate contributions to social participation in their work. This can be done on an individual level, but also on a collective level, for example by making connections between resources available in a neighbourhood and people living in this community.

10.11 A contextual community approach

Van Ewijk (2008) strongly advocates a contextual community approach. He refers to social professionals as '... builders, as bridging professionals, or even as (social) architects, creating a social fabric to hold communities and societies together. In this contextual approach we are de-categorizing, de-labelling and deconstructing, because in the micro context people are more individualized and personal. Social professionals in contexts do not usually start from a category, or a target group, but from a context felt as problematic, and intervene for improvement or do everything to sustain a certain supportive context.' (2008, p. 12)

A contextual community approach can also be placed in the context of a changing society in which active, participatory citizenship is sought to be revitalized. Citizen-based perspectives are nowadays promoted throughout the European Union. This citizen- and community-orientation aims at activation, social responsibility, and self-determination related to social rights and related obligations. Here the social professional has a mission, a social assignment to implement a concept of citizenship (Dente, 2007). Van Ewijk (2009a/b), and Van Ewijk, Wilken, Verhagen & Menger (2009) have introduced in terms of this new professional orientation, the notion of *citizenship-based social work*. Van Ewijk (2010, p. 69) defines this as a field of action, knowledge, and research that 'aims at integration of all citizens, and supports and encourages self-responsibility, social responsibility and the implementation of social rights'. A citizenship-based approach implies that social professionals aim at strengthening and supporting individuals and their informal networks. They never replace these networks, but add to them whenever necessary.[109]

Putnam's (2000) notions of bridging and bonding from his theory on social capital can be useful here.[110] According to Putnam, two powers are necessary to create social participation and cohesion in a local community: bonding and bridging. *Bonding* represents the reinforcement of mutual ties among citizens, where norms of reciprocity and trust are important. This usually takes place among citizens who share a common identity, for example through historical roots, religion, or culture. These local communities are relatively small *communities-in-the-community*, and are characterized by informal solidarity. Examples are neighbourhood associations, sport clubs, church communities, political parties, and consumer groups. *Bridging* is the externally focused force that can be found in networks that connect people to external resources (information streams, labour market, educational opportunities, governments, and so on). Via bridging, a connection is created between different groups and organizations in society. This creates conditions for

---

[109] Wilken and Den Hollander (2005) argue in favour of a comprehensive approach in which the professional is both working at an individual level, offering care and support, *and* at a community level, working in and with communities in order to raise the level of mutual support and care. In the support model I elaborated in an earlier paper (Wilken, 2005; 2007), a close collaboration is promoted between professionals who work mainly individually with specific groups (e.g. people with psychiatric or intellectual disabilities, forensic populations) and professionals who are engaged in community work (e.g. in community centres, schools. and housing corporations). Research shows that this collaboration at the level of a determined geographical area such as a neighbourhood of a town, can improve chances for participation and social inclusion, thereby contributing to the well-being of people in vulnerable social positions (Wilken and Dankers, 2010). The role of 'intermediary professionals' is important for facilitating processes of connecting people on a community or social network level. By increasing the strengths of social networks, people with a chronic disease or a disability do not only receive more informal support, but also have more opportunities to make a contribution to others (Brettschneider & Wilken, 2007).

[110] According to Putnam (2000, p. 19), social capital "refers to the connections among individuals - social networks and the norms of reciprocity and trustworthiness that arise from them".

social participation. According to Putnam, this concerns 'weak ties', where no specific reciprocity and trust are needed. This network is synonymous with modern society. The network is necessary as nourishment and carrier for the local communities. Via this network, citizens are connected to each other. The network society as a whole can, however, only exist if citizens are aware of their mutual interdependence and their common interests that must be served by society as a whole. An example is safety. Safety comes about, on the one hand by *bonding*, within the own small community, but on the other hand by *bridging*; the resources of the larger community are needed, for example the police and the juridical system. The same goes for health and social care.

Professionals can perform both bonding and bridging activities in order to help people in a socially marginalized position to connect to the community and to become part of *social capital* (Wilken, 2005; Oudenampsen, 2004). Bonding activities are aimed at connecting the individual to social networks in the community. Bridging provides access to resources needed for both individual well-being, and becoming part of communities.

10.12 A normative-reflective professional

Returning to the core identity of the professional, it can be concluded that the notions discussed in the logic of good care require a specific type of professionalism. Good care, as it is described in this book, has a normative foundation, since it is based on a number of moral principles belonging to the ethical foundation which I described previously, and on the values belonging to the tenets discussed earlier (presence, shared perspective, diversity, recognition, autonomy and vulnerability, and empowerment). This requires a specific sensitivity to all the elements of these tenets. Although sensitivity can also be (only) present at an intuitional level ('providing care from the heart'), I think that professionalism also requires being aware of what is experienced on a level of rational awareness. This requires reflection and the availability and constant development of a body of knowledge.[111] I consider a body of knowledge as consisting of values, skills, and both professional and personal experiential knowledge. All this knowledge is 'embodied' in the person of the professional.[112] Values are often hidden in the actions of the

---

[111] See Schön (1983), and Schön and Rein (1994) on different forms of reflection.
[112] See Polanyi (1958; 1967) on tacit knowledge.

professional, or, as Pols (2004) puts it: Professionals 'enact' values. Values obtain a concrete form in daily activities.

Part of this awareness entails reflecting on the own values involved in the practice. These values also have to be confronted with values rising from the person and the context. Kunneman (1996) describes this as 'a reflective attitude with respect to content of questions and dilemmas which are coming forward'. This takes place via making conscious and argued accounted connections between (a) the quality of the own existence; (b) the content of the work; and (c) the larger cultural and social context, considered in the context of the quality of the own professional actions as experienced by clients. Professionals in social professions participate in caring for 'the good life' of their clients (Nussbaum, 1993; Ricoeur, 1992). Therefore, they constantly find themselves in a tension field between the personal life world of the client and the world of systems, justice, solidarity and private interests. Being able to make moral judgements is an important aspect of modern professionalism (Driessens & Geldof, 2008; Van Doorn, 2008).

For Kunneman (1996), normative professionalism is closely connected to the notion of equality. The professional is not superior to the client. Kunneman (1996, p. 300) states the following in this regard: 'Ultimately professionals and clients are involved in a related project, namely leading a meaningful life in which they can experience their personal value because they can be of actual meaning for others. Searching reflectively for notions about meaningful life and personal value, together with others, over and over again, forms the core of normative professionalism in social professions.' Normative professionalism is not only determined by the way professionals are shaping the interference between their work and their existence, but also in the way they relate to the cultural and societal context in which the questions of clients appear.

A central question in the discourse on good care is: Is what I am doing as a person and a professional beneficial to the person I am serving? In order to answer this question, conceptions of 'beneficiality' should be reflected upon. These conceptions are formed by the norms and values of the professional and the client, but also from the community and the society. Norms and values can be consistent or conflictive. Because in every situation there is a new constellation, it requires constantly finding a relation between the own beliefs, the beliefs of the client and his or her environment, the beliefs of the community (including the service agency and the professional group), and the beliefs of society. Jacobs (2010) states that this requires a continuous dialogue about values between different stakeholders involved in a particular practice. Professionals have to support clients to make good choices, which do not only serve an individual interest, but also the collective interest of the community.

The normative values of the discourse on good care form a beacon, but will at the same time be constantly contested, because of this ever-changing dynamic. Therefore, normative professionalism is not a static situation but a continuous learning process. Jacobs, Meij, Tenwolde and Zomer (2008, p. 12) describe normative professionalization as 'the realization of the power field of different norms (societal, organizational, professional, and personal) in which the professional finds himself, and the search for the right basis for justifying the professional acting, which can vary per situation and requires deliberation (before, during and after)'. Van Houten (2008, p. 34) states that normative professionalization implies that 'equality and diversity, attention, responsibility and competence, are central fixed points', thereby adding a moral content to the notion of normative professionalization, which is consistent with the theories developed in this chapter. Central to this are the moral character of the professional actions and the reflection on these actions. This morality is defined by an open character and a high dialogical content. The morality is aimed at the promotion of quality of life, which requires a good understanding of the judgement of the client about his or her own quality of life.

In the process of normative professionalization, in terms of the tenet of shared perspective, there is an intrinsic tension between 'rooting' and 'shifting' (Jacobs, 2008, p. 46), i.e. the interchange of inner and outer perspectives (Van der Laan, 2006). Rooting refers to being rooted in one's own culture, and the lifestyles, working styles, rituals, values, and language belonging to that culture. Shifting means opening up to and entering other cultures. In the discourse on good care, the bottom-up approach (also referred to as a 'social environment perspective') is favoured, which starts from the perspective of the client. At the same time, the professional should not disappear from the perspective of the client. In order words: The professional has to remain rooted in his or her own culture, although this culture is in constant open interaction with the culture of clients (tenet of diversity).

10.13 Towards a 'new social professional'

In this article I explored the identity of a 'new social professional', using insights from studies analyzing experiential knowledge of service users. In summary, the new social professional can be characterised as:

- A relational professional, able to connect, understand, and acknowledge;

- A contextual professional, able to work in different contexts. He is able to work within the context of different physical and cultural environments; in the context of policy, laws, regulations, and institutions; able to operate in the tension field between the world of individuals and the systems world of institutions and bureaucracy;

- A bonding and bridging professional, able to connect people and resources; able to strengthen social networks;

- An empowering professional; encouraging, supporting development, strengthening individuals, groups and communities;

- A professional promoting social rights and citizenship, ensuring protection and mobilizing resources;

- A reflective professional, able to use an ethical framework to take a sound moral position; I agree with Banks (2011) that social justice is a core ethical value. This includes a commitment to distributing welfare and health services fairly in accordance with need, and challenging oppressive power structures. It also entails questioning the power and interests of governments, public service employers, and social professionals themselves that cause them to ignore or accept inequalities and oppression. Banks states: 'Social workers have the right, power, and duty to promote what they regard as good and ethical practice and to challenge and resist inhumane, degrading, and unjust practices and policies.' (2011, p. 13)

- A learning professional, working on the basis of multiple knowledge resources (scientific, practice, and experience based), and able to learn in a continuous way.

The 'new social professional' is able to take a firm personal and professional position, but at the same time taking different perspectives into account: the perspective of the client, his environment, and the perspective of the community and the society. Weighing moral dilemmas are an inevitable part of the job. The social professional is an 'embedded' professional. He or she is able to be in the 'front line', being a fellow human being and a fellow citizen, working side by side with people in need of support. At the same time, the professional is able to maintain a helicopter view, putting daily reality in a broader perspective. He or she is able to create and keep a hopeful future orientation, contributing, over a longer period, to reach sustainable results with regard to self-reliance, participation, and social cohesion.

It is obvious that the identity pictured in this publication has a highly idealistic character. This 'ideal' professional does of course not exist. But the elements of a theory of good care can serve as beacons for the development of the social professions in our time.

Bibliography

Baart, A. (2001). *Een theorie van de presentie*. Utrecht: Lemma.

Banks S. (2011). Ethics in an age of austerity: Social work and the evolving New Public Management, *Journal of Social Intervention: Theory and Practice* – 2011 – Volume 20, Issue 2, pp. 5–23

Brettschneider, E., & Wilken, J.P. (2007). *Hoezo, een netwerk? Onderzoek naar de aandacht voor sociale netwerken in de verstandelijk gehandicaptenzorg.* Amsterdam: SWP / Kenniscentrum Sociale Innovatie.

CIVICUS (2005). *Civil Society Index Methodology.* http://www.civicus.org/new/media/CSI_Methodology_and_conceptual_frame work.pdf

Cameron, C. and Moss, P. (2007). *Care work in Europe: current understandings and future directions.* London and New York: Routledge.

Diamond, L.J. (1994). Toward Democratic Consolidation. *Journal of Democracy* - Volume 5, Number 3, July 1994, pp. 4-17

Doorn, L. van (2008). *Sociale professionals en morele oordeelsvorming.* Utrecht: Kenniscentrum Sociale Innovatie, Hogeschool Utrecht.

Driessens, K., & Geldof, D. (2008). Normatieve professionaliteit in het sociaal werk. *Alert, 34*(2), 66-75.

Ewijk, H., van (2008). Social change and social professionals. *European Journal of Social Education, 14/15,* 9–19.

Ewijk, H., van (2009). Citizenship-based social work. *International Social Work, 52*(2), 158–170.

Ewijk, H., van, Wilken, J.P., Verhagen, S., & Menger, A. (2009). Debating and deepening citizenship based social work. *Ensact Conference social action in Europe, different legacies & common challenges* (Abstract book) (p. 218). Dubrovnik: Ensact.

Ewijk, H. van (2010). *European Social Policy and Social Work. Citizenship-based social work.* London and New York: Routledge.

Ghorashi, H. (2006). *Paradoxen van culturele erkenning: Management van diversiteit in Nieuw Nederland.* Amsterdam: Vrije Universiteit.

Heijst, A. van (2005). *Menslievende zorg: Een ethische kijk op professionaliteit.* Kampen: Uitgeverij Klement.

Honneth, A. (1995). *The struggle for recognition: The moral grammar of moral conflicts.* Cambridge: Cambridge University Press.

Houten, D. van (2008). Professionalisering: Een verkenning. In Jacobs, G., Meij, R., Tenwolde, H. & Y. Zomer (Eds.), *Verkenningen van normatieve professionalisering* (pp. 16–35). Amsterdam: SWP.

Israel, B. A., Checkoway, B., Schulz, A., & Zimmerman, M. (1994). Health education and community empowerment: Conceptualizing and measuring perceptions of individual, organizational and community control. *Health Education Quarterly, 21*, 149–170.

Jacobs, G. (2001). *De paradox van kracht en kwetsbaarheid: Empowerment in feministische hulpverlening en humanistisch raadswerk.* Amsterdam: SWP.

Freedberg, S. (2009). *Relational theory for social work practice: A feminist perspective.* New York: Routledge.

Jacobs, G. (2010). *Professionele waarden in kritische dialoog: Omgaan met onzekerheid in educatieve praktijken.* Tilburg: Fontys Hogescholen.

Jacobs, G., Meij, R., Terwolde, H. & Zomer, Y. (2008). *Goed werk: Verkenningen van normatieve professionalisering.* Amsterdam: SWP.

Kal, D. (2001). *Kwartiermaken· Werken aan ruimte voor mensen met een psychiatrische achtergrond.* Amsterdam: Boom.

Kunneman, H. (1996). Normatieve professionaliteit: Een appel. *Sociale Interventie, 5*, 107–112.

Knight, B., Tandon, R. & Hope Ch. (2002). *Reviving democracy. Citizens at the heart of governance.* London and New York: Routledge.

Laan, G. Van der (2006). *Maatschappelijk werk als aandacht: Inbedding en belichaming.* Amsterdam: SWP.

MacIntyre, A. (1985). *After virtue.* London: Duckworth.

Meininger, H. P. (2007). *Verhalen verbinden: Een narratief-ethisch perspectief op sociale integratie van mensen met een verstandelijke handicap.* Inaugural lecture, Vrije Universiteit, Amsterdam.

Nussbaum, M. (1993). *The quality of life.* New York: Oxford University Press.

Oudenampsen, D. (2004). Sociaal kapitaal: Investeren in het samenleven van gehandicapte en niet-gehandicapte burgers. *Passage 13*(1), 9–17.

Polanyi, M. (1958*). Personal knowledge: Towards a post-critical philosophy.* London: Routledge.

Polanyi, M. (1967). *The tacit dimension.* New York: Anchor Books.

Pols, A. J. (2005). Enacting appreciations: Beyond the patient perspective. *Health Care Analysis, 13*(3), 203–221.

Putnam, R. (2000). *Bowling alone: The collapse and revival of American community.* New York: Simon & Schuster.

Regenmortel, T. van (2002). *Empowerment en maatzorg: Een krachtgerichte psychologische kijk op armoede.* Leuven: Acco.

Ricoeur P. (1992). *Oneself as another.* Chicago: University of Chicago Press.

Schön, D. (1983). *The reflective practitioner: How professionals think in action.* London: Temple Smith.

Schön, D., & Rein, M. (1994). *Frame reflection: Toward the resolution of intractable policy controversies.* New York: Basic Books.

Tronto, J. (1993). *Moral boundaries: A political argument for an ethic of care.* New York: Routledge.

Wilken J.P., & Den Hollander, D. (2005). *Rehabilitation and recovery: A comprehensive approach.* Amsterdam: SWP.

Wilken, J.P. (2005). Op weg naar een zorgzame samenleving: Voorwaarden voor vermaatschappelijking en participatie. *SPH, Tijdschrift voor Sociale en (Ortho)pedagogische Functies. 10*(63), 4–7.

Wilken, J.P. (2007). *Zorg en ondersteuning in de samenleving: Voorwaarden voor succesvolle vermaatschappelijking van de gehandicaptenzorg.* Amsterdam: SWP.

Wilken J.P., Ravelli A. & Van Doorn L. (2009). Aansluiten bij het perspectief van de cliënt. Betekenisgeving en ervaringsleren als professionele kernwaarden, In: Ravelli A., Van Doorn L., 2009. & Wilken J.P. (red.) *Werk(en) met betekenis. Dialooggestuurde hulp- en dienstverlening.* Bussum: Coutinho.

Wilken, J.P. (2010). *Recovering Care. A contribution to a theory and practice of good care.* Amsterdam: SWP.

Wilken, J. P. & Dankers T. (Eds) (2010). *Schakels in de buurt. Op weg naar nieuwe vormen van zorg en welzijn in de wijk.* Amsterdam: SWP.

11. The interactive social worker

Harrie Staatsen

11.1 Introduction

In the previous chapters, the professors based at the Research Centre for Social Innovation have contributed to a greater visibility of social work. In their contributions, substantial clues are to be found to form an outline of the interactive social worker. With this I mean a social worker who constructs social work in different roles, in a state of continuous interaction with other professionals and citizens. In this concluding chapter I will further develop the outline of the interactive social worker.

I will begin by describing the core task of social work, and will then delve into the construction of social work. Within social work there are different images of man and society associated with norms and values which have a more or less binding effect. Often we can speak of an invisible hand, one that also guides the professional actions of a social worker. Not only is social work itself guided by this invisible hand, it simultaneously concerns the people who suffer from the direction this invisible hand directs them towards. The concept of the self-responsible active citizen who is well able to direct his own life in a market society, may also have an oppressive effect. In this perspective, the social worker is a normative professional; in the transition from welfare state to a neo-liberal market society, he works with the normative imperative of active citizenship. In this chapter I will argue that giving support to active citizenship will be particularly promising when it is links the interest of interest of individual citizens to a common interest. I will illustrate this with the example of citizens' initiatives in the *Soesterkwartier* area in the city of Amersfoort. I will conclude this chapter with the statement that change processes in education are related to the guided change processes in the professional practice of the social worker. Joining the professional practice with the educational practice is thus important in several respects.

11.2 Core task of social work

The core task of social work has long been to promote human development by influencing behaviour and social relations. This takes place within different social environments. Both the individual development as well as the social environment are, in relation to each other, object of change-oriented influence. The people this influence is aimed at are for a large part, as this book shows, physically, mentally, or socially vulnerable. The level of vulnerability together with the surrounding social environment, determines the chance of individual and social development. In whatever social environment one lives, social work will professionally try to find ways for people to develop themselves individually and socially, as fully as possible. In this book, Wilken and Van Ewijk connect this core task of social work, to promoting self-reliance, social participation, and strengthening social cohesion. In their view, by connecting these points of view, social professionals work in a context-oriented manner.

The development of man and his environment are inextricably linked and influence each other. People define the quality, direction, and sense of individual and social development, in continuous interactions. When people's physical, mental, and social potential develop in a right balance, they can become authentic and autonomous individuals able to give direction to their own lives and that of others, of their own accord. When there are physical, mental and social limitations to a greater or lesser degree, taking direction of one's life can become problematic.

To a large extent social work is aimed at preventing individual and social limitations and problems. Prevention by, for example, early recognition, customized support, education, quick referral, etc. reduces the chances for one's loss of self-direction and meaningful coexistence with others. When problems or limitations emerge, social work, first and foremost, offers support with developing and retaining control over people's own lives. The direct surroundings of the person are immediately involved in this action. Hans van Ewijk argued in chapter 3, that social work needs to hold on to the principle of people's self-direction as much as possible. The initial requirement for this is the support of people from the direct environment; neighbours, family, and friends can provide this support. Only when this support is not sufficient, professional care and assistance comes into play.

11.3 The scope of social work

In the course of time, social work has gained form and content in many places in our society, in various sectors, job types, and functions. The social worker usually has a connection with a specific discipline. In addition, there is further specialization in the field with regard to target group, methodology, and methods. This allows social workers to more or less, determine their own substantive position, and the way in which they contribute to the role of social work in our society.

The communication on the development of social work would benefit from a clear vision on the scope of its content, for which a theoretical and methodical basis needs to be laid in the training of social workers. This range of professional behaviour can be visualized on a continuum from mostly preventive to therapeutic behaviour. Prevention means both, preventing problems that can occur in the individual and social development, as well as the prevention of the deterioration of existing problems. The preventive action extends over many aspects of individual and social development. The development of educational programmes, not only on parenting, health, living together in solidarity, and setting up a neighbourhood watch, but also in the field of cultural development and community building can be part of this. Also, mild forms of care and assistance, such as parenting support, housing advice, child care by elderly in the neighbourhood etc., are to a large extent prevention-oriented. At the other end of the scale, fixed problems are at the heart of (therapeutic) treatment. These problems usually have an individual and a social component, and a physical, mental, or social background, or a combination of these. Not only the treatment of problems, but also learning how to handle permanent problems, and actively participating in society again, are part of this type of professional behaviour.

11.4 The construction of social work

Within the scope of social work, several professions play a role, each having their own professional practice. When the expertise of social professionals in collaboration with others, is connected to a demand for individual or social development, we can speak of the construction of social work. All kinds of professionals involved with the individual and social development of people – from general practitioner to local policeman, from social worker to psychiatrist, from welfare worker to care coordinator, from football coach to family coach – can participate in the practice of social work. With the increasing appeal to the problem-solving capacities of citizens themselves, non-professionals such as family members, informal carers, and volunteers contribute significantly to the construction of social work.

Thus, the social worker deals with development questions in interactive connections. A first interactive connection is established with the person(s) that has (have) the development question. The question is not always well visible or might be directed to the wrong address. In trusted proximity, the social worker interactively examines the nature of the question, and in cooperation a goal is formulated, as well as the process of getting there. On this basis, the social worker starts working, both together with other disciplines as well as in meaningful connection with the surrounding social environment. Social work is in this way, interdisciplinary, both internally as well as in connection with others.

The construction of social work does not proceed in a linear fashion, since it is part of a surrounding influential context. In essence thus, the same happens to social work as to those who use social work: in its own development it is the object of change-oriented influence. In the context of on-going social changes, the function and content are not only determined by social work itself, but also by the surrounding social context of political, economic, and legal practices. Under this influence, social work has become highly differentiated in the past decennia. Social work had become involved in a growing number of individual and social development issues; partly because of its own development, partly at the invitation of the government. The government, as a funder of social work, started posing consecutive demands on the structure, costs, and content of social work within a short period of time. This was simultaneously accompanied by increasing demands in the field of quality control and legitimacy. In today's times of cutbacks on public spending and a changing social policy, social work is under great pressure.

Besides government-funded social work, more private social work has also emerged, which has to operate as a profitable company. This has caused, the necessary, competition to appear in the field of social work, which has made it subject to the growing influence of market principles. Due to these developments, the active role of citizens as designers and co-creators of what's at issue in social work, has been pushed into the background over the past decades.[113] In processes of policy-making, citizens are merely bystanders. The buying and selling of 'welfare products' has become, intentionally or not, the essence of welfare policies, with organizations as manufacturing companies. Over the past years, the government has started deciding what is good for the people, and this structurally forms an obstacle for citizens to solve problems themselves. Active citizenship has proved to be more an ideology than reality. But this can be different.

---

[113] See the report *Burgerkracht* (Civilian strength) by the *RMO* (Council for Social Development)

11.5 Images of man and society as the focal point of social work

Linking citizenship with the core task of social work makes clear that change-oriented influencing of human development has images of man and society at its foundation, whether explicit or not. An image of man and society is a normative image which is connected to essential values and norms. Those values are often rooted in different traditional or modern ideological and religious paradigms. The values form the basis for the norms: precepts which, whether or not enforcing, determine humans and their coexistence.

An image of man and society is often not very well defined. Over the course of time it is given new shape and meaning repeatedly, and it can be of guiding significance to large or even very small groups of people. In our late-modern market society, in which humans live in fast-changing networks, the previously collectively accepted images of man and society have become more differentiated and individualized. In addition, fundamental subcultures hold on with conviction to their own image of man and society, which only changes at a very slow pace. In many areas of society, guiding values and principles are developed. Within politics, the economy, law, education, the arts, health care, and social work as well, values and norms give direction to people's thinking and actions. Values and norms offer people both a guidance for their own behaviour, and a framework for analyzing the behaviour of others. This also counts for the social worker, both in his role as professional as well as in his role as a citizen.

In *Discipline and Punishment*, Michel Foucault (1975) describes the double effect of norms. On the one hand a norm is based on formal equality between people, aimed at normality, but on the other hand, this formal equality can also be a basis for differentiation. A norm is compelling since everyone has to fulfil it; at the same time a separation is made between those who do and those don't meet the norm. When the values and norms are anchored in the shared common culture, they start to form 'an invisible hand' which guides human development and human coexistence. This invisible hand offers a firm grip when open, but when closed it can be a fist. In our strongly culturally differentiated society, there are multiple images of man and society. Because of the ongoing processes of individualization, rationalization, and secularization, these images have gotten a more personal character and their contents are shared by smaller groups of people.

Social work is confronted with the effect of the invisible hand in different ways. Not only is social work guided by it, but it also deals with people who suffer from the direction the invisible hand guides them to. The image of the self-responsible active citizen who is well able to take direction of his own life in a market society, can have an oppressive effect. A social worker who has internalized this image as the absolute truth will, guided by the hand, most probably work with people with a YAVIS label (young, attractive, verbal, intelligent, successful). People with the unattractive HOUND label (homely, old, unattractive, nonverbally dumb) will most probably fall out of his view.

11.6 Social worker: a normative professional

Professionally, the social worker continuously makes choices that are based on the assessment of the situation. This assessment is partly shaped by internalized values and norms. Besides the values and norms that the social worker uses as a citizen and the ones arising from the organization that one works in, there are also professional values and norms that the social worker has adopted himself. Intuitively and/or consciously, this set of values and norms is constantly involved in the assessment of situations and the making of professional choices. It is of utmost importance that the social worker is aware of this normative nature of his profession, and that he continuously engages in a reflection on how his professional acting is determined by it. Critical reflection on professional behaviour is necessary to make the invisible hand visible. Feedback from the people using social work (the clients) and from colleagues that one works together with, is of great importance here. Also in continuing education, the social worker can gain insight to his professional behaviour and develop himself innovatively.

11.7 The normative imperative of active citizenship

In recent decades the welfare state has reduced its spending, for both financial and ideological reasons. Financially, the welfare state seemed to have become unaffordable, and ideologically, the (excessive) care from the cradle to the grave could take away people's impetus for activity. The government withdrew and gave way to the rapidly developing market society. This gave more space to the liberal ideology of the active citizen acquiring a livelihood out of enlightened self-interest. Thus the citizen became responsible for his own problems. The relation between a withdrawing government and citizens' personal responsibility is clearly described by Evelien Tonkens (2009, transl. eds.): 'Less governance in this context means, almost automatically, more self-responsibility for individual citizens. It is not the government which has to support people and get them out of trouble, but people have to save themselves. They have to take care not to fall into trouble, and if they do, they have to get up themselves.'

A logical continuation of this social development is the articulation of 'active citizenship', in which not only the relation between government and citizen is redefined, but also that of a new normality. 'Citizenship' says something about the behaviour of citizens. It not only deals with legal, but also with moral rights and obligations. The addition 'active' refers to the normative imperative of actively participating in society. What *good* active citizenship means, is part of a debate in which citizenship is connected to values and norms. In order to achieve active citizenship, it is important for citizens to be motivated towards it, to be competent, and to be invited and challenged by it in their social environment and surrounding society. Through its core task, social work can play an important role in the development of active citizenship. A first step would be to investigate whether people are sufficiently equipped and motivated to be involved in active citizenship. Secondly, it is important to see if there is enough space and challenge within the social environments of people for the development of active citizenship. Finally, we need to investigate whether active citizenship can be connected to personal and common interests.

In *The theory of moral sentiments* (1753), Adam Smith formulated his ethical position which, combined with the ethical core of *The wealth of nations* (1776), can *mutatis mutandis* be applied to the ethics of the active citizen in our society. We learn from the first book that a just society is the result of citizens sensibly pursuing their self-interest. This self-interest, the engine of a flourishing capitalist society, must be seen within the context of the responsibilities of the citizen. Self-interest is not based on egoism, but on care for others from a well understood own position (theory of moral sentiments). As it appears from Adam Smith's descriptions, self-interest is not a neutral concept. In it's connection to the care for others, it gets a positive connotation.

Human interests are always at the foundation of human behaviour. When interests are conflicting or intertwined, it can lead to problems. When personal interests coincide with the common interest, a positive synergy emerges. If the social worker is capable of connecting personal with common interests, 'suitable active citizenship' can develop.

11.8 Suitable active citizenship pays off

Suitable active citizenship pays off. I want to make this clear on the basis of an example of good practice. In the *Soesterkwartier* area in Amersfoort, the residents have taken direction of their neighbourhood into their own hands. The management of the municipality of Amersfoort has turned its all-important role as director of neighbourhood development into that of a partner of the residents who indicate the direction of the development themselves. For example: initial plans of demolishing houses that were still usable were redirected to the renovation of the houses. The demolition of a workshop for train maintenance was cancelled on the basis of plans proposed by the neighbourhood. The workshop, now regarded as an industrial heritage site, has become a 'traffic garden' for children. In addition, a project for energy supply was set up. Solar panels were placed on the roof of the local school, so that the school can now generate its own power supply. Currently, there are plans for the placement of a windmill in the area, so that the whole neighbourhood can provide for its own energy requirement. There are also plans in the making, for healthy food production and car sharing. Eventually, other goods and services that are of importance to the neighbourhood can be produced similarly, in a sustainable and cheaper way by the neighbourhood itself.

In *Productie door de burger* (Production by the citizen, transl. eds.), Jurgen van de Heijden (2011) reports on these initiatives. He has, as in other places in the Netherlands, designed the energy project in this neighbourhood together with the citizens. In his book he gives two suggestions to stimulate active citizenship and social entrepreneurship:

1. Finding and strengthening the kinds of social entrepreneurship that are already present in the neighbourhood. You can do this by visiting the neighbourhood, or by referring to the municipal guidebook. It is important to find out where the movement is, and then make a network analysis in which active people can be connected to each other.

2. Stimulating people towards social entrepreneurship. This involves a more demand-oriented approach. In a network analysis of the residents and the social organizations it is important to identify available expertise and connect this to questions present in the neighbourhood.

For both methods it is important to slowly build on what is already there. This example makes clear that, when self-interest (in this case in retaining one's own home, and in free energy supply) is connected with the common interest of a connected neighbourhood in a sustainable living environment, it pays off in both material and nonmaterial respects.

11.9   Professional practice and educational practice of social work

In the vocational training towards becoming a social worker, the professional practice of social work plays a central role. Within this training, students are exposed to current professional practice in the field and learn how to work effectively through research and critical reflection. Through this professional exposure, students develop professional competencies. From the very start of the training programme, the student performs relevant professional tasks in realistic learning environments. Right from the beginning, the student takes part in the construction of social work. So, the professional and educational practice of social work are closely intertwined. This asks from the professional practice, that actively training new colleagues form an integral part of people's profession. From the educational practice, this calls for taking responsibility in the active execution of professional tasks. This means that the execution of concrete professional tasks is central to every realistic learning environment. Such an approach will benefit both the professional as well as the educational practice. Offering and executing modern professional tasks is the common responsibility of both the professional as well as the educational practice.

The core task of social work is substantially similar to the core task of the related vocational training Both practices deal with change-oriented influence. It is important to pay attention to these parallel processes in the training programme. Professors and students can mirror the professional practice. In this sense, the role of the professor can be compared to that of the social worker, and the role of the student to that of the clients in social work. Educators and students can identify with these different roles very closely, and make a transfer to the professional practice based on common critical reflection on the experiences within the change-oriented learning process. Critical reflection is also needed with respect to the images of man and society and their invisible effects; thus also with regard to the normative imperative of active citizenship. This means that educators and students can and must debate on the meaning of good and suitable active citizenship, based on their own development. The results of this debate should be given practical shape in both the educational as well as the practical practice. In this way as well, these two practices can coincide to a great extent.

11.10 Outline of an interactive social worker

The following outline is not a picture of all that a social worker should be able to do, but more a picture of what a social worker should learn. What one needs to learn is an extension of the normative imperative of active citizenship: the student needs to actively master something, and the professor needs to actively 'unmaster' himself. To participate as a social worker in professional practice, in my opinion you need to learn to be able to do the following:

1. Search in immediate interactions with people for active development challenges within their social environments, aimed at suitable active citizenship and the manner in which it can be achieved.

2. Implement (start, adapt, evaluate) change-oriented development approaches, together with other professionals and citizens, aimed at active citizenship within different social environments.

3. Anchor individual and social changes towards suitable active citizenship, within different social environments.

4. Independently as well as together with other experts, critically reflect on the meaning and value of the social worker and social work for continuing and past change processes within different social environments.

5. Actively contribute to the innovation of existing professional practices, aimed at suitable active citizenship, based on published results of applied research.

6. Interactively maintain and develop own professional competencies through education (in self-learning teams) and supervision.

7. Interactively educate and guide students of social work.

Bibliography

Achterhuis, H. (2010). *De utopie van de vrije markt*. Rotterdam: Lemniscaat

Buijs, G., Dekker, P. & Hooghe, M. (2009). *Civil society, tussen oud en nieuw*. Amsterdam: Amsterdam University Press.

Diekstra, R., Berg, M. van de & Rigter, J. (red.) (2004). *Waardenvolle of waardenloze samenleving*. Uithoorn: Karakter Uitgevers B.V.

Foucault, M. (1975). *Surveiller et punir*. Parijs: Gallimard.

Heijden, J. van de (2011). *Productie door de burger*. Delft: Eburon.

Hortulanus, R., Eijken, J. van & Staatsen, H. (2011). *Hulpverlening die er toe doet*. Onderzoek naar implementatiemogelijkheden van een nieuwe vorm van casemanagement in de leerling-zorg binnen de regio Alblasserwaard/ Vijfheerenlanden. Utrecht: LESI, Universiteit Utrecht.

Jong, S. de (2009). *'De lastige burger', Dienstverlening in een tijd van ontbrekend burgerschap*. Van Duuren Media B.V.

Karskens, M. (2008). 'Bewaken en Pronken'. Goed Burgerschap en de kennissamenleving. In *Burger in uitvoering. Jaarboek KennisSamenleving* (deel 4) (pp. 27-52) Amsterdam: Aksant.

Karskens, M. (2008). The Political Frontiers of Europe as a Civil Society. *Limes, 1-2*, 186-198.

Lans, J. van der (2008). *Ontregelen. De herovering van de werkvloer*. Amsterdam: Augustus.

Lans, J. van der (2010). *Eropaf! De nieuwe start van het sociaal werk*. Amsterdam: Augustus.

Raad voor Maatschappelijke Ontwikkeling (2011). *Burgerkracht De toekomst van het Sociaal werk in Nederland*. Den Haag: Raad voor Maatschappelijke Ontwikkeling.

Smith, A. 1937 (1776). *The wealth of nations*. New York: Random House, Modern Library.

Smith, A. 1976 (1753). *The theory of moral sentiments*. Indianapolis, Ind: Liberty Classics.

Spangenberg, F. & Lampert, M. (2009). *De grenzeloze generatie en de eeuwige jeugd van hun opvoeders*. Nieuw Amsterdam Uitgevers.

Tonkens, E. (2009). *Mondige burgers, getemde professionals*. Amsterdam: Van Gennep.

Veerman, C. (2010). *Differentiëren in drievoud , omwille van kwaliteit en verscheidenheid in het Hoger Onderwijs*. (report by Advisory committee Veerman, commissioned by the Ministry of Education, Culture and Well-being).

Winter, M. de (2011). *Verbeter de wereld begin bij de opvoeding*. Amsterdam: SWP. Samenleven

List of contributors

Lia van Doorn studied pedagogy at the Utrecht University (UU). She worked among other at the Department of General Social Sciences (ASW) of the UU and at the Dutch Institute for Health and Welfare (NIZW). Since 2007 she is a professor attached to the Research Centre for Social Innovation of HU University for Applied Sciences Utrecht. E-mail: lia.vandoorn@hu.nl.

Hans van Ewijk, theologian and cultural psychologist, was professor 'Social Policy, Innovation and Professional Development' at the HU University for Applied Sciences Utrecht, and is now extraordinary professor 'Social Work Theory' at the University for Humanistics, and visiting professor 'International Social Policy and Social Work' at Tartu University, Estonia. E-mail: hansvanewijk@planet.nl

Jef van Eijken studied adult educational theory at the University of Amsterdam. He worked as community worker, college professor and course manager MWD and SPH. Since 2001 he has been actively involved with the development of lectorates, the Research Centre of Social Innovation and the Pedagogy program at the HU University for Applied Sciences Utrecht. E-mail: j.vaneijken@chello.nl

Ben Fruytier studied sociology at the Catholic University of Nijmegen, currently Radboud University. Till 2000 he worked at the IVA Institute for policy research and consulting. Currently he is a professor at the research group Organizational configurations and Work relations. He also works as Associate Professor of Organization and Human Resource Issues at Radboud University Nijmegen. E-mail: ben.fruytier@hu.nl.

Rob Gründemann is professor at the research group Organizational configurations and Work relations. He carries out research in the field of work participation, with a specific focus on lower educated employees. He also works as senior researcher/consultant at TNO. E-mail: Robert.gründemann@hu.nl

Jo Hermanns is together with Anneke Menger professor Working With Mandated Clients at the HU University for Applied Sciences Utrecht. He is also professor of Pedagogy and extraordinary professor at the Kohnstamm Chair at the University of Amsterdam.

Doorje Kal was prevention worker social psychiatry from 1992 till 2002. In that capacity she initiated the *Kwartiermaken* project, on which she received her post-graduation degree from the University for Humanistics in Utrecht. Since June 2011, she is extraordinary professor Kwartiermaken, described as 'making space for otherness'. E-mail: doortje.kal@hu.nl

Maarten van der Linde studied history at Utrecht University. He worked as professor and researcher at the Horst Academy in Driebergen. Nowadays he works a history professor at the Insitute for Social Work of the HU University for Applied Sciences Utrecht, and he is also extraordinary professor 'History of social work' at the same institute. E-mail: maarten.vanderlinde@hu.nl

Anneke Menger is together with Jo Hermanns professor Working With Mandated Clients at the HU University for Applied Sciences Utrecht. This research group has been made possible by the support of three probation services. She studied social sciences and management at the Groningen University. She published on working with mandated clients, in particular in rehabilitation work, such as *Het Delict als Maatstaf* ('The Fact as Basis', with Louis Krechtig) and *Walk the Line* (with Jo Hermanns). E-mail: anneke.menger@hu.nl

Harrie Staatsen is a sociologist. He worked as a researcher in psychiatry and care for the mentally handicapped. In recent years he taught sociology and worked as executive educational innovation in the field of Social work at the HU University. He is currently active as a researcher and consultant in projects in the professional education and practice of Social work. E-mail: Harrie.staatsen@hetnet.nl

Stijn Verhagen, social scientist, is professor Participation and Social Development. He previously worked as a consultant at the Council for Social Development and he was professor and PhD-student at Utrecht University and the University of Amsterdam. Stijn publishes among other on integration, social support, active citizenship and social prevention. E-mail: stijn.verhagen@hu.nl

Jean Pierre Wilken, social scientist, is professor Participation, Care and Support. He is involved with the participation of people in a vulnerable position in all fields of society, such as district and neighbourhood, work and leisure. He published extensively in the field of psychosocial rehabilitation and social support. E-mail: jean-pierre.wilken@hu.nl

www.ingramcontent.com/pod-product-compliance
Lightning Source LLC
Chambersburg PA
CBHW032135020426
42334CB00016B/1174